THE JEWISH PEOPLE

HISTORY · RELIGION · LITERATURE

THE JEWISH PEOPLE

HISTORY • RELIGION • LITERATURE

THE ORIGINS
OF THE SYNAGOGUE
AND THE CHURCH

KAUFMANN KOHLER

Edited

BY

H. G. ENELOW

ARNO PRESS
A New York Times Company
NEW YORK • 1973

Reprint Edition 1973 by Arno Press Inc.

Reprinted from a copy in
The Newark Public Library

THE JEWISH PEOPLE: History, Religion, Literature
ISBN for complete set: 0-405-05250-2
See last pages of this volume for titles.

Manufactured in the United States of America

Library of Congress Cataloging in Publication Data

Kohler, Kaufmann, 1843-1926.
    The origins of the synagogue and the church.

    (The Jewish people: history, religion, literature)
    Reprint of the 1929 ed. published by Macmillan,
New York.
    Bibliography: p.
    1. Judaism—History—Post-exilic period. 2. Jews.
Liturgy and ritual—History. 3. Church history—
Primitive and early church. 4. Kohler, Kaufmann, 1843-
1926. I. Enelow, Hyman Gerson, 1876-1934, ed.
II. Title. III. Series.
BM165.K65 1973   296'.09   73-2213
ISBN 0-405-05277-4

THE ORIGINS
OF THE SYNAGOGUE
AND THE CHURCH

DR. KAUFMANN KOHLER

THE ORIGINS
OF THE SYNAGOGUE
AND THE CHURCH

BY THE LATE
DR. KAUFMANN KOHLER

Edited with a Biographical Essay
BY
H. G. ENELOW

THE KAUFMANN KOHLER MEMORIAL VOLUME

New York
THE MACMILLAN COMPANY
1929

SET UP BY BROWN BROTHERS LINOTYPERS
PRINTED IN THE UNITED STATES OF AMERICA
BY THE CORNWALL PRESS

PREFACE

AT its annual meeting held at Cape May, New Jersey, on June 25, 1927, the Alumni Association of the Hebrew Union College resolved to establish a special fund in memory of the late Dr. Kaufmann Kohler, to be devoted to the publication of scholarly works on Judaism. As the first publication, it was decided to issue Dr. Kohler's own volume on *The Origins of the Synagogue and the Church,* on which he was known to have worked for many years, and the manuscript of which he was in the act of revising when he passed away.

When the editor undertook to prepare the manuscript for the press, he did so from a desire to help in the enterprise, rather than because he felt himself the best man for the task, or equal to it. Dr. Kohler's work covers such a wide range, that it would have required much more time and very much more learning than the editor possessed, in order to give it such full and minute revision as it probably would have received from its author, had he been allowed to finish it. Some additional chapters planned by the author, on the Mission of the Church and of the Synagogue, were left unwritten. As it is, the editor has confined his work to a revision of the style of the actual text, and to such consolidation in the final chapter of the extant material as seemed proper and desirable. He has refrained from obtruding upon the work any references to other men's views on the various subjects it deals with, or to the literature that has grown up since the manuscript was first prepared, and also from excision of occasional repetitions. Even as it stands, Dr. Kohler's work is sure to win the appreciation of scholars and to prove stimulating to students of the subject.

Our thanks are due to members of Dr. Kohler's family, who in various ways have assisted in the production of this volume, and especially to Miss Rose Kohler for her careful typewriting of the difficult manuscript, and to Dr. Max J. Kohler for numerous suggestions, as well as constant interest and help. The portrait appearing as a frontispiece is based upon an artistic photograph made by Mrs. Doris Ulmann. Rabbi Joseph Marcus was kind enough to verify the references. At the request of the Publication Committee and of members of Dr. Kohler's family, the editor's biographical essay was included. This paper appeared originally in the American Jewish Year Book for the year 5687 (1926-1927), and is reprinted in its original form, except for some slight corrections and additions.

The Committee of the H. U. C. Alumni, in charge of this publication, consisted of the following gentlemen: Dr. Marcus Salzman, Chairman; Rabbi Morris M. Feuerlicht, and Rabbi Jacob Tarshish.

H. G. E.

A BIOGRAPHICAL ESSAY

"THE HOLY ONE," according to the Rabbis, "does not raise a man to leadership without first trying and testing him." Dr. Kohler, at the time of his death, on the 28th of January, 1926, was universally regarded as the foremost exponent of Reform Judaism. But to that high position he had risen after a life of toil and struggle in behalf of his ideals. "His is an intellect," Dr. Schechter said, "devoted entirely to what he considers the truth, and a heart deeply affected by every spiritual sensation: he delights to engage in what he considers the Battles of the Lord." All his life Dr. Kohler gave to the quest of truth, to the defense and furtherance of his faith. "You can judge," he wrote as a young man, "what an irresistible compulsion to reach clearness and truth drives me on." From that time forth he never wearied, and when more than fourscore years old he might have repeated the words of the octogenarian biblical hero, Caleb the Kenizzite, longing to conquer yet another mountain: "I am as strong this day as I was in the day that Moses sent me; as my strength was then, even so is my strength now."

I

In his early youth, none would have dreamt of him as a future leader of Reform Judaism. Everything in his antecedents and environment seemed to pledge him to strictest Orthodoxy. He was born, in the year 1843, on

the 10th of May, at Fürth, Bavaria, which, with its rabbinic academy and Hebrew printing-press, had formed,
for many generations, a stronghold of Orthodoxy. His
maternal ancestry and his relations included several
rabbis of the old school. Moreover, all his teachers
were of the same group: first, disciples of R. Wolf Ham-
burger, the head of the famous Fürth Yeshibah, who preferred to see that old establishment, founded by one of
his ancestors, go to pieces rather than put secular studies
into its course, as the government in 1826 had decreed;
and then, successively, Dr. Marcus Lehmann, of May-
ence, R. Jacob Ettlinger, of Altona, and, finally, R. Samson Raphael Hirsch, of Frankfort on the Main.

To all those masters—famous in the annals of modern
Orthodoxy—young Kohler had gone for learning and
inspiration, and it was Rabbi Hirsch, the most active and
attractive of them all, that had made upon him the deepest impression. "The man who exerted the greatest
influence upon my young life," he wrote after many years,
"and imbued me with the divine ardor of true idealism
was Samson Raphael Hirsch." When at Frankfort,
Kohler was in his twenty-first year; at that time he was
still so whole-heartedly devoted to Orthodoxy that he
never visited a Reform synagogue, nor, though two sons
of Geiger were fellow-students of his at the Gymnasium,
did he go to hear Abraham Geiger, whose *Urschrift* had
been out for several years and who was just then giving
his masterly lectures on Judaism and its History, the first
volume of which was issued in 1864.

What changed Kohler's attitude were some discoveries
he made soon after entering the University of Munich.
Various causes, or experiences, serve in different individuals to shake the foundations of an old inherited faith.
In the case of Kohler it was philology, a subject he took up

at the university. In his study of Arabic, it dawned upon him that his old adored teacher, Samson Raphael Hirsch, was wrong in regarding Hebrew as the original language of the human race and in basing much of his teaching on that assumption. Dr. Kohler never forgot the dismay with which that sudden realization filled his soul. It was a blow to the faith, the ideas, he had imbibed from his parents and masters. Nor could Rabbi Hirsch, to whom he went for help, do more than assure him that he would get over his doubts in course of time, and that they were an inevitable part of experience—"the torrid zone" in one's journey through life.

But his doubts did not disappear. On the contrary, at the University of Berlin, to which he removed, they grew even more intense and perplexing, while the lectures of Professor Steinthal on psychology and ethnology served more and more to oust the simple notions of religion and history upon which he had been brought up. Those were sad days for him—days of spiritual anguish—especially as there was none to assist him with counsel and guidance. Zunz and Steinschneider were lecturing in Berlin, but he found them cold and uncongenial; he was not made for bibliography. Fortunately, he neither neglected his talmudic studies, nor allowed himself to fall into the mood of skepticism and irreligion which many others embraced. While his Orthodoxy was gone, the spirit of faith remained a vital force within him.

II

The effect of his university days we find in Dr. Kohler's first printed work, *Der Segen Jacobs,* which appeared in 1867. It was the thesis he submitted at the University of Erlangen for his doctor's degree, but it attracted much more attention than such theses usually gain. For one thing, it showed a great deal of learning, both rabbinic and classic. Upon the study of the Blessing of Jacob it brought to bear a variety of knowledge gleaned in many fields, from the talmudic Midrash to Hellenic mythology. Then, it employed boldly the critical method, trying to determine the period of Hebrew history to which the Blessing belonged and the conditions it reflected. Incidentally, it gave an outline of the development of the God-idea in ancient Israel, and sought to show that the prophetic movement represented a continuous progress of ideas and was reflected in the Pentateuch, as well as in other parts of the Bible. All this, including the assumption of tribal polytheism among the pre-Mosaic Hebrews, was bound to please some as well as to irritate others. Yet, the most striking thing about that work, I think, was the Introduction, in which the author discussed the conditions of his own age and demanded more attention on the part of leaders to its spiritual needs.

"One is moved to write," says the young author, whom I am translating, "by a feeling of discontent with the present and what it offers. On the one hand, discontent with science, which is so ready to regard itself as finished and closed, while, as a matter of fact, we see everywhere mere beginnings toward a better state of knowledge, and with every branch of knowledge coming forward as an enemy to all the others, presuming to displace and supersede all others; and, on the other hand, discontent with life, which has been torn into so many contradictions, breaking up men in their religious, political, and social aims into ever new parties by such catchwords as Forward or Backward, Liberal or Conservative, without attempting to bring about unity or harmony. However, as concord and unity must emerge from the strife of contrasts, it rests upon every one who would work for a fairer future to contribute his share." "Above all," he demands, "is it not necessary to try to achieve such unification and harmonization in the realm of religion? Is it not true that representatives and teachers of religion have helped to create the sad disunion of the present and are still nourishing the unholy strife? In the name of religion, everything that is old and traditional is called holy, while all that is new is as such condemned, as well as all progress. In the name of religion, men are not allowed to think, to gain spiritual independence and maturity. That foolish principle has served to transplant crass ignorance and pollution to Jewish soil, also; a principle, the harshness and cruelty of which is felt in its full force by him only who, through love of truth and in the service of faith and by a sense of deep union with Judaism, has struggled for freedom of thought and has had to pay for it dearly step by step." "Shall the young generation," he asks, "attain freedom through frivolity, or shall not its education rather aim from the outset to transform external religious forms into inward religiousness, the naïve customs of the fathers into conscious morality? Is it not imperative that children be taught nothing in the name of religion which, the next hour, would be contradicted or nullified by the teacher of the natural sciences? Shall we, by our attitude, help to make religion ridiculous, or undermine it?"

"Religion," he argues, "is eternal. Man will never be able to dispense with it. It can never be displaced by cold philosophic statements or ethical abstractions. Mankind can never dispense with the higher unity of action and thought, of will and duty, yes, with the idea of a Deity which has given to the free will its ethical laws and to the world of the senses its natural laws, no matter what different forms the Deity might take on in the conception of the individual. Religion, however, must try to adopt the form in which it can best serve the struggle of the age towards truth, unity, and ethical freedom, and thus connect the traditions of the past with the ideals of the future. And what are the ideals of the future of mankind, if not those which Judaism, or to speak more generally, Prophetism, put forth more than twenty-five hundred years ago, namely, that the time would come when men, united by a love of peace and truth, would regard and love one another as the children of one God?"

Surely, an unusual preface, this, to a doctor's dissertation! It was the combination of enthusiasm for practical work with the critical study of the past that probably earned for the author the anathema of his old teacher, Dr. Lehmann, as well as the ardent commendation of that matchless champion of both historic study and progressive effort, Abraham Geiger.

Diverse things have been written about "The Blessing of Jacob." Dr. Emil G. Hirsch said that it marked the beginning of an entirely new conception of revelation (which, in view of Geiger's many years of prior work, I doubt); Dr. Kohler himself regarded it as the first disclosure of the existence of the prophetic element in the Pentateuch, and as the unacknowledged source, in that respect, of Kuenen's History of the Religion of Israel. One thing, however, is certain: its publication destroyed the author's prospects for a rabbinic position in his own country. His best friends and admirers could see that much. At Fürth there was nothing short of consternation at the news that a book by one of its native sons had been put under the ban by Dr. Lehmann. Dr. Loewi, an old friend of Kohler's, leader of the local "neologues," who had hoped to put him into the rabbinate of Nuremberg, upbraided him for imprudence. Even Geiger, it would seem, could see no hope, and advised him to prepare for an academic career. Dr. Kohler actually entered the University of Leipsic for that purpose, taking up further studies in Oriental philology. But, after all, one cannot thwart nature. He was not made for an academic career. Though he diligently studied Semitic languages, and wrote articles for Geiger's magazine on some minute philological themes with all the punctiliousness of a born grammarian, his spirit was not content. He could not confine himself to the past, nor to the lure of Semitic particles. It was the preacher in him that demanded expression; the man of spiritual action, of religious leadership, strove to the fore through his academic activities and disquisitions. "There was in me," we read in his Reminiscences written on his seventy-fifth birthday, "something of that fire of which the Prophet Jeremiah says that it cannot be quenched."

III

There was but one solution—America. Dr. Geiger warmly recommended him to the leaders of Reform Judaism in America as a desirable acquisition; he himself, on the strength of Geiger's introduction, corresponded with Dr. Einhorn, a native of his own province, and wrote to Dr. Samuel Adler (the letter was recently published by Dr. David Philipson). Finally, he was invited to become the rabbi of Congregation Beth-El of Detroit. When he reached these shores, on August 28, 1869, he was met by Dr. Einhorn, whose daughter, Johanna, he married a year after his arrival, and whose successor and biographer (not to say apostle) he was destined to become later on.

Just a week after landing, on Saturday, the 4th of September, 1869, he preached his Inaugural Sermon at Detroit, in German, taking as his theme, The Qualities of a God-called Leader of Israel. It was based on the call of Moses, and as we read it, we not only admire its maturity and force, but also we can see why it had proved impossible for Dr. Kohler to remain in the seclusion of collegiate pursuits. He felt the call, we are told, to enter the service of God. He felt the call of the God of the Spirits—*Elohe Ha-ruhoth;* Go lead thy people, become a leader of the community of Israel, lead young and old to the flaming God-mountain, into the sanctuary of Religion! Moses he took as his model, discerning in him two spiritual qualities—humility and compassion—and two mental qualities, namely, an historical sense for the old, and a frank, sympathetic understanding of the tasks and achievements of the new age, of the demands of the present and the future.

It is not on record what the Jewish pioneers of Michigan thought of that lofty address and prophetic program. But it is said that they were pleased with his ministry, and that among them he even achieved some minor practical reforms. I have heard it stated that one of his meritorious acts in Detroit was to abolish the *tallith*. But whether that is so or no, it was not in that direction that lay Dr. Kohler's forte, or desire. His main concern was the Reform idea. Into its exposition and defense, he put all his strength and ardor. He was distinctly the intellectual champion of the significance and purpose of Judaism as construed by Reform. And in that capacity he revealed himself soon after he came here, not only to his congregation at Detroit, but to the entire country. He attended the Rabbinical Conference at Philadelphia in 1869. Moreover, he promptly began to contribute to

the Jewish journals, to one of which—*The Jewish Times*
—he had indeed sent at least two essays before leaving
Fürth, writing on both historical and contemporary questions, but especially on the need and meaning and legitimacy of Reform. None could doubt but that an important force, as Geiger put it, had been added to Judaism
in America.

IV

From Detroit, after two years, Dr. Kohler was called
to the pulpit of Sinai Congregation of Chicago. Reaching that city soon after the fire that had laid it waste,
he turned his Inaugural Sermon—preached on the 11th
of November, 1871—into a message of comfort and
hope. As text he took the quickening words of the
sixty-first chapter of Isaiah: "To give unto them a gar-
land for ashes, the oil of joy for mourning, the mantle
of praise for the spirit of heaviness." That vibrant
verse he developed into a threefold message for the
desolate city, forecasting its great future and urging it
to seek salvation through hope, solace through love, and
freedom through faith, while aiming to found its new
grandeur upon a spirit of communal solidarity and righteous living. One can easily imagine the salutary effect
the address must have had upon the melancholy mood
of his new congregation.

In Chicago, we are told, he was the first to introduce
Sunday services. But, again, it was not the Sunday service as such that concerned him. What he wanted was
an opportunity for teaching and vitalizing the Jewish
religion, and making it an active influence in the lives
of the people. His chief aim was to show that Judaism
was not a mere relic of the past, that its truths were
still alive and necessary, and that it was in harmony with

the intellectual forces of the new age. He started a service on Sunday mornings because that seemed a good time to assemble the people, in view of the decay of synagogal attendance on the Sabbath, but neither then, nor later on, did he waver in his adhesion to the sanctity of the historic Sabbath.

It was for the promotion of the Reform idea of Judaism that he inaugurated the Sunday service, and the keynote he struck in the address he delivered at the opening service, January 18, 1874, and called "The New Knowledge and the Old Faith" (*Das neue Wissen und der alte Glaube*). The title probably was suggested by David Friedrich Strauss's then recent work on the *Old and the New Faith,* and the theme, by the lively discussion on the relation of Science and Religion which was going on at the time, as a result of Darwin's epoch-making works on the *Origin of Species* and the *Descent of Man,* published in 1859 and 1871 r spectively. Dr. Kohler sought to show that the new physical sciences, with the doctrine of evolution taught by Darwin, were not necessarily a menace to religion; that they could not be expected to remove or supersede religion; that, on the contrary, the more one learnt of the marvels of Nature, the more genuine must grow one's adoration of God; and that, finally, Judaism, which had always been an unshackled and spiritual religion, had nothing to fear from the spread of knowledge. Dr. Hirsch has rightly praised that address for its clarity and comprehensiveness; and even to-day it has not lost its value.

Religion and science, Dr. Kohler argued, were not rivals, but partners in the spiritual life of mankind. Like sun and moon, each had its place in the sky of the human spirit. Increase of knowledge does not mean diminution of the content of faith. The light of faith must shine ever more brightly in the sunlike radiance of science. Religion and science must illumine each other, and become as one. Not mutual belittlement, but reconciliation and unity, is their goal. Harmony of mind and spirit—of the whole man—that is their aim.

While paying tribute to the achievements of science and its contribution to human enlightenment, he pointed out its inadequacy to satisfy the human spirit. "Is it not strange and significant," he asks, "that just during the ascendancy of the physical sciences a weary melancholy vein of resignation has possessed the cultured circles of society? While our age celebrates the proudest triumphs of the intellect, marching forward with steam and electric power; while progressive intelligence keeps on uncovering new inexhaustible sources of well-being and extending ever farther the goal and outlook of the future, the pessimism of Schopenhauer and Hartmann has become the popular wisdom of the day, and the dreary philosophy of Buddha, the sad fate of dissolution into Nirvana, into dreadful nothing, finds a deep echo in the hearts of men."

He could see no peril to Judaism in modern science, which culminates in the conviction that the world was not created by one act, but has evolved, and that man also was not created perfect, but has grown gradually. That he regarded as the essence of what was then the new Darwinian doctrine. And shall that teaching lead to atheism? On the contrary. "I have a higher conception of the wisdom of the Eternal than if I believed that He must from time to time rush in to help or improve His own work; for, the eternal laws of Nature are His eternal wisdom, His immutable will. He were not the Eternal were He forced ever to change His will."

Nor does man forfeit his distinctive place in creation,

he thought, by the acceptance of the evolutionary teaching. The distinction of man lies in his capacity for growth. "The beast remains standing where Nature has placed it; man does not remain in the same position. He is driven by the creative forces farther and farther from his root, away from his natural origin toward the higher, the infinite; away from the transient shell towards the eternal. If nothing else, this would prove that more of the creative energy and the creative mind inheres in him than in his fellow-creatures. As all Nature, reaching from the inanimate upward toward living forms finally attains to man, the crown of creation, so man, with whom a new empire of the spirit seeks to be born, strives toward God, the Highest. In Nature, development takes place toward the external; in the spirit, it is inward. Thus, everything that stamps man as man—language, reason, art, the sciences, morality, and religion—our entire culture, has grown from rude beginnings into ever higher perfection."

Is not such a view of the world, he demands, which regards advancement and development as the law of Nature and of the spiritual life, and which says to man: Strive upward and forward; triumph over the lower world from which thou didst spring; not behind thee but before thee lies Paradise!—is not such a view of the world the fairer praise of the Creator? Does not such continuous progress prove the sway of a supreme wisdom and goodness, which leads all toward completion? And does not such a view harmonize entirely with our own religion, the history of which is perennial progress and the goal of which is the highest ideal for the future of mankind? Is it not in accord with our particular conception of religion, which beholds its essence not in form but in reform, which sees its vital force in the

eternal renewal of Judaism, and its Messianic mission
in the movement toward a perfected mankind? "We do
not die to the old faith," he concludes; "we let the science
of the new age quicken our spirit anew and declare before
the world the works of God and the goal of mankind."
Eight years Dr. Kohler remained at Sinai Congregation, and they were full of activity. Energy was one of
his characteristics; Reform Judaism his passion. He
longed to expound the contents of the history and the
religion of the Jew in the light of Reform, and during his
many years of study at rabbinical colleges and universi-
ties he had stored up a fund of knowledge which now
came to his aid and fed his literary fecundity. His sermons often sought to elucidate important phases of the
Jewish past, and the adaptation of old doctrines and
practices to the new conditions. They invariably blended
the academic with the practical, the research of the
scholar with the fire of the preacher. Nor was their
effect limited to his own congregation. Many of his
addresses, in both German and English, appeared in the
Jewish journals of those years. *The Jewish Times,* published in New York, is full of them. Besides, he wrote
occasionally on purely academic themes. His interest in
scholarly work never abated, especially in the study and
interpretation of the Bible, the beauty and glory of which
he was always eager to make known to the people.
Thus, he published, in 1878, a new German translation
of the Song of Songs, accompanied by a scholarly analysis of its content and style, and dedicated it to Dr. Einhorn and Dr. Samuel Hirsch, on the occasion of the
marriage of the former's daughter to the latter's son,
Emil G. Hirsch. No less devoted was Dr. Kohler to the
religious education of the young, which, like other heroes
of Reform Judaism, such as Geiger and Holdheim, he

treated as one of his chief tasks. In behalf of the young, he began, in 1876, to publish a history of biblical times, under the title, *A Jewish Reader for Sabbath Schools,* and later became editor of *The Sabbath Visitor,* which he filled with a mass of historical and ethical material, just as still later, in 1899, he issued a *Guide for Instruction in Judaism,* which has gone through many editions.

v

When in the year 1879 (less than four months before his death) Dr. Einhorn retired, it was quite natural that Dr. Kohler should be made his successor as rabbi of Temple Beth-El in New York. Here, with the same zeal and ardor, he continued his work as exponent of Judaism from the standpoint of Reform. "The Principles and the Purpose of Reform Judaism"—that was the subject of his Inaugural Sermon which he delivered, in German, on the 6th of September, 1879—the one hundred and fiftieth anniversary, as it happened, of the death of Moses Mendelssohn. He was still convinced, as he was when he wrote the preface to the Blessing of Jacob, that Judaism is a religion which had gone through a process of development in the past and was capable of further evolution, that it is a mobile and not a fixed faith, that it contained a most valuable spiritual message for modern man, and that, moreover, Religion, as such, was needful to mankind, with nothing else to take its place. Judaism, he felt, was the religion of the future. "The idea of progressive Judaism alone," he affirmed, "has given us the consciousness of a lofty mission, the victorious confidence and expectation of an incomparably great future, of which no current of culture or fashionable philosophy can rob us any more!" Ethical Culture, he was certain, was no substitute for religion, though

just then it was being thus played up, to the delectation
of numerous New Yorkers.

This was the doctrine Dr. Kohler was trying to spread,
when Dr. Alexander Kohut, soon after his arrival in
America in the year 1885, attempted to make naught of
all the efforts of Reform Judaism, by declaring it to be
no Judaism at all. He who disowns on principle the
statutes and ordinances of Mosaico-Rabbinical Judaism,
he proclaimed, forfeits the name of Jew. Dr. Kohut's
renown as a scholar was calculated to give weight to his
utterance and to jeopardize the work of Reform Judaism.
Immediately, Dr. Kohler took up the challenge. Though
late in the season, after the Confirmation Service, when
people begin to scatter for the summer, he gave a series
of sermons under the general title, "Backward or Forward?", in which he offered a new and fervid exposition
of the evolutional nature of the Jewish religion and of
the demand for a continuance of the process of adjust-
ment, and for a reconciliation of the ancient faith with
the knowledge and the needs of the new age. Throughout these addresses, however, Dr. Kohler showed again
some of his inherent traits: he never attacked his opponent personally, he denied not his linguistic erudition
nor his right to his own convictions, he showed no lack
of reverence for the past. On the contrary, piety to
him was part of true progress; the two went together.
But so much the more positive was he in the defense of
his own position.

Those sermons, originally given in German, were published by Dr. Kohler's Congregation in an English version. But they had an even more important sequel.
They led to the Pittsburgh Rabbinical Conference, which
Dr. Kohler convened in the autumn of the same year,
and which adopted a declaration of principles that is

still regarded as the most authoritative corporate declaration of the doctrine and aim of Reform Judaism. No
wonder the Central Conference of American Rabbis, on
the occasion of Dr. Kohler's eightieth birthday, in 1923,
issued a reprint of the proceedings of that historic Conference as a tribute to its author.

During his New York ministry, Dr. Kohler gave himself freely to the various tasks engendered by metro-
politan life. The Jewish community was growing, particularly as a result of European persecutions; needs were
increasing. Of course, Dr. Kohler sought to stimulate
the charitable activities of the community; first, his heart
was sensitive and generous, and, then, as a scholar he
knew that philanthropy or social service (or whatever
might be the label of the moment) had always formed
an integral part of Jewish religion and conduct. Often
he spoke and wrote on the conception of charity in
Judaism, and on its history. Nevertheless, Dr. Kohler
never allowed himself to become a mere adjunct to other
people's jobs; or a mere advertiser of other people's
laudable endeavors. He never lost sight of the substance
of his rabbinic function, namely, to conserve Judaism—
the Torah—by study and instruction, by the kind of
teaching upon which ultimately all practice depends.

The multitude of essays and addresses he kept on
printing witness to his unceasing diligence. *The Jewish
Times, The Jewish Reformer* (which he edited and the
caption of which he had adorned with miniature portraits
of Mendelssohn, Geiger, and Einhorn), the *Zeitgeist,*
and other periodicals, are filled with a variety of his contributions on both historical and polemical topics. In
every important controversy his voice was heard:
whether it be on the Sabbath, or Sunday service, the
establishment of a synod, or mixed marriages, or the

reception of proselytes, or the relation of the Jewish laws of marriage and divorce to civil legislation. Great figures of Jewish history frequently formed his theme: from Moses to Mendelssohn, from Hillel to Zunz, fom Philo to Lazarus. Repeatedly, also, he wrote on the history of the Jewess, and her relation to Judaism. On the other hand, he produced some original critical studies, such as his essays on the pre-Talmudic Haggada (in the *Jewish Quarterly Review*) and on the Origin and Basic Forms of the Liturgy (in the *Monatsschrift*), and his edition of the Greek text of the Testament of Job, with an English translation and exegetical notes (in the Alexander Kohut *Semitic Studies*). Besides, he edited, in 1880, a volume of Dr. Einhorn's *Selected Sermons,* a second edition of which he brought out in 1911, with a fine biographical essay, in honor of the centenary of Dr. Einhorn's birthday, which had occurred in 1909.

His great literary opportunity, however, came with the publication of the *Jewish Encyclopedia,* which, under the management of Dr. Isidor Singer, began to appear around the year 1900. Dr. Kohler was one of the chief supports of that magnificent project, and some of its most important and authoritative pages were written by him. He was the editor of the departments of Philosophy and of Theology, in both of which, for encyclopedic purposes, a good deal of pioneer work had to be done. But, besides, he himself contributed some three hundred articles, especially on Pharisaic and Hellenistic Judaism, and on the origins of Christianity, subjects he had studied with particular devotion and construed from a standpoint of his own.

VI

Before the *Encyclopedia* was completed, in the year 1903, Dr. Kohler was elected to the presidency of the Hebrew Union College. That event was regarded by some as one of the ironies of history. They had not forgotten the feud which existed between Isaac M. Wise, the founder of the College, and the leaders of Reform Judaism in the East. Dr. Kohler was supposed to have belonged to the latter group. Fortunately, neither Rabbi Wise nor Dr. Kohler was a fanatic. Whatever their differences, they had not been blind to each other's merits. As a matter of fact, it was Dr. Kohler who had delivered the Sabbath address at the first graduation of the Hebrew Union College, as he had also presented some important papers at the meetings of the Central Conference of American Rabbis, founded by Rabbi Wise, and taken a leading part in the making of the Union Prayer Book, issued by the Conference, incorporating in it a good deal of Dr. Einhorn's book of prayers. Dr. Kohler's coming to the College, therefore, was not as illogical as to some it appeared. At any rate, it was hailed with joy by those who were jealous for the maintenance of high academic and spiritual ideals at that institution.

Nor were they disappointed. Dr. Kohler breathed new life into the College, amplifying and improving its course of studies, and setting before it his own high academic standards. But it was the spirit of the College he cared for most, which he sought to express and to stimulate in every address he delivered, whether within its own walls or elsewhere. Some of those utterances found their way into the volume called *Hebrew Union College and Other Addresses*, published in the year 1916, as a companion to Dr. Schechter's *Seminary*

Addresses—volumes, by the way, that, standing side by side, aptly commemorate the friendship which, despite doctrinal differences, existed between these two illustrious leaders. During his presidency, the College moved to its new buildings, the dedication of which was graced by the presence, and enlivened by an address, of Dr. Schechter, while the number of students increased, in spite of the difficulties that some new enemies of the President and of Reform Judaism tried to create.

More and more the College came to feel the benign influence of Dr. Kohler's personality. Both the faculty and the students delighted to honor him whenever occasion offered. In honor of his seventieth birthday, in 1913, the faculty issued a volume of *Studies in Jewish Literature,* with contributions by European and American scholars, including a bibliography of his writings, while the students got out special numbers of their journal on the occasion of his seventy-fifth anniversary, in 1918, and again on his retirement, in 1921, after eighteen years of service.

Though absorbed in the work of the College, Dr. Kohler found time for other important activities. For the Central Conference of American Rabbis, which, on his election to the presidency of the College, had made him its own honorary head, he prepared several learned papers, such as on Assyriology and the Bible, on the Origin and Function of Ceremonies in Judaism (in which he defines the place of ceremonies in religion, and while recognizing the foreign origin of some old Jewish ceremonies and their obsoleteness, insists upon the need of suitable ceremonies to the conduct of the religious life) ; on the Harmonization of the Jewish and Civil Laws of Marriage and Divorce; on the Mission of Israel and its Application to Modern Times; and on the Theological

Aspect of Reform Judaism (in opposition to the proposal made by a certain scholar that the Conference prepare a creed of Reform Judaism for final adoption by a Synod). In the latter paper the author offered a thorough critique of old Jewish creeds, as well as of the new one proposed, and took the position that any attempt at formulating a creed for one section of Judaism, with the exclusion of the rest, was a dangerous proceeding, which should by all means be discouraged, as it tended to create a schism, in antagonism to the spirit and tradition of Judaism.

Moreover, it was to the Conference that he originally presented the biographic essay on Dr. Einhorn, which later was incorporated in the Memorial edition of Dr. Einhorn's *Selected Sermons*. Dr. Kohler also took a leading part in the defense of Reform Judaism, which was being attacked just then from various quarters. Withal, he continued to produce occasional critical studies, as, for instance, on the Creed of Maimonides—a German version of his Conference paper on the subject, on the Zealots, and on the Documents of Jewish Sectaries (discovered by Dr. Schechter). Besides, from 1908 to 1915, he acted as one of the editors of the English Bible issued by the Jewish Publication Society, which had previously printed his own translation of the Book of Psalms. Similarly, he served as a member of the Jewish Classics Committee of that society.

VII

One of the most gratifying results of Dr. Kohler's connection with the College was the publication of his work on *Jewish Theology*. In addition to fulfilling the duties of the presidency, he acted as professor of theology and of Hellenistic literature. In that capacity, he was led to coördinate the many studies in these branches which he had carried on for many years, and to prepare them for systematic presentation. There was need for such a work, the lack of which Zunz had deplored a century before. The Berlin society for the promotion of Jewish knowledge invited Dr. Kohler to prepare it as part of a series it was publishing, and when it appeared, in the year 1910, it was recognized forthwith as an important contribution to Jewish literature.

A large work it is, with a long title: *Outline of a Systematic Theology of Judaism on an Historical Basis.* But the title is justified by its contents. Indeed, judged by the wealth of its material, it is succinct. No wonder the late Professor Neumark—whose vast erudition made no spatial compromises—was amazed at its brevity. "Questions," he says quaintly, "the full discussion of which would require several volumes, are kept in evidence by concise and exact linguistic formulations." Dr. Neumark, also, commended it to the student-reader for "the complete references to the sources in the Notes." "For the expert reader, however," he adds, "the all-important fact is decisive that the presentation itself shows so minute a familiarity with the sources and the scientific literatures devoted to the same, that no scholar, ever so great and recognized, is supposed to be possessed of it as long as he did not actually demonstrate it *ad oculos.*"

As a matter of fact, Dr. Kohler's work tried to cover every aspect of Jewish theology, on both the theoretic and the practical side. Divided into an Introduction and three main parts, it seeks, first, to define the general concepts of theology and of Judaism, then to determine the essence of Judaism and its basic beliefs, and, in more than fifty chapters, to present the Jewish teaching concerning God, Man, and the Mission of Israel. Every chapter is pervaded by Dr. Kohler's central view concerning the history and the nature of Judaism.

Jewry and Judaism, to him, belong together. Without Judaism, Jewry is a body without a soul. It is a long, eventful history Judaism has had—spiritually and intellectually eventful, as well as politically—having come into close contact, and reciprocal action, with numerous currents of thought. Within Judaism itself, various tendencies and mental types have found expression—legal and lyrical, national and universal, ritualist and rationalistic. "But one thing is clear," according to Dr. Kohler, "the core and center and purpose of Judaism (as they appear in Scripture and in the liturgy of the Synagogue in the form of teaching and hope) is the doctrine of the One only holy God and of the upbuilding and spread of His Kingdom of truth, righteousness, and peace in the world, and the development and propagation of that doctrine is indissolubly linked with it as the historic mission of the Jewish people." Judaism is a progressive religion, in the sense that it has passed through a process of evolution, while its goal is to hallow the life of the Jew, to fill it with spiritual radiance and ethical power, and to make Israel the priest-servant of mankind for the purpose of bringing about in the end the kingdom of God.

No phase of religious thought or practice is overlooked in Dr. Kohler's work. Whether it be divine love and justice or human duty, whether it be charity or revelation or immortality, whether it be the life of the synagogue or the relation of Judaism to other religions, all is discussed. Everywhere there are indications of the author's learning, but no less so of his temperament. While it is designed as an historic portrayal, the personal element is not absent. The entire book, which appeared in an English version in 1918, is written with warmth, with devotion and reverence, *con amore,* with such blend of love and reason as its author regarded as peculiar to Judaism itself, and, in spite of its polemic against non-Jewish doctrine, with generous recognition of the worth and work of other religions. It formed a fitting consummation to Dr. Kohler's years of toil in that field.

VIII

Retiring from the active presidency of the College, Dr. Kohler returned to New York. But that did not mean either withdrawal of interest from the College or cessation of literary work. On the contrary, he straightway set about certain new tasks. The Dante anniversary, in 1921, revived his interest in certain studies he had made of that poet, who appealed to the esthetic element in him, as well as the theologic. One of the fruits of his new leisure was a book on *Heaven and Hell,* published in 1923, wherein he traced Dante's eschatological conceptions back to various older creeds and mythologies. It was an essay in Comparative Religion and folklore; a return, in a way, to an old love of his university days. For the *Hebrew Union College Annual* he wrote an essay on the Origin and Composition of the Eighteen Benedictions and their relation to certain early Christian prayers—again a comparative study. But, above all, he devoted himself to a work which he had had in mind for many years, namely, on the Beginnings of the Synagogue and the Church, and their Interrelation.

That was a subject with which, in its diverse phases, he had dealt off and on for several decades, and concerning which he held definite views. The Synagogue he regarded as originally a creation of the biblical Hasidim, or Saints, from whom, in the course of time, sprang the

Essenes, who, in their turn, produced the first Christians. Jesus, he believed, was a disciple of the Essene ascetics, if not an actual member of their sect. At first, the Essenes were merely members of the Pharisaic group bent upon a rigorous exercise of religious duties and cultivation of the mystical virtues; but gradually they adopted certain concepts from alien sources and ended by being disowned by the Pharisees. Drifting more and more away from interest in the present life and into speculation about the hereafter, the Essenes inspired a good deal of what is known as Apocalyptic literature, the heroes of which were great figures of the past, such as Abraham, Enoch, and Moses. Out of their midst sprang the Christian Church, with its emphasis on the other world and with Jesus as its hero.

This subject, which Dr. Kohler had presented fragmentarily in previous writings, he meant now to treat as a whole. True, the theory of the interconnection of the Hasidim, the Essenes, and the early Christians was, as far back as 1867, rejected by Joseph Derenbourg (in his famous "Essay on the History and Geography of Palestine") as an attempt to explain the unknown by something equally unknown and obscure; and his view was shared by Abraham Geiger. But that did not daunt Dr. Kohler. He had actually finished his work, and revised half of it, when he died. The last article from his pen, however, which appeared before he passed away, was a contribution to the Jubilee Volume of the *Hebrew Union College Annual*, 1925, where, among other things, he advocated the establishment at the College of a Chair in the History of Religion, or Comparative Religion. It would, indeed, form a proper tribute to his memory if such a chair were created and associated with his name.

IX

"They are happy men," says Francis Bacon, "whose natures sort with their vocations." Dr. Kohler, I think, belonged to that class. Calling and character in his case went together. He was a born preacher, a trained scholar, and, withal, an indomitable idealist. The exalted dreams and hopes of the idealists never lost their hold upon him. It is a great thing, says the Roman moralist, to play the part of one man: *magnam rem puta unum hominem agere.* Such unity marked Dr. Kohler's life. "The Lord is my banner!" *Adonay nisi*—with that cry he began and closed his career.

The persistent unity of his thought was part of his greatness, but also of his romantic nature. A romantic he was, like his teacher, Samson Raphael Hirsch, though their goals lay far apart, and he himself disliked the term. To the one, romance meant a return to the past, a retention of the past, by no matter what fanciful means. To Dr. Kohler romance meant freedom, action, unhampered pursuit of truth. It meant re-forming of the past, spiritual mastery of the present, and adventure into the land of the prophetic future. A knight of the spirit was he. He believed in progress, and never ceased extolling it, whatever the say of latter-day cynics. It was man's distinctive mark, he held with Robert Browning.

> Progress, man's distinctive mark alone,
> Not God's and not the beasts': God is, they are;
> Man partly is, and wholly hopes to be.

Nor was his belief in the Mission of Israel blighted by recent attacks. Ideas and ideals live, he asserted.

His undying, undiminished enthusiasm, also, was part of his romantic nature. Others, though buoyant and fervid at the outset, have their disillusionments, their seasons of doubt, even bitter moments. Not so Dr. Kohler. One of those was he of whom the Psalmist says that in old age also they flourish. In his autumnal garden the roses of faith and hope still continued to bloom. He was active, ardent, enthusiastic to the very last—personifying, as well as professing, the deathless romance of the Jew.

H. G. Enelow

INTRODUCTION

"THERE is a time to tear down, and a time to build up; a time to cast away stones, and a time to gather stones together," says the Preacher. Ever since the beginning of our era of scientific and historical research we have been busy tearing down whatsoever seemed obsolete, lifeless and meaningless in religious practice, and have cast aside outgrown views and concepts that no longer appeared in harmony with the advanced thought of the cultured. The whole tendency of progress and freedom became destructive and antagonistic to the traditions and customs of the past; and faith, the soul and essence of religion, in contrast to mere reason, was sapped to the core. The consequence was gross materialism, predominance of selfishness and unbridled passion, and the increase of vice and crime in society. Obviously, however, a reaction is setting in and a more sober and salutary view of life is taking hold of the upper classes, of the leading men and women of to-day. True, the swing of the pendulum goes too much to the side of conservatism, so as to encourage, here and there, bigotry and fanaticism in the ruling Church. Still, idealism is gaining its way, and God and the things of the soul are being regarded more seriously. We have reached an age of reconstruction and regeneration in matters of faith. Religion is again becoming the controlling power of humanity; in the same measure it is recognized as the true arbiter in place of dogma.

Yet this must needs lead to a higher unity. However

slow this process will be—and what is a century when, "in the sight of God, a thousand years are but as yesterday when it is past?"—the various creeds must in time coalesce and grow into an all-encompassing faith in God and humanity, having the Messianic goal, the divine Kingdom of truth and righteousness, in view. It is to this end that Synagogue and Church, mother and daughter, must work together. This requires mutual understanding and an appreciation of each other's aims and achievements in history, despite the wide gulf that kept them apart during all the past centuries, despite all the discord and hatred, the persecution and tyranny displayed by the one, and all the unparalleled suffering and humiliation encountered by the other. For are they not branches of the same tree of life? Have they not, each in her own way, a common providential task to accomplish and a common historical goal in view? And since the great Jewish thinkers of the Middle Ages, such as Maimonides and Judah Halevi, had the vision and the courage to declare Christianity and Mohammedanism to have been selected by divine Providence as agencies to lead mankind ever nearer to the prophetic goal of one God and one humanity, all the more does it behoove us to-day, with our larger historic view of the past and our wider outlook into the future, to bring the relationship and kinship of Synagogue and Church to greater recognition.

It is well-nigh admitted by the Christian world that neither coercion nor persuasion will ever deflect the Jew from his unfaltering loyalty to his ancestral heritage. Nor is uniformity in matters of belief expected where the trends of mind and sentiment have throughout the ages been so wide apart. Still, there is undeniably a growing demand among the more enlightened for a closer approach, for a common meeting-ground and a coöperation in all matters pertaining to the moral and social uplift of man, and this can best be attained upon the basis of our common historic past. After all, it was the Hebrew Scripture, the so-called Old Testament, which molded and inspired both the Synagogue and the early Church, while the authors of the New Testament were, like Jesus, its central figure, Jews. Yea, the very names *Synagogue* and *Ecclesia*—the older name for Church retained only in the French, *l'Église*—are almost identical, being the Greek translations of the Hebrew *Edah* and *Kahal,* the "Congregation" or "Assembly" of the Lord, Aramaic *K'nishta* and Hebrew *K'neset,* terms used for the religious community of the Jews and of the early (Syrian) Christians. Only at a later time did the Christian Church adopt the name Ecclesia for its religious assembly, while the Jews and the Judeo-Christians adhered to the name Synagogue.[1]

As the message once came to Ezekiel the prophet: "Son of man, take thee one stick, and write upon it: For Judah;—then take another stick, and write upon it: For Joseph; and join them for thee one to another into one stick, that they may become *one* in thy hand!" so, we trust, some day another great seer will arise, pronouncing the message of reconciliation and reunion of Judaism and Christianity, blotting out hostility and prejudice forever, while rebuilding humanity on the foundation of faith in the one and only God of justice and of love. In the meantime mutual understanding and enlightenment must, while pointing to the common origin, bring us ever nearer to the goal.

[1] The name Church is derived from the Greek Kyriakon (doma) —the House of the Lord, which was adopted by Western Christianity, in place of the name Ecclesia, during the fourth or fifth century.

CONTENTS

PAGE

PREFACE v

A BIOGRAPHICAL ESSAY BY H. G. ENELOW . vii

INTRODUCTION xxxiii

BOOK I

CHAPTER

I. THE BEGINNINGS OF JUDAISM AND THE
   SYNAGOGUE 3

II. THE RESTORED TEMPLE AND ITS RULING
    PRIESTHOOD 7

III. THE LAIC CHARACTER OF THE SYNAGOGAL
     MOVEMENT 14

IV. THE PSALMS AND THEIR AUTHORS . . . 18

V. THE DEVOTIONAL ASSEMBLIES IN THE BABY-
   LONIAN EXILE AND THEIR LEADERS . . 25

VI. THE HASIDIM, THE MEN OF PRAYER . . 29

VII. THE ZADDIKIM AND HASIDIM IN THE PSALMS
     OF SOLOMON 33

VIII. THE EXCEEDING PIETY OF THE HASIDIM . 36

IX. THE HASIDIM, THE EMINENT CHARITY
    WORKERS 39

X. THE HASIDIM AND THE ORIENTAL OR MYS-
   TIC LORE 43

XI. THE HASIDIM AND THE SACRED NAME . . 49

XII. THE SH'MA YISRAEL AND ITS RESPONSE, A
     HASIDEAN INSTITUTION 53

XIII. THE TEFILLIN (PHYLACTERIES) AND THE
      ZIZIT (FRINGES) 61

CONTENTS

CHAPTER		PAGE
XIV.	THE DAILY PRAYERS OR THE EIGHTEEN, RESPECTIVELY, SEVEN BENEDICTIONS	65
XV.	THE SEVEN BENEDICTIONS FOR THE SABBATH AND HOLYDAYS	79
XVI.	THE SABBATH AND HOLYDAYS AS DEVELOPED BY THE HASIDIM	81
XVII.	THE MUSAF PRAYER	89
XVIII.	THE HALLEL AND OTHER PSALMS IN THE LITURGY	90
XIX.	THE READING FROM SCRIPTURE	92
XX.	THE BENEDICTIONS IN THE SYNAGOGAL LITURGY	95
XXI.	PROSTRATION AND ADORATION	100
XXII.	THE KEDUSHAH OF THE SCHOOLHOUSE, AND THE KADDISH	103
XXIII.	THE MAAMADOT SERVICE	106
XXIV.	THE HASIDIM AND THE PHARISEES	108
XXV.	THE ESSENES	117
XXVI.	PHARISAISM AS A SYSTEM	134
XXVII.	THE THREE CARDINAL PRINCIPLES OF JUDAISM DISTINCTIVE OF THE SYNAGOGUE	138
XXVIII.	THE PHARISAIC ETHICS	146
XXIX.	THE PHILANTHROPIC ACTIVITY OF THE SYNAGOGUE	151
XXX.	THE HOLYDAYS OF THE SYNAGOGUE AND THEIR MEANING	153
XXXI.	THE IDOLATOR, THE STRANGER, AND THE PROSELYTE	157
XXXII.	THE PHARISAIC ESCHATOLOGY	164
XXXIII.	THE APOCALYPTIC LITERATURE	170

BOOK II

CHAPTER   PAGE

I. THE CONDITIONS OF JEWRY BEFORE THE RISE OF CHRISTIANITY 203

II. JOHN THE BAPTIST 206

III. THE JESUS OF THE GOSPELS AND THE HISTORICAL JESUS 211

IV. THE BEGINNINGS OF THE CHURCH . . . 232

V. THE ESSENES AND THE EARLY CHURCH . 238

VI. THE EARLY CHURCH AND THE SADDUCEAN AUTHORITIES 241

VII. THE SO-CALLED APOSTOLIC LITERATURE, COMPRISING THE TEACHING AND THE LITURGY OF THE EARLY CHURCH 247

VIII. PAUL, THE APOSTLE TO THE HEATHEN, AND THE CHRISTIAN CHURCH 260

IX. THE GNOSTIC SECTS 271

NOTES 277

BOOK I

THE ORIGINS OF THE SYNAGOGUE AND THE CHURCH

CHAPTER I

THE BEGINNINGS OF JUDAISM AND THE SYNAGOGUE

All beginnings of things are wrapt in darkness. Deep down in the soil, beneath the surface, all new life germinates, hidden from the eye of the observer. Then all of a sudden, on a warm spring day, the new vegetation sprouts forth from the ground, after it had been slowly growing and ripening during the long winter season under the frost-decked cover. The same process takes place in history, where the great movements which give rise to new epochs come to view unobserved in their origins and first stages. Thus, the so-called four centuries of silence which lie between the fall of Babylon and the Maccabean era, forming the seed-time of the new religious life of Israel, seem all of a sudden to have given rise to new forms and views, while in reality they have nurtured, amidst the great national crisis in the innermost depth of the people's soul, that spiritual growth which came as a new creation to the light of day. This was the cradle period of Judaism. And because its working is concealed from our view, owing to the lack of information in our Biblical sources concerning this period, a wide chasm yawns between pre-exilic Israel and post-exilic Judaism across which our historians would not venture to build the bridge.

3

True enough, Rabbinic tradition, based upon the acceptance of the so-called Oral Law along with the Written Law as divinely revealed to Moses on Mount Sinai, evades the difficulty by assuming that an authoritative body of one hundred and twenty men, consisting of the last three prophets, Haggai, Zechariah, and Malachi, and the first generation of Scribes with Ezra and Nehemiah at their head, known as the Men of the Great Synagogue, formed the direct line of successors to Moses, Joshua, the Elders and the Prophets, thereby connecting the pre-exilic and post-exilic periods. But this artificial chain of tradition, presented in the first Mishnah of Abot, was obviously constructed for the purpose of entwining the Soferic, or Rabbinic, interpretation of the Mosaic Code with the Written Law; it ignores the real factors of the process of development of the Law. It takes no cognizance of the priesthood of either the first or the second Temple, to whom the Pentateuchal Code chiefly owes its existence, as well as its early execution; and moreover it represents the Prophets, the pronounced opponents—down to Ezekiel, the priest-prophet—of the whole priestly ritualism, as the recipients and transmitters of the Law. For us this chain of tradition has no historical value whatsoever.. It is not only in striking contrast to the results of modern Bible criticism, which sees in the Pentateuchal Code the work of many centuries from Moses to Ezra, but it also assumes the existence of an organized body, such as the Men of the Great Synagogue at the time of Ezra and Nehemiah, of which no trace can be found anywhere. All that we know is that an assembly of eighty-five men, enumerated in Neh. 10:2-29, signed the constitution of the new Judean Commonwealth. These, together with the men mentioned in Neh. 8:4-7 and 9:4-5, and the last three prophets, possibly made up the number of one hundred and twenty,[1] and this probably led the Rabbis to the assumption of a permanent Great Assembly to which the various Synagogal institutions were to be ascribed.

All the more surprising is the fact that so few modern historians who follow the records of Josephus and the New Testament, instead of the Talmudic sources, in regard to the post-exilic period, pay due attention to the beginnings of Judaism, and particularly to its most genuine creation, the Synagogue, which by far eclipsed in power and influence the Temple of Jerusalem and gave birth to both the Church and the Mosque. True, the people during the Exile, despite the strong denunciation of the priesthood and of animal sacrifices by the great pre-exilic prophets, were anxious to see the Temple restored, as Ezekiel had foretold, believing that only there God's presence would be manifested; and, after the promulgation of the Mosaic Code by Ezra the Scribe as the sole regulative power of the new commonwealth, the Temple with its hierarchy did indeed become the central and dominating force of the people and their religion, besides which the Synagogue, called as it was "the little sanctuary," after Ezek. 11:16, could at best claim only a secondary rank. Still, the real dynamic and spiritual power, the fashioner and constant refashioner of Judaism in the various lands and ages, was the Synagogue, the house of common prayer and public instruction in charge of the pious and learned men from among the laity, who finally wrested the Torah from the priesthood and created the religious democracy of Judaism. Here the Law was expounded and developed in the spirit of progress so as to adapt it to the ever new requirements of time and environment. Here the people's loftiest hopes and aspirations were voiced in the divine service.

Here the soul of Judaism found its truest expression in continuity with the prophetic spirit of old. In striking contrast to the imposing priestly pomp of the Temple with its animal sacrifice and smoke of incense, for which also Haggai and Zechariah zealously waited, there loomed up in the Synagogue a new and simple form of worship which, together with the appealing popular method of reading and expounding the Scripture to the assembly, invested the Jewish religion with a spirituality unknown and undreamt of before, and gave it that democratic character which enabled its influence to become world-wide, going far beyond the boundaries of state and nation. Indeed, the genius of Israel, which produced the prophets, the true exponents of religion for humanity, created in the institution of the Synagogue what no religion previously had possessed, a house of real communion of the soul with God, "a house of prayer for all peoples."

Where, then, shall we look for those men, endowed with a divine spirit that prompted them to find this altogether new way of bringing the people nigh to their God and making them realize that they were indeed "a congregation of the Lord," "a kingdom of priests and a holy nation"? The Rabbis and other ancient writers, lacking the modern historic sense, ascribed the institution of the Synagogue to Moses.[2] Nor is the problem solved by the attempt of Leopold Loew to identify "the house of the people," in Jer. 39:8, with the Synagogue, or by the similar theory of Dr. Samuel Krauss that the Synagogue was originally a communal house.[3] The question is not in what place the devotional assemblies were held at first, but how, when, and by whom they were started so as to become a permanent institution; and to this no satisfactory answer has, I think, as yet been given.

CHAPTER II

The Restored Temple and Its Ruling Priesthood

The great unknown author of the last chapter of Isaiah, called the Trito-Isaiah, certainly strikes a deeper note of religion than was common, when he begins: "Thus saith the Lord: The heaven is My throne, and the earth is My footstool; where is the house that ye may build unto Me? and where is the place that may be My resting-place? For all these things hath My hand made, and so all these things came to be, saith the Lord; but on this man will I look, even on him that is humble and of a contrite spirit, and trembleth at My word." Here no room is left for a sacrificial cult and a privileged priesthood; only an upward look of man to his Maker, such as is implied in prayer, is demanded. All along, however, religion had been the concern of a class of men privileged to approach the Deity with sacrifice and similar rites of worship. Such were the priests. Nor was it different with ancient Israel. It was only the great prophets, proclaiming the God of Sinai as the God of justice, of mercy and holiness, demanding righteous conduct instead of sacrifices, that gave religion a new meaning. They deprecated priestly ritualism, insisting instead on pure morality in action and thought. But this view was far beyond the grasp of the people, who, prone to idolatry, remained deaf to the words of the prophets until they were chastened by one catastrophe after the other. Then they repented of their constant backslid-

7

ings. The Northern Kingdom was entirely swept away by Assyria's conquerors; only the little Kingdom of Judah, greatly diminished, became "the saving remnant." Its dominant priesthood, the house of Zadok, then undertook, in the name of Moses, the ancient lawgiver, to remold the inherited legislation so as to eliminate as far as possible the vestiges of idolatrous practices and render Israel a nation "Holy unto the Lord," giving it a religious, instead of a merely political, character. This reform was brought about under King Josiah by the promulgation of the Book of Deuteronomy in which, on the one hand, the prophetic principles of justice, love and holiness were to a large extent embodied, and, on the other, the claims of the Jerusalemic priesthood, as sole functionaries at the altar, were upheld, to the exclusion of all other places of worship and their priesthoods. The ideas voiced in Deuteronomy prevailed in the end, and Babylonia became the iron furnace from which Israel emerged, like a phoenix rising from the ashes, regenerated as the people of Judaism.

But then two prophets of widely different types and views arose to determine its course. On the one hand, there was the priest-prophet Ezekiel, who in his vision of the Dry Bones foretold the resurrection of all Israel, having its Jerusalemic Temple, with its sacrificial cult in charge of the Zadokites, as its center. Moreover, he offered a system of ritualism of his own, which subsequently gave rise, first, to the Holiness Code in Leviticus, and, then, to the Priest Code adopted by Ezra and further developed in the form in which we now have it in the Pentateuch. On the other hand, there was the unnamed Seer of the Exile, the so-called Deutero-Isaiah, who, soaring to the highest realms of prophetic vision, beheld Israel's destination amidst its dispersion over the globe to consist in becoming "a light to the nations and a covenant interlinking all the peoples on earth"; "the covenant of the Lord," and its very afflictions to be designed for the healing of the nations. With his universalistic views, conceived under the influence of the world-wide conquests of Cyrus, the broad-minded Persian king, this prophet would dispense with priests and sacrifices, while pointing to Zion as the future religious center of humanity. But such lofty anticipations were, like those of the ancient prophets, beyond the reach of the people in general, and only formed the hope and outlook of a distant future.[1]

As a matter of fact, the national restoration, with its sacerdotal center of religious life, became the sole object of the Exile, and the whole history of the past was accordingly construed in this light. Even the tabernacle in the wilderness was portrayed after the pattern of the Solomonic Temple, and the sons of Zadok, the first high priests officiating there, were, as the only legitimate priests, transformed into the sons of Aaron, the brother of Moses the lawgiver. They alone were declared (in the Holiness and Priest Codes) to be admissible to the priestly office, whereas the other Levites who officiated as priests at the now tabooed shrines were, in accordance with Ezek. 44:6-14, reduced to subordinate functions outside of the sanctuary. Thus the Temple became, as among other nations, the monopoly of the priesthood, and their hierarchical system was fully outlined in the Priest and Holiness Codes. The laity was, at the penalty of death, excluded from the sanctuary and from any participation in the rites of worship, or from having any share in the preparation of the holy incense. At the same time no provision whatsoever was made for common prayer or any form of worship by the laity. Thus the ancient pagan principle of the priest's aloofness from the people was retained, and the distinction between things sacred and profane, between clean and unclean, based upon the primitive taboo system and underlying the Levitical purity laws, not only remained in force but grew in rigidity under the priestly dominion, assuming a position far superior to the ethical laws.

And this hierarchical system invested the Sadducean priesthood with all the power and authority of the Law, and made it the embodiment of sanctity, which was the inherent claim of all Israel as "a kingdom of priests and a holy nation." Already in prophetic and pre-prophetic times the priests usurped the rights of the laity, demanding a share of all its possessions, and now all this was fixed by strict regulations of the Priest Code. Above all did the high priest, as the chief of the sanctuary, obtain powers which even the king in his best days did not possess. He claimed the prerogative of offering from his own treasury, as his personal gift on behalf of the people, the daily burnt-offerings ordained by the Law,[2] stressing the term, "Thou shalt offer," which the Pharisean teachers applied to the people.[3] But especially significant were the functions of the high priest on the Day of Atonement on which all the sins committed by the people, aside from those pertaining to the sanctuary, were to be expiated by him.[4] Though the rite concerning the goat to be sent out to Azazel, the demon of the wilderness, believed to dwell in the ravines of the rock Bet Haduda near Jerusalem, is but a strange revival of paganism—the goat to be offered to the Lord at the Temple being a later addition—the day's service culminated in the high priest's entrance into the Holy of Holies, where, upon the lid of the holy ark, called the Mercy-seat, the Deity, invisible to the eyes of common

mortals, was enthroned in mysterious darkness. Wrapt
in the smoke of incense kindled by him before entering,
lest he be struck by the awful sight,[5] he performed there
the rite of atonement for the sanctuary, his own household and the people at large, while making confession of
their sins. He then solemnly pronounced the ineffable
Name, while declaring the whole Congregation of Israel
to be free from guilt. Upon hearing the Name pronounced in awe, all prostrated themselves and blessed the
glorious Name of the Lord. There he also offered a
solemn prayer for the prosperity of the land during the
coming year; but he was especially warned not to tarry
too long in this awful place, lest he frighten the people
waiting outside.[6] As a matter of fact, particularly
worthy high priests, such as was Simon the Just, claimed
to have had on this occasion visions of the Deity, or to
have heard a voice of prophetic character, as did John
Hyrcanus.[7] The pronunciation of the sacred Name
while blessing the people[8] remained during the Temple
time the exclusive privilege of the priests.

In conformity with Deut. 17:8f., 33:10, the priests at
first constituted the High Court of Justice at the
Temple; and in the hands of the high priest as the head
of the High Court lay the regulation of the Calendar,
just as the Pontifex Maximus at Rome fixed the same
each month. After the appearance of each new moon,
the high priest proclaimed the new month, and so was
the beginning of each year in spring fixed by him with a
view to the state of the crops.

Strange to say, the Zadokite priesthood, with the exception of Ezek. 43:19, 44:15 and 2 Chron. 31:10, is
nowhere mentioned in our Biblical and post-Biblical records, and only Dr. Schechter's fortunate discovery of a

Temple hymn in the Hebrew Ben Sira, 51, 12f., in which
God is praised for having "chosen the sons of Zadok to
be priests," has evidenced the fact that the ruling priests
before the Maccabean era belonged to the house of
Zadok; thus confirming the opinion long ago expressed
by Abraham Geiger that they were identical with the
Sadducees spoken of by Josephus and the New Testament, as the ruling priestly aristocracy. To these belonged Simon the Just, Ben Sira's contemporary, praised
alike by him and the Talmudic records for his many
excellent traits as a loyal high priest. It was only under
the deteriorating influence of Syrian paganism that the
Sadducees degenerated into an arrogant and disloyal
party, so as to become in Talmudic tradition a heretic
sect. As long, however, as they remained loyal executors
of the Torah there was no dispute as to their higher
rank. In fact, they strictly adhered to a literal execution
of the Law, whether in regard to the beginning of the
seven harvest weeks and their festal conclusion with the
Pentecost [9] or in regard to the principle of retaliation,[10]
seldom yielding to common sense in the execution of Justice[11] unless forced to do so by the Pharisees when they
came to power. The peculiar rites of lustration, so
indicative of priestly sanctity, and particularly the preparation of the ashes of the Red Heifer for the purification
of unclean persons [12] so puzzling to the Rabbis, were not
merely strictly observed by the priests, but further extended in practice.[13] Moreover, as if they were cast in
a different mold to form a class of their own, if not a
higher caste, the ruling priesthood would marry within
their own class only, or at best with the old patrician
families.[14] In their arrogance they indulged in saying:
"Stand by thyself, come not near to me, for I am holier
than thou." [15] Allied as they were with the aristocracy

of wealth, they boasted all the more of their aristocracy of blood.

The great change came when their disloyalty under the Syrian reign brought about the revolt of the Hasidim, the pious men from among the laity who, by their democratic views and their interpretation of the Law in the spirit of progress, succeeded in pushing the Sadducean views and practices aside as "heretical." The destruction of the Temple put an end to the whole Sadducean party, including the Boethusians, the *homines novi* created by King Herod, the son-in-law of Simon Boethus, who had endeavored to revive the Sadducean practices. Afterwards the very meaning of the two party names was forgotten, as is shown by the legend told in Abot de-Rabbi Nathan c. 5.[16]

CHAPTER III

The Laic Character of the Synagogal Movement

A quaint legend in the Talmud [1] relates that the men of the Great Synagogue, under the leadership of the prophet Zechariah, resorted to the use of the ineffable Name in order to banish the Evil Desire which was wont to seduce the people in the Holy Land to the practice of idolatry. Yet, no sooner had they done so than they found that without the Evil Desire, which engenders animal passion, the sexes would not commingle, the hens would not lay, and the whole order of earthly life would come to a standstill. So they gave up the fight against the Evil Desire in general and retained the ban only against idolatry.

There is a deeper truth hidden in this strange story. It is the recognition of the striking fact that the Jews of the period of the second Temple manifested an altogether different religious spirit from those of the first. Out of the fiery furnace of the Babylonian captivity emerged a new people, no longer prone to idolatry, or "rebellious," as Ezekiel repeatedly called them. Realizing with bitter remorse the truth of the stern prophetic warnings, "they turned to the Lord in the land of their captivity" and "sought Him with all their heart and with all their soul," as stated in Deut. 4:27f.; 30:1-10. Still, as they lived in "the land of the stranger," which according to the prevailing view was regarded as unclean,[2] they felt themselves "cast off by their God." [3]

Their priests could not approach Him after the prescribed mode of worship, nor offer any expiatory sacrifice for them, and they could only anxiously wait for the
time of the restoration of the sanctuary on His holy
mountain, as predicted by Ezekiel.[4]

But here the point of a new departure was reached in
Judaism, of which all records fail to take due notice
and which marks a new epoch in the history of religion.
There were those who in their deep yearning for God
felt the need of entering into closer personal relation
with Him without the mediatorship of priesthood and
sacrifice, by simply pouring out their soul to Him in
prayer, as did Jeremiah and many a man of God before.
And here we notice that just as Moses in Egypt went
out of the city to commune with God in prayer,[5] or as
Ezekiel in Babylonia received his visions on the River
Chebar, so did the pious men there try to find a new
way of communing with God in turning their faces
toward the site of the Temple in Jerusalem. This was
done not only by Daniel,[6] but is strikingly brought out
also in the Dedication Prayer of King Solomon,[7] which
was composed in the Exile, as is evidenced by the following paragraph:

If they sin against Thee and Thou be angry with
them, and deliver them to the enemy, so that they
carry them away captive unto the land of the
enemy, far off or near, yet if they shall bethink
themselves in the land whither they are carried
captive, and turn back, and make supplication unto
Thee . . . if they return unto Thee with all their
heart . . . and pray unto Thee *toward their land,
which Thou gavest unto their fathers, the city which
Thou hast chosen, and the house which I have built
for Thy name;* then hear Thou their prayer and

their supplication in heaven Thy dwelling-place, and maintain their cause; and forgive Thy people . . . and give them compassion before those who carried them captive.[8]

It is plain that this prayer, which contains no reference to the sacrifices to be brought in the Temple, but speaks only of the prayers to be offered by the people *toward* the holy land and the holy city with its Temple, has only the practice of the people in the Exile in view, a practice kept up by the Jewish people ever since. And it is not improbable that the words of Trito-Isaiah 56:7: "My house shall be called a house of prayer for all peoples," are to be taken in the same sense that the nations all over the world shall direct their prayers toward the Temple at Jerusalem as their religious center —the *Kiblah*—as in the Temple proper prayers were not offered by the people.

At any rate, the spirit of devotion and prayer which made itself felt in the early period of the Exile led to the beginnings of the Synagogue.[9] Thus, the people, lamenting over the fall of Zion, assembled on the shores of the streams of Babylon for their devotional prayer and song,[10] and from Zech. 7:5f. we learn that on the memorial days of their great national disaster the people held devotional assemblies amidst fasting and prayer.

Still the question with which we are chiefly concerned is: To whom are we to ascribe the introduction of regular prayer in these assemblies, no matter whether they had specific places arranged for them or not? After all, we must not overlook the important fact that, however highly we estimate the achievements of the ancient prophets for Judaism as the unique ethical force of life, however powerful their appeal to the human conscience, it is none the less true that when Amos dwelt upon God's

stern reign of justice, or Hosea pointed to His inexhaustible mercy and forgiveness, and Isaiah portrayed
in unique impressiveness His sublime holiness, they failed
to voice the essential need of religion, which consists in
the soul's yearning for a Power higher than ourselves,
in whom alone we can find rest and peace amidst life's
vicissitudes. While denouncing in the most vigorous
terms the priestly cult in the Temple as routine performance, which, instead of promoting righteous conduct,
rather encouraged unrighteousness, they did not, as they
might have done, emphasize all the more the value of
sincere devotion and true worship and thus bring out
the positive side of religion as the concern of the individual. Even Jeremiah, who in his life of trial learned
to seek God in prayer, has only words of reproach for
the Temple and its priesthood, but hardly a syllable in
favor of common devotion. Only the distressing conditions of the Exile brought about a change; and so we
find devotional assemblies longing for words of comfort,
such as were offered by the great seer of the Exile.[11]
Here, indeed, the souls of the people are stirred to seek
God in penitence and prayer, and there are those elect
ones who are especially responsive to the appeal and
destined to form the nucleus of a regenerated Israel.[12]
And this spirit found its deepest resonance in that unique
branch of Jewish literature which has exerted the mighti-
est influence upon religion by giving expression to the
human longing and yearning after God, namely, the
Psalms.

CHAPTER IV

The Psalms and Their Authors

True enough, prayer and song in connection with the sacrifices were not peculiar to Israel. Not to speak of the invocation of the Deity at every shrine of worship by the priest or any person ministering at the altar, there is the ancient Babylonian liturgy which formed the prototype of the Psalms in its form of composition and its diction. All the more puzzling is the fact that the Mosaic Code nowhere provides for this higher element of worship alongside of sacrifice; nor was such a provision made at the rebuilding of the Temple after the Exile. Obviously the need of such was not yet felt by the people. Also individual prayers, such as Hannah offered at Shiloh's sanctuary, to judge from the story, must have been rare. Singularly enough the older term for praying was *he'ethir,*[1] which means offering the smoke of sacrifice; and some such sacrifice, instead of prayer, was resorted to in a time of pestilence, as we learn from 2 Sam. 24:25; Num. 17:9-15. Even the usual word for prayer, *hithpallel,* which means asking God for intercession, we find primarily used for prayers in behalf of others, as in the case of Abraham and Moses, Samuel and Isaiah, Jeremiah and Job.[2] At any rate, regular prayers by the people were unknown in the pre-exilic period. Wellhausen[3] thinks that Jeremiah, in wrestling with God in his great trials, gave rise to the spirit of prayer and devotion which pervades the Psalms, and thus became the true father of prayer. Be that as it may, the deep yearning for God and the perfect trust and confident hope voiced in the Psalms are found nowhere else in literature. Such words of faith as are offered in Ps. 73:25-28: "Whom have I in heaven but Thee? and beside Thee I desire none on earth. . . . The nearness of God is my good," have no parallel anywhere, nor can the Penitential Psalm 51 be compared with the so-called Penitential Psalms of Assyria, not to speak of the Prayer of Moses, Ps. 90, the Creation Psalm, 104, or the unique description of God's omnipresence, in Ps. 139.

The Psalmists opened for all time the floodgates of devotion and prayer by voicing, in accents of lyric power and beauty before unheard of, the various emotions of the human soul, its deepest longings and its highest aspirations, its sighs of woe and contrition and its rapturous songs of thanksgiving and joy. While sounding forth, as it were, with their harp and lyre the whole keyboard of the human heart, echoing now its saddest notes of distress and despair, of bitter remorse and dismay, and then again its most serene accords of hope, trust and peace, they carried the worshiping assembly upon wings of devotion to the very throne of Him who dwelt no longer upon the Cherubim of the Ark, as of old, but, as Ps. 22:4 has it, upon the praises of Israel. Thus, the sacrificial cult of the Temple was more than replaced by the spiritual outpourings of a devout assembly, and the road was paved to the Synagogue with its congregational hymns and prayers.

Now before asking for the authorship of the Psalms, we must distinguish between the older ones, which were the outpourings of individuals who in some way or other yearned for divine help and offered their thanksgiving for having obtained it, and the later ones, which were either composed in their entirety for the Temple or the Congregation, or were by alterations, insertions and additions transformed into Temple hymns, the Ego there standing for the Congregation of Israel. To the former belong most of those in the first three books, which have retained their individual strain without undergoing essential alterations. A small number of these, however, are real Temple hymns, and they take little, if any, cognizance of the sacrificial cult. In fact, Pss. 40 and 51 directly oppose it; Ps. 69:31 does so indirectly, and the rest, with the exception of the King Psalms 20 and 66:13-15, ignore it, dwelling instead on the songs and prayers. Others again, such as Pss. 15, 24:1-6, 18 and 19, stress the ethical and spiritual side of religion. Nowhere, in fact, is the spirit of the Priest Code or the priesthood voiced in any of these, and we can think of the Psalmists only as the successors of the prophets.

It is unnecessary to-day any longer to argue that the headings of the Psalms, which ascribe them to King David in accordance with the Books of Chronicles, have no historical value. They were written at a late period when the Psalter had become a Temple hynmal in charge of the Levitical guilds of singers. But it has been well pointed out by Graetz in his valuable Introduction to his Commentary on the Psalms [1] that, in view of the Levites officiating as singers under Ezra and Nehemiah, we have every reason to surmise that the Levitical singers were also the poets, as was the case throughout antiquity. This is indeed confirmed by the fact that the authors of the Psalms refer to their own song and play on the harp and the lyre, while praising God amidst the Congregational worship. Graetz, however, commits an error fatal to his theory in assuming that these Levites

functioned during the first Temple. This is contradicted
first of all by the Book of Deuteronomy, which still
identifies the Levites with the priests, and then most
decidedly by Ezekiel who, as we have seen, shows the
Levites to have been the former priests of "the high
places" who were degraded to inferior positions outside
of the Temple, but he knows nothing as yet of their
having been appointed to be singers at the Temple, as
we find them in the Books of Chronicles. But the matter
offers a different aspect when we think of the Levites
during and after the Babylonian Exile. To them the
terms *Ebionim* and *Aniyim*—"the poverty-stricken"—
used frequently by the Psalmists, actually apply, since,
owing to their inferior status, they were so reduced in
circumstances as to be constantly harassed by the arrogant ruling class of priests and other superiors, as is so
vividly described in the older Psalms. Moreover, their
very depression and misfortune tended to arouse in them
the deeper emotions, the spiritual side of religion, which
the Zadokite priesthood lacked. Being descendants of
the Northern priesthood, which no doubt came into
closer contact with the Syrian or Assyrian culture than
did the ones in the South, many of these Levites were
more apt to cultivate and develop the art of music and
song, or Psalmody itself, than were the priests who had
officiated at the Temple of Jerusalem. Others, again,
had more time and opportunity to devote themselves to
the study of the national literature than had the Zadokite priesthood, for whom the punctilious observances
of the Temple rites was the paramount task. Hence
we see the Levites, who had hesitated both under Zerubabel and Ezra to join the priests in their return to
Palestine but afterwards came there in larger numbers,
distinguish themselves as *Mebinim*, "the teachers," either

in music and song or in the Law.[5] Obviously the author
of Ps. 137, when referring to the songs of Zion, speaks
as a member of the Levites. But most characteristic is
the exilic song, Pss. 42-43 (which John P. Peters [6] with
fine critical acumen ascribed to a former priest of the
sanctuary at Dan, near the source of the Jordan, who,
in his longing for the living God, prayed for the *Urim
We-Tumim* oracle to lead him back to God's holy mountain). Every line of this magnificent lyric poem indicates the singer's thorough familiarity with the peculiar-
ity of the wonderful spot and its rushing cataracts. And
what is especially significant is that, instead of referring
to the sacrificial cult practiced there, he speaks only of
"his song which was with him day and night," and with
his harp he offers God his thanksgiving hymn.[7] Surely
only a Levite could have spoken thus. Likewise, the
words: "I will sing unto the Lord," in Pss. 13:6, 27:6,
28:7, or the Korahite's words in Pss. 47:2, 8, 57:8,
59:17, 61:9, 69:31 must decidedly be ascribed to the
Levites.

As Graetz has pointed out,[8] two names stand out con-
spicuously in the older Psalms: the *Anavim,* "the devout
ones"; and the *Hasidim,* "the saintly ones." The
former, as was shown by Rahlfs [9] in his suggestive little
work, *Ani and Anav in the Psalms,* derived their name
from their submissiveness to God's decrees as "they,
under the influence of the Exile and its hardships, became
true followers of the prophetic teachings, and with
implicit faith in God bore their affliction in humble recognition of the divine justice, looking confidently forward to the ultimate triumph of their cause." They
formed, says Rahlfs, the nucleus of regenerated Israel,
typifying Deutero-Isaiah's "Servant of the Lord" who

"gave his back to the smiters and his cheek to the revilers," and he ascribes to them with convincing arguments Pss. 9-10 in the original form; Pss. 12, 25, 36, 37 and 49, not to speak of others he mentions. Besides these are the *Hasidim,* "the saintly ones," the men of faithfulness and piety.[10] Whether used in the singular or in the plural, the term *Hasid* always denotes the faithful one, the saintly or pious one, and is with few exceptions, such as Ps. 50:5, applied only to the Levites. Especially instructive are Pss. 89:20 and 132:9, 16, where the priests are represented as "clothed with victory" (*Zedek,* an allusion to the sons of Zadok) and the Levites as "the Hasidim who shout for joy."

Evidently, then, the Levites had taken a prominent part in the composition of the Psalms long before the Psalter was made the Temple hymnal under the direction of the Levitical singers' guilds. We also find them placed by Ezra at his side to open the service with prayer and also to assist him in the reading and expounding of the Book of Law,[11] and the very form with which they opened the service remained typical for the Synagogue and likewise for the Church service. In all likelihood these Levites, among whom the sons of Asaph are especially mentioned as functioning with their instruments alongside of the priests under Zerubabel and Joshua the high priest,[12] appeared first at the devotional assemblies of the laity before they were admitted to Temple functions, in which they well-nigh eclipsed the priesthood by their music and song. Later on the Zadokite priests, in their jealousy, did their utmost to keep them down; but they were too firmly entrenched in their position as musicians and singers to be subdued, and the Chronicler, himself a Levite, shows them to have been standing in the foreground of the Temple service. And here the question arises, What became of them when the Temple sank? This must be answered in the next chapters, where the Hasidim loom up as the spiritual power of the Synagogue.

CHAPTER V

THE DEVOTIONAL ASSEMBLIES IN THE BABYLONIAN EXILE AND THEIR LEADERS

The Mosaic Codes, beginning with Deuteronomy, speak of Israel not so much as a political nation as they do of the Congregation, *Edah,* or "the Assembly, *Kahal,* of the Lord" in the sense of a religious community— names which correspond with the Aramaic *K'nishta,* the Hebrew *K'neset,* and the Greek *Synagoge* (Synagogue) and *Ecclesia* (Church) (French *l'Église*). As a religious community Israel survived after the downfall of the nation. In speaking of "the Congregation," or "the Congregations," or of "the Assembly of the people," the "Assembly of the holy ones," or "of the saints" (Hasidim) by which "God is exalted" or "praised," the Psalmists have in view devotional assemblies of the people, not the Temple which then no longer existed. Only before a large assembly of pious laymen did the prophets utter their powerful denunciation of the sacrificial cult with its special appeal to the priests as God's faithful ones (Hasidim); and the same may be said of Pss. 49 and 78. So are all the Deutero-Isaianic addresses best understood when taken as appeals to audiences that were to be won for the higher prophetic ideal and a more spiritual concept of Israel's truth. The same holds good also of the exhortatory portions of Deuteronomy, such as 10:12—11:32 and 29:9—30:20. Moreover, in the numerous passages inserted in the prophecies of Isaiah,

25

Micah and Jeremiah, and containing Deutero-Isaianic
ideas of Israel as the priest-people, we can find only the
higher aspirations of the few elect, in contrast to the
hopes of the people for a restoration of the Temple,
denounced by Ezekiel and his school. Yet this was but the
result of a laic movement started among "the devout"
and "saintly ones" who "trembled with awe at the word
of God." [1]   In the course of time these became the
creators of the Synagogue, and, nurtured as they were
by the spirit of the ancient prophets, they succeeded
afterwards in introducing the reading of their "words of
comfort" alongside of the Torah, at "the dismissal" of
the Congregation, "the *Haftarah,*" in order to have
the Messianic hope voiced for the encouragement of the
people amidst the tribulations of the Exile.   Later on the
real origin of the Haftarah was forgotten and all sorts
of conjectures arose about it. [2]

As to the reading from the Torah, its origin as a
rule is ascribed to Ezra, the Scribe, but it apparently
dates from the Exile, as the very fact that the people in
unison asked Ezra to bring the book of the Law of
Moses and have it read to them [3] seems to show that such
reading was not altogether an innovation. The Torah,
or the Book of Law, had from of old been in charge of
the priests who, like the Scribes, functioned as the
teachers and custodians of the Law, as we learn from
Deut. 31:9, 24. [4] From these, then, emanated the guild
of the Soferim, the Scribes, who compiled and from time
to time revised or recomposed the Codes of Law. As
the name *Sofer* denotes, they were primarily those skilled
in writing and then became the professional bookmen. In
all likelihood it was due to their efforts that in place
of the archaic Hebrew alphabet, still in use among the
Samaritans, and found in ancient Hebrew inscriptions

and on coins of a later period—the old pictorial form to which the letters owe their Phœnician names—our square letters, called the Assyrian script and adopted from the Aramaic writing, were introduced. The change probably intended to give the sacred Scripture a more dignified hieratic character in contrast to the writing of the common people (*Hediotot*). The Talmud says that Ezra was prompted by the holy spirit to make the change, according to Ezra 4:7.[5] Such a change, however, is not the work of one man, but must be regarded as a gradual process extending over a considerable period. As a matter of fact, the simple square letters were more adapted to the multiplication of copies of the Book of Law for general use in the various Synagogues.

No matter, then, whether Ezra the Scribe had any predecessor or not, in the official decree of King Artaxerxes he is called "the priest, the scribe of the Law of the God of heaven."[6] In this capacity he came to Jerusalem with the Book of the Law of Moses and had it read before the people assembled "before the broad place that was before the water gate,"[7] and the very choice of this public square, instead of the Temple mount, is significant enough to indicate its connection with the exilic devotional assemblies.

Whatever his share was in the composition of the Book of Law, it is certain that it was not the complete Pentateuch which he read, as a comparison of Neh. 8:14-18 with Lev. 23:40, and especially the omission of the Day of Atonement, amply shows. Evidently the work of the composition of the Code was continued by his successors until it reached the final form in which it has come down to us, and we may well assume that he was not the first scribe engaged in the great work. After the Code had received the final form at the hand of the

Soferim, they endeavored to harmonize the many differences and contradictory passages by their interpretation of the text, but at the same time they occasionally
corrected it, as the Talmudic tradition still speaks of the
Tikkune Soferim, the textual corrections of the Scribes;
but in these the late translators of the Scripture still had
a hand, as is amply shown by Geiger.[8] But these Scribes
introduced also many new precepts and practices in
accordance with the requirements of the time, and their
teachings, called *Dibre Soferim,* were laid down in Halakic rules forming part of the Oral Law and were afterwards codified in the Mishnah.[9] Considering all this, we
come to the conclusion that the devotional assemblies of
the Babylonian Exile had, on the one hand, the Hasidim
as the men of prayer and song, and, on the other, the
Soferic readers and expounders of the Law as leaders;
and we find both combined in the Maccabean time.[10]

CHAPTER VI

THE HASIDIM, THE MEN OF PRAYER

Sufficient attention has not been paid to the remarkable fact that the pre-exilic writings contain but few genuine prayers, and that only since the Exile have public and common prayers held a conscipuous place in the life and literature of the people. The prayers put into the mouth of King David[1] and into that of King Jehoshaphat,[2] Ezra's prayer[3] and Daniel's,[4] have the true ring of prayer. Add to these those in Ben Sira 36:1-17; 51:1-12ff.; Tobit 3:1ff.; 8:5ff.; 13:1-18; Judith c.9; 13:4ff.; 16:2ff.; 1 Macc. 4:31ff.; 2 Macc. 14:35-36; 15:22f.; 3 Macc. 2:2f.; 6:2f.; Baruch 2:11f.; 3:8; the Prayer of Manasseh, and the various prayers in the Book of Enoch and the Baruch Apocalypse. They all lead us to surmise that they owe their origin to a special class of men, namely, the Hasidim, such as had "the high praises of God in their mouth and a two-edged sword in their hand,"[5] powerful personalities of the type of Jose ben Joezer (misspelt *Razis* in 2 Macc. 14:37), the leader of Separatism and father of the Jews (Hasidim?), whose tragic death as martyr is also alluded to in Gen. R. 61:18 and likewise in Enoch 90:8 as "the lamb that was dashed to pieces."[6] Most prominent as a hero of prayer was the popular saint Onias, the Circle-drawer, called thus for having a ditch dug around him while praying. Much against the Pharisean rule represented by Simeon ben Shetah, the Pharisean leader, he used the ineffable Name

29

when invoking God for rain in a time of great drought.[7]
A remarkable passage in Gen. R. 13, 7 says, with reference to Gen. 2, 5: "There was no man as yet on earth to
make the creatures worship God as did Elijah and
Onias the Circle-drawer by bringing down rain from
heaven through prayer." Josephus,[8] relates that "Onias,
a righteous man, beloved of God, who was known as
having successfully prayed for rain in a great drought,
during the siege of Jerusalem where Aristobulus and his
faction were within the city, was asked by Hyrcanus and
his party, who were encamped outside, to make impreca-
tions against the former in order to bring about their
defeat, but instead he prayed: 'O God, King of the Universe, since they that stand now with me here are Thy
people, and those that are besieged are Thy priests, I
beseech Thee that Thou mayest neither hearken to the
prayers of those against these, nor bring to effect what
these pray against those!' whereupon he was stoned to
death by the wicked Jews about him." His two grand-
sons, Abba Hilkiah and Hanan the Hidden One, were
also endowed with the miraculous power of bringing
down rain by their prayers.[9]

As to the use of the sacred Name in prayer by the
Hasidim, the following Talmudic passages may be
quoted. Commenting on Ps. 36:11,[10] Abba bar Kahana
(about 300 of the Christian era) says: "Continue Thy
lovingkindness unto them that know Thee"; this refers
to the Men of the Great Synagogue and the generation
of martyrs of the Hadrianic persecution who knew how
to make use of the sacred Name. Thus, when it says
of Ezra that he blessed Y H V H, the great God,[11] it
means that he pronounced the great Name. And of the
ten Martyrs of the Hadrianic persecution, Haninah ben
Teradion is singled out as having in public made use of

the sacred Name and having thereby brought divine punishment upon himself, his wife and his daughter,[12] as this practice is severely denounced by the Pharisean authorities.[13] On the other hand, Joshua ben Levi says in the name of Phinehs ben Yair, both adepts of Hasidean lore: "The prayers of Israel are not answered in this world because people do not know the use of the ineffable Name, but in the world to come God will impart to them that knowledge, for it says: 'My people shall know My name,' [14] and likewise: 'Because he hath known My name, he shall call upon Me, and I will answer him.' " [15] Eminent among the last of the Hasidean wonder-workers, the *Anshe Maaseh,*[16] was Haninah ben Dosa. He was summoned by both Johanan ben Zakkai and Gamaliel II to pray for their sick sons, and he prayed like Elijah with his head between his knees, in the upper chamber of the house, to be secluded from the people, and both lads recovered.[17] He was frequently called upon to pray for the sick, as we learn from the Mishna.[18] He is likewise mentioned among the numerous heroes of prayer who brought down rain in seasons of drought,[19] and his fame as a worker of miracles is reflected in numerous Talmudic legends.[20]

It was evidently owing to the fact that these Hasidim and Anshe Maaseh, the "wonder-workers," were looked upon by the people as "rain-makers" that they took a conspicuous place in the popular festivities of the water-libation on the Sukkot night, which symbolized the heavenly blessing of seasonable rain, and in which the holy spirit played a prominent part.[21]

Of the ancient Hasidim the Mishnah [22] tells that they "spent an hour in profound meditation before praying in order to fill their heart with intense devotion to their Father in heaven while communing with him." A similar statement is made regarding the three daily prayers in the Didascalia 7, 24. Neither would they allow themselves to be interrupted in their prayer even by the greeting of a king or by a serpent coiling around their heel.[23] Especially noteworthy is the advice of R. Ammi, in Palestine in the fourth century,[24] to apply to a renowned Hasid whose prayer is regarded as efficacious in case one's own prayer has not been heard by God. In like manner says his contemporary Samuel ben Nahmani:[25] "When on account of Israel's sins rain is withheld, let some venerable person, like Jose the Galilean, be asked to offer prayer for the people, and rain will come."

CHAPTER VII

THE ZADDIKIM AND HASIDIM IN THE PSALMS OF SOLOMON

In connection with the Hasidean prayers, it seems proper to pay special attention to the collection of prayers under the title of the Psalms of Solomon, originally written in Hebrew and preserved in Greek, which have only in recent times been brought to light.[1] Composed apparently for the Synagogue between 80 and 40 B.C.E., they form a collection of prayers made at random without any chronological order and seemingly dropped and forgotten after the destruction of the Temple. Many of them give vent to the indignation of the people against the Maccabean usurpers of the monarchy who desecrated the Temple and the priestly office by their flagrant crimes and vices, while declaring the Roman invasion to be the manifestation of God's judgment upon the great sins of the nation and its rulers. But they also voice the people's fears and anxieties in view of the siege of the holy city and the Temple by Pompey, and likewise the joy and triumph over his tragic end in far-off Egypt, and the confident hope in God and His Anointed, the Messiah from the house of David. Occasional reference is made to the Resurrection and the Day of Judgment, but nowhere is the restoration of the Temple with its sacrifices mentioned. A number of the Psalms are individual prayers or thanksgivings; one contains a prayer that the *Shekinah,* the Divine Presence, be not removed from Israel, and another contains a prayer for relief from an imminent calamity, such as a great drought, followed by a corresponding thanksgiving for the relief that came.

Throughout the whole collection, the Hasmonean rulers are spoken of as the sinners guilty of acts of unrighteousness, of incest and secret sins, of violation of the Temple and of oppressing the righteous. Ps. 4 is especially directed against the hypocrites who sit in the pious council, yet "commit secret sins at night, lurking in lust for any woman they see," and are severe and cruel in judgment. In contrast to these depraved Sadducean priests and nobles there are depicted the righteous who fear God, confide in Him, show true love for Him and His Law, look upon His chastening as a blessing and, believing in free will, lay great stress on repentance. They bear the mark of life for eternal salvation, whereas the wicked bear the mark of destruction. The last two Psalms dwell on the advent of the Messiah, the son of David, who will purge Jerusalem of all heathenism and render the people holy by his reign of righteousness, his words being like the words of angels ("the holy ones").

Now, considering that we find here the Pharisaic views pronounced in opposition to those of the Sadducees, modern translators of these Psalms and others take it for granted that they are the product of Pharisean writers, though the name Pharisee nowhere occurs in them. Instead, we find two names constantly mentioned as representing those views: "The Righteous" and "The Saints," corresponding exactly to the *Zaddikim* and the *Hasidim* of the thirteenth of the Eighteen Benedictions. The former apparently represent the bulk of the God-fearing and law-abiding community, as in Isa. 60:21 and many Psalms, and also in Josephus and in Talmudic writings, in contrast to the unrighteous; though occasionally the name is used for the outstanding perfect men of the age. Distinct from these are the Saints, who represent a higher degree of loyalty and devotion; hence they are also called "saints of God" or "of the Lord." [2] They are identical with the saints of 1 Macc. 2:42, described as "the valiant men of Israel who willingly offered themselves for the Law." They are such as "make atonement with a trespass-offering"—compare the *Asham Hasidim* in the next chapter—for any offense committed unconsciously, "and afflict their soul with fasting in order that the Lord may purify the saintly man and his house." [3] "They rise from their sleep and bless the name of the Lord." [4] Nay more, "They praise His name with rejoicing in the midst of them that know His righteous judgments." [5] So, "His praise is in the mouth of His saints." [6] "The saints give thanks in the assembly (*ecclesia*) of the people," whereupon "the Congregations (Synagogues) of Israel glorify the name of the Lord." [7] Accordingly these gatherings for prayer are called "the assemblies—Synagogues—of the saints." They alone believed in the power of the holy spirit, [8] and, like the Hasidim of the Davidic Psalms, they are "the poor and needy." [9] Evidently, then, these Hasidim were in continuity with those of the Davidic Psalms, the men of prayer, and to them the Psalms of Solomon must be ascribed. We thus come to the conclusion, also, that the real founders of the Synagogue were not the Pharisees as a body, but their leaders, the Hasidim.

CHAPTER VIII

THE EXCEEDING PIETY OF THE HASIDIM

Apparently the author of Ecclesiastes was already familiar with the rigorous ways of the Hasidim when he says: "Be not righteous overmuch," [1] and when he speaks of those who would not take an oath or bring offerings to the altar.[2] Of course, we can think here only of the Essenes as described by Josephus and Philo. On the other hand, we have in the Psalms of Solomon just come across the saints who would make atonement for unknown trespasses,[3] and they are specifically mentioned in the Talmud[4] as the *Ancient Hasidim*. These same Ancient Hasidim are recorded as having been extremely scrupulous regarding the Biblical commandment of the Fringes [5] and the possible desecration of the Sabbath through childbirth.[6] Neither would they, even at the peril of death, allow the killing of snakes and scorpions infesting them on the Sabbath day.[7] A certain Hasid on noticing a broken fence in his vineyard on Sabbath had decided to have it repaired at the close of the day, but considering this decision a matter of business forbidden to contemplate on Sabbath, according to Isa. 58:13, he desisted from making the repairs altogether, and, behold, he was rewarded by having a tree of wondrous fertility grow up in his field which made him rich for life.[8] Similarly, we are told of Abba Jose ben Simai of Shihin that, when fire had broken out in his yard on the Sabbath and the men of the military camp of Sepphoris under his supervision had come to extinguish it, he, against the opinion of the Pharisean teachers, would not allow them to do so, whereupon rain fell down from heaven and extinguished the flames; but nevertheless he compensated the men and their commander for their proffered aid.[9] Apart from the rigorous observance of the Levitical purity laws in general enjoined by the Ancient Elders, somehow identified with the Ancient Hasidim by Frankel[10] and I. H. Weiss,[11] the Hasidim were especially severe in dealing with woman in her menstruous state and would not have her paint her eyelids and rouge her face, nor adorn herself with a colored dress, lest her attractiveness induce her husband to have intercourse with her while the Law[12] says that she should remain separate. Only R. Akiba, favoring the milder Pharisean practice, warns against having her appear repulsive to her husband, which might induce him to divorce her.[13]

Regarding Idolatry also, the Hasidim went so far as to prohibit even looking at things or persons, taking literally the words: "Turn ye not unto the idols."[14] So would the Hasid R. Menahem or Nahum ben Simai, called the "Sons of holy men," not look at Roman coins with pictures of the emperors engraved thereon.[15]

Above all, they observed caution lest any injury be caused to anybody by allowing thorns or broken pieces of glass to be left in their fields.[16] Their leading principle in all these matters is expressed in the oft-recurring sentence: "Keep away from whatever is ugly and like unto it."[17] On this principle is also based the prohibition of raising sheep and goats, as they graze upon the fields of others and do damage there.[18] For the same reason we are told that Abraham's cattle would go about only muzzled,[19] and the ass of Hanina ben Dosa and that of Phineas ben Yair, both known as Hasidim, stood out as models.[20] In fact, it was taken for granted that God would cause no damage ("stumbling block") to come to anyone through the righteous, either directly or through their cattle, Phinehas ben Yair being given as example.

Another principle of the Hasidim was that, instead of keeping strictly to the letter of the Law, one should go beyond the line in order to do the right and the good.[21] In fact, there existed collections of Hasidean teachings, called *Mishnat* or *Megillat Hasidim,* in which the principle is expressed of doing more than just strictly following the letter of the Law. Compare the story of Joshua ben Levi, to whom the prophet Elijah would not appear when he failed to observe the Hasidean rule not to surrender any fugitive of the Government even at the peril of one's life.[22] The ethical maxim in Aboth 5, 10 tells: "He who says, 'Mine is mine and thine is thine' is a mediocre character, or selfish like the men of Sodom; but he who says 'Mine is thine and thine is also thine' is a Hasid." In the same spirit Jesus says to his disciples in Matt. 5:30: "Except your righteousness exceed the righteousness of the Scribes and Pharisees, ye shall in no wise enter into the kingdom of heaven."

CHAPTER IX

THE HASIDIM, THE EMINENT CHARITY WORKERS

Zealous as the Hasidim were in the performance of
any divine commandment, as is shown, for instance, in the
story of the forgotten sheaf which caused an unnamed
Hasid to offer a thanksgiving for the privilege of fulfilling the Law,[1] their foremost concern was to do the
works of charity and personal service, *Zedakah* and *Ge-
milut Hesadim*, which are declared to be equivalent to
all the divine commandments together.[2] Seeing R. Joshua
ben Hananiah greatly distressed at the sight of the
Temple ruins, R. Johanan ben Zakkai said to him: "We
have in our work of charity the same means of atonement as were the sacrifices at the Temple; and besides
(referring to Hosea 6:6), 'I desire mercy, *hesed,* not sacrifice'"; and, referring to Ps. 89:3, taken to mean "The
world is built on mercy," he pointed to Daniel,[3] *Ish
Hamudot,* "the man of compassion," according to Theo-
dotion's translation. For Daniel not merely told
Nebuchadnezzar: "Break off thy sins by almsgiving, and
thine iniquities by showing mercy to the poor,"[4] but he
is said to have spent his time in works of benevolence,
now rejoicing the bride on her wedding day and then
paying honors to the dead, but principally giving alms
to the poor.[5]

This is an allusion to the organized charities in charge
of the Hasidean brotherhoods, *Haburot.*[6] Of the
brotherhoods at Jerusalem we are told by R. Eleazar,
the son of Zadok, an eye-witness to the destruction of

the Temple, that they divided the discharge of the duties
of benevolence among themselves, one party attending
to the festive meals at betrothals or weddings, the other
to the festivities of a new-born son, another going to a
house of mourning or to the collecting of the bones at
the mortuary, while a difference arose between the
Ancient Hasidim and those of a later date as to whether
the house of joy or that of mourning had a prior claim.[7]
In Ab. de-R. Nathan, c.8,[8] the Hasidim who go out to
release the imprisoned and ransom the captives are
spoken of as "those that fear God," and on the following
page we learn of their going forth in pairs to release
women prisoners, and in c.3, 17, of one Hasid going out
in a ship to attend to charity work and, in c.3, 16, of
another who provides for the poor.

How well organized their charity was may be learned
from Tos. Peah 4, 8-14, and that it goes back to very
old time is shown by the Mishnah Kid. 4, 5, according
to which those in charge of the charities belonged to the
old patrician families with whom alone the priests of the
Temple time would intermarry. The place for the collection and the distribution of charity was the meeting
house of the city council, *Heber Ir,* and the charity
department seems to have had the special name *Heber Ir
Betobah,* "the City Council for Kindness." [9]   The
Babylonian Jewry kept up the rule of Tos. Peah 4, 9,
that there should be no community without an alms box
and a soup kitchen.[10]   The collectors of charity were
called *Shluhe Mizwah,* "those sent forth for the duty (of
benevolence)," corresponding to the Apostles in the New
Testament, who were originally collectors of charity, as
were the so-called Jewish Apostles also in later times,[11]
and were always sent forth in pairs lest they be suspected
of dishonesty.[12]

I have elsewhere[13] referred to the striking similarity between Matt. 25:31-46 and Midr. Teh. to Ps. 118:17, in which the various kinds of benevolence are enumerated concerning which individuals or nations would give account on the Day of Judgment. Such are, in the former passage, the feeding of the hungry and giving drink to the thirsty, offering shelter to the homeless and clothing the naked, visiting the sick and ransoming the captive; in the latter, there are mentioned besides the first two the bringing up of orphans and different other works of benevolence, while the idea that whatsoever is given to the needy is given to God is expressed also in Mid. Zuta to Cant. 1:15 with reference to Num. 28:2: "My bread." Besides the six kinds of charity mentioned in Matt. c.25, the Church took over from the Hasidean practice the burial of the dead. But the Didascalia 4, 1-2, has *ten:* (1) showing to the orphan the care of parents; (2) to widows the care of husbands; (3) providing for the marriage of women of suitable age; (4) for the poor craftsman, work; (5) for the incapacitated, some assistance; (6) for the homeless, lodging; (7) for the hungry, food; for the thirsty, drink; (8) for the naked, clothing; (9) for the sick, visitation; and (10) for the prisoners, rescue. The Deuteronomic verse 13:5: "After the Lord your God shall ye walk" is interpreted in Sotah 14a, to mean that we should perform acts of benevolence such as God did when He clothed the first man, or visited Abraham in his sickness, or consoled Isaac in his mourning, and buried Moses on Mount Nebo.

It is especially instructive to compare the words in Matt. 6:19f. and Luke 12:33f.: "Lay not up for yourselves treasures on earth, where moth and rust consume them, and where thieves may break through and steal them, but lay up for yourselves treasures in heaven, where

neither moth nor rust consume, and where thieves do not
break through nor steal," with the ancient Talmudic
story relating to King Monobaz, the husband of Queen
Helene of Adiabene, who became a Jewish proselyte.[14]
When reproached by the princes of his house for his
great generosity, he said to them: "My fathers have laid
up treasures where human hands may grasp them, I,
where no human hand can reach them; my fathers laid
up treasures of Mammon, I, treasures of the soul; my
fathers laid up treasures for this world, I, for the world
to come." It is plain that the Jewish sentences are more
original and rest on actual occurrence. As a pattern of
philanthropy Abraham was held up as one who, to
strangers coming from all sides, offered hospitality under
his terebinth, which remained the symbol of philanthropy
for the Christians also, as is learned from the story of
St. Jerome,[15] and Abraham was said to have received the
lesson from Shem—Malkizedek.[16] In the Testament of
Job,[17] Job is represented as the type of a philanthropist
excelling even Abraham. Many of the old Hasidim
went so far as to distribute their whole fortune among
the poor, like the Essenes and the early Christians; but
the Synod of Usha, in the middle of the second century,
decreed that no one should spend more than a fifth part
of his possessions for charity.[18]

CHAPTER X

The Hasidim and the Oriental or Mystic Lore

The great change that took place in Judaism during and after the Babylonian Exile, owing to its contact with Babylonia and Persia, was one that has affected the entire religious thinking of the world. It is Edward Meyer, who in his *Geschichte des Alterthums* [1] and in his special work *Die Entstehung des Judenthums,* has pointed out what a mighty influence the universalism of the Persian Empire under Cyrus and the ethical tendency of the Zoroastrian system with its cosmic and eschatological views exerted particularly on Judaism, by offering a far wider outlook upon life than was known before. The rapturous glorification of Cyrus by Deutero-Isaiah, who hailed his advent as that of God's anointed, destined to bring the deep mysteries of the world to the light of day, [2] is the best indication of the realization that a new era of religious life was dawning in consequence of the victories of the great world-conqueror whose reign was one of tolerance and liberty to the oppressed nations. The grossly sensual and brutal gods of heathendom, who led their worshipers to the very abyss of moral depravity by their obscene idolatrous rites, had to give way to a more spiritual deity adored as the good "God of heaven," of light and truth, to Ahura Mazda, the supreme, if not the only god of the Persians, whose counterpart Angrimainyus, the principle of evil and darkness, was after a long combat finally to be subdued and annihilated by him. This system was ethical in its import, inasmuch as it made its followers strive for the defeat of all evil powers without and within, and for the triumph of the good and the true.

Of course, the exilic seer, while contrasting the Persian dualism with Israel's pure monotheism as established by the great prophets, was all the more emphatic in declaring Israel's God to be both "the Former of light and the Creator of darkness, the Maker of peace and the Creator of evil," the first and the last besides whom there is no other God.[3] Nevertheless, the Jewish leaders of thought could not but feel that they lived in a more congenial atmosphere while observing that, in place of the animal sacrifices offered everywhere to the Deity, the Mazdean priests practiced forms far less offensive to the eye and the heart in offering the Homa juice, the sacred water and fire with some cooked meat, but chiefly prayers, though these were rather taken to be means of averting the evil powers lurking everywhere. At any rate, prayer and song predominated, so as to give the worship a more spiritual character.[4] Above all, it was the outlook into a future life after death which invested the Mazdean religion with a higher character and thereby greatly enhanced the belief of those initiated, enlarging their vision and scope. The whole cosmic system presented life as a great world drama, the end of which was to be the triumph of the good principle over the evil one, whereby "death would be swallowed up forever";[5] the resurrection of the dead to be followed by the final judgment which would vindicate the righteous. In this great world-struggle lasting six or twice six millennia, the Persian savior (*Saoshyant*) would, with his associates, aid Ahura Mazda in crushing Angrimainjus and his hosts. This Persian system was adopted by the Jewish leaders of thought, the Hasidim, and the *Messiah* became for them the World-Savior who would combat and finally annihilate Satan "the wicked one." [6] Thus the entire Messianic hope of Judaism underwent a change, while at the same time the Jewish angelology and demonology was formed under Perso-Babylonian influence. Nay more, the whole concept of the hereafter, so gloomy in the realm of Sheol, was transformed into one of hope in consonance with the spirit of a higher, all-readjusting divine justice.

But this transformation of thought took place only in the minds of a select class of men eager to imbibe the more or less occult wisdom of the Mazdean priests, whereas the people at large and the official priesthood, the Sadducees, rejected the innovation. These new ideas were introduced by the Hasidim as divine mysteries handed down to the initiated from the hoary past by such men as Enoch, Noah and Shem, the men of vision singled out in the Apocalyptic writings and occasionally in the Talmud. We must bear in mind that the psychological process by which the foreign views were assimilated in olden times was not one of reason and speculation, but one of spiritual ecstasy and mysticism, combined with a certain apotheosis of the heroes of the past.

So was the heavenly throne-chariot of Ezekiel's vision (referred to also in 1 Chron. 28:18 and Ben Sira 49, 8), as soon as it was brought into connection with the chariot of the Persian Mithra, Ahura-Mazda's charioteer, made a subject of secret lore under the name of Maaseh Merkaba. [7] Similarly, the Creation chapters in Genesis, Proverbs c.3; c.8, and Job cc.37-38 were, in connection with Persian and Babylonian, and later on also Greek, concepts, turned into cosmogonic secrets, *Masseh Bereshit*, to be taught only in esoteric circles consisting of but

two or three. Hence, already Ben Sira 3, 20, followed
by the Mishnah and Talmud Hag, *l.c.,* warns against
"intruding into that which is beyond and above," before
or after, as it is the glory of God to conceal things.[8] To
the category of the secret lore belongs also the inquiry
into the future life. Interpreting the verse Cant. 1:4:
"The King hath brought me into his chambers," the
Midrash says: "God will bring Elihu ben Barachel the
Buzite[9] to have him reveal unto Israel the chambers,
the secrets of Behemot and Leviathan"[10] and Ezekiel to
have him reveal the secrets of the Merkabah.[11]

A legend in Sanh. 94a relates that Metatron, the
prince of the world, asked God to grant King Hezekiah's
wish to know the Messianic time, but God answered:
"Mine, Mine is the secret."[12] Only privileged students
of the Scripture discussed, and not without personal risk,
these secrets. When Jonathan ben Uziel, "the greatest
of Hillel's eighty disciples," translated the Prophets
(with his paraphrase), a flame emanated from him which
burned every bird flying above him, and a heavenly voice
was heard saying: "Who revealed My secrets to My
children?"[13] Similar stories were told about R. Johanan
ben Zakkai, the other great disciple of Hillel, and his
disciples.[14] Of the four famous schoolmen of the following century—Simeon ben Azzai, Simeon ben Zoma, Elisha
ben Abuyah, and Akiba—we are told[15] that they entered
—that is in their ecstatic vision—into Paradise,[16] and
behold, the first-named was struck dead, and to him the
verse was applied: "Precious in the sight of the Lord
is the death of His saints";[17] the second became men-
tally afflicted, and to him was applied Prov. 25:16: "Hast
thou found honey? eat so much as is sufficient for thee,
lest thou be filled therewith, and vomit it"; the third
one uprooted the plantations—that is, he apostatized—

and to him was applied Eccl. 5:5: "Suffer not thy mouth
to bring thy flesh into guilt"; but Akiba, the last one,
entered in peace and came out in peace, and to him was
applied Cant. 1, 4: "The King has brought me into His
chambers; we will be glad and rejoice in thee." As a
matter of fact, some of these died as martyrs of the
Hadrianic persecution, and in the Geonic period their
fellow-martyrs were made the heroes of the Merkabah
vision describing for us the celestial Hall, the *Hekalot*,
in elaborate forms after the pattern of Enoch. When
once written down, these apocalyptic visions lost more
and more their esoteric character. As shown by Mayer
Friedmann in the Introduction to his Sedar Eliahu,[18] the
Hasidim of the Tannaitic and Amoraic periods appear
as the men of vision conversing with angels and demons
and particularly with the prophet Elijah, called also
Abba Eliahu, or spoken of as the "Aged One," a teacher,
or monitor, and helper of men. Specially favored with
apparitions were Simeon ben Yohai, the mystic; Jose ben
Halafta, the historian; R. Meir among the Tannaim,
and Joshua ben Levi among the Amoraim. Most prominent in a later period was Rab Anan, a disciple of Rab
of the third century, to whom the Seder Eliahu Rabba
and Zuta, full of sayings of Elijah, is ascribed.[19]

The chief aim of the Hasidim was the attainment of
the Holy Spirit through fasting and prayer; by it
the great uncommon things were to be accomplished.
Phineas ben Yair, the famous Hasid and wonder-worker
of the second century, enumerates ten grades of holiness
leading up to the Holy Spirit.[20] When prophecy ceased,
it was regarded by the Pharisean school as a feeble substitute for it,[21] and later on the Heavenly Voice, *Bat-Kol*,
took its place. Such a heavenly voice was heard at *Bet
Gedi* near Jericho—possibly the seat of the Essene col-

ony—in regard to Hillel as worthy of the Holy Spirit, and at *Jabneh*, in regard to Samuel ha-Katan, a disciple of Hillel.[22] The Holy Spirit was ascribed to the ancients before Abraham,[23] and in Num. R. c. 15, at the close, we are told that in the future all Israel will be endowed with it. A more universalistic character is ascribed to the Holy Spirit in Seder Eliahu,[24] where the author says: "I call heaven and earth as witnesses that Jew or Gentile, man or woman, bondman or bondwoman will be endowed with the Holy Spirit, each according to his conduct."

The terms Holy Spirit and Shekinah are often interchanged in some passages quoted above. In Suk. 28a all the eighty disciples of Hillel are said to have been worthy of having the Shekinah rest upon them. Interesting is the saying of R. Akiba regarding necromancy: [25] "If he who starves himself for the sake of obtaining the spirit of impurity is successful, how much more ought he to succeed who starves himself for the sake of obtaining the spirit of purity? But our sins separate us from the living God."

CHAPTER XI

The Hasidim and the Sacred Name

In primitive times the invocation of the name of the Deity was believed to possess a sort of magic power forcing the Deity to accomplish the wish of the worshiper, and it also consecrated the place of worship. Thus, the Name of Yahveh was actually "placed" or "made to rest" upon His house or altar. In this sense the verse Ex. 20:21 is to be understood: "In every place where thou shalt (the Masoretic 'I shall' is a Soferic emendation) mention My Name, I will come unto thee and bless thee." Quite significant is the remark of Simeon ben Azzai:[1] "Throughout the laws on sacrifice the sacred Name is exclusively used to counteract the ways of the heretics," with which Josephus *Ant.* II, 12, 4 should be compared: "Moses asked God for His sacred Name in order that when offering sacrifice, he might invoke His presence at the sacred act." It is always the invocation of the sacred Name that makes the prayer, the blessing or curse effective.[2] So was the greeting done *with*, not *in* the Name of *Yhvh*.[3] Regarding oaths Deuteronomy says repeatedly: "Thou shalt fear *Jhvh* thy God . . . and by His Name shalt thou swear,"[4] commenting upon which Temurah 4a says: "When thou fearest the Lord thy God, then thou mayest swear by His Name." God himself sweareth by His great Name.[5] In blasphemy, also, the penalty of death is inflicted only on the pronunciation of the sacred Name having been heard by

the witness.⁶ Later on the very word *Nokeb* was taken
to mean simply the pronunciation, and it was declared
to be forbidden under penalty of death by heaven.⁷
Notice, also, the word *Ha-shem* in Lev. 24:11, instead
of Y H V H.

Only the priests in the Temple were allowed to pronounce the sacred Name and were enjoined to do so
when blessing the people, in accordance with Num. 6:27:
"And they shall put My Name upon the children of
Israel, and I will bless them." ⁸

Reverence for "the great, the glorious and awful
Name" is especially inculcated in Deut. 28:58 and in
32:3: "For I will proclaim the Name of the Lord;
ascribe ye greatness unto our God," the implication
being ⁹ that, whenever the Name is mentioned by the
leader in prayer, the Congregation should respond with
the words: "Blessed be His glorious Name!" More
about this in the next chapter.

In post-exilic time, the use of the name Y H V H was
more and more restricted and finally altogether with-
drawn from common use. Hence the later books of
Scripture and the Korahite and Asaphite Psalms use
Elohim instead. The priests, when pronouncing the
Name in their blessing, did it in a whisper—"swallowed
it up." ¹⁰ For the people at large the name *Adonai*, "the
Lord," was introduced as a substitute both in the reading and the translation of the Scripture, as is shown by
the Septuagint and the Targum. And while this sub-
stitution guarded the Name from profane use, it formed
at the same time the highest triumph of Jewish monotheism, inasmuch as it proved the most powerful means
of rendering the Biblical God for all readers of the
Bible *the* God and Lord of the world. For as long as
Yahweh—or Jehovah, as the name was erroneously read

—was viewed as the proper Name of Israel's God, there adhered to Him a more or less tribal character, but as soon as He is spoken of as the Lord (Adonai), He has ceased to be merely the God of one nation and has become the universal God.[11] But henceforth the four-lettered Name, called *Shem Ha-Meforash* or *Shem Ha-Meyuhad,* "The Name set apart for God"—compare Wisdom of Solomon 14:21, "the incommunicable Name" —assumed a more mystic character, invested with magic power, as we saw above when speaking of the prayers of the Hasidim, whereas the Pharisean teachers forbade the use of the Name for magical purposes.[12] An ancient Baraita [13] says: Formerly the quadruliteral Name (the "twelve-lettered Name" is apparently a late alteration) was transmitted to everybody, but when the insolent ones increased it was transmitted only to the discreet ones (*Z'nuim*) among the priesthood, and they merged it in the melodious song of their priestly brethren." [14] Later on the instruction in the pronunciation of the Name was still more restricted, according to R. Johanan of the third century. The magic use of the Name, however, was already condemned by Hillel when he said: "He who makes use of the *Crown* perishes." [15] The word for Crown, *Taga,* is explained correctly in Ab. de-R. Nathan (I [16]) as referring to the sacred Name, though it was afterwards referred to the crown of the Torah.[17] However, as was stated above, the Hasidim made frequent use of the sacred Name, and the belief in its magic power is very frequently expressed throughout the Talmud, the Midrash and the Targum.[18]

Especially interesting is the Noahic passage: [19] And this is the charge of Kasbeel (the angel of the oath) who showed to the holy ones the head of the oath, the hidden Name. . . . Through that oath the heaven was established, and the earth founded above the water, and the sea placed within its bound, and the depths made fast, and the sun, the moon and the stars made to complete their course, and likewise the spirits of the water and winds, the chambers of the hail and hoarfrost, of the rain and the dew. . . . Through this mighty oath they are all preserved.[20] In the Book of Enoch, Metatron, the prince of angels, is represented as having learned from God Himself the mystery of the Shem ha-Meforash by which "the heavens and the earth, the sea and the dry land, the mountains and hills, the streams and fountains, Gehenna and the Garden of Eden were created, and man and beasts, the fowls of heaven and the fishes of the sea, Behemot and Leviathan, and all the creeping things of the water and dry land were formed." And he revealed the mystery to Moses, who transmitted it to Joshua, by whom it was transmitted to the Elders, and so it was handed over to the Prophets, and then to the Men of the Great Synagogue, to Ezra the Scribe, and then to Hillel, and finally to R. Abahu and R. Zera, who entrusted it to the men of faith, the mystics, who were to cure by it the various diseases in accordance with Ex. 15:26. Thus, we see how the Sacred Name was used by the whole line of the Hasidean mystics for magical purposes and especially for cures with the help of prayer.

CHAPTER XII

THE SH'MA YISRAEL AND ITS RESPONSE, A HASIDEAN INSTITUTION

The most prominent and most characteristic feature of the entire Synagogal literature, the one which centralized and consolidated it for all time, is the solemn Scriptural verse which became the creed and the rallying cry of the Jew all over the world: "Hear, O Israel, the Lord our God, the Lord is One." [1] This Deuteronomic verse, forming as it were the keynote of the entire teaching of Judaism, embodies both the fundamental belief and the historic mission of Israel. It corresponds to the words of Zech. 14:9: "And the Lord shall be King over all the earth; in that day the Lord shall be One and His name One." Yet only men of a true religious genius, imbued with the holy spirit, could select out of the 5845 verses of the Pentateuch—as Professor Steinthal once wrote [2]—this one verse as the watchword of the Jew wherewith to challenge all the religious and philosophical systems of the world. Such were the Hasidim.

Naturally the question comes home to us *when* and *where* was this solemn declaration of Israel's unique belief in the only One God, implying the pledge to live, and if needs be, to die for it, rendered the central idea and leitmotif of the Synagogue? It is inaccurate to ascribe its introduction, in common with the Eighteen Benedictions and other prayers, to the Men of the Great

53

Synagogue, as Zunz[3] and others do. For, while these were acknowledged to be a Rabbinical institution, the recital of the Shema every morning and evening was, in distinction to the Prayers,[4] taken by all the ancients as a Mosaic commandment derived from Deut. 6:7 and 11:19, as shown in the Mishnah Ber. 1, 3, where the schools of Shammai and Hillel differ only in regard to the mode of recital, but never doubted its Mosaic character.[5] Josephus,[6] when ascribing to Moses the commandment "to remember God's benefit bestowed upon Israel at their deliverance from Egypt, and this twice every day, both when the day begins and when the hour of sleep comes on," has the same passage in view, obviously referring to the three portions of the Shema, Deut. 6:4-9; 11:13-21 and Num. 15:37-41, as only the closing verse of the last one speaks of the deliverance from Egypt. But the introductory sentence to the Shema in the Septuagint Deut. 6:4, which reads: "And these are the statutes and ordinances which the Lord commanded to the children of Israel in the wilderness as they went forth from Egypt," seems to indicate that in the Alexandrian Synagogue the Shema was read with this introduction.

It needs, however, no special argument to prove that although the Soferim connected the recital of the Shema with the Scriptural passage, just as they connected the putting on of the Tefillin and the fixing of the Mezuzah with the following verses, the real origin as well as the purpose of the Shema recital must be sought elsewhere. Evidently the name given it by the ancient teachers, *Kabbalat Ol Malkut Shamayim,* "the Acceptance of the yoke of God's sovereignty," clearly states that its object was to be the declaration of Israel's fundamental belief in God's unity in opposition to the polytheism of the pagan world. But then we must ask ourselves, At what period in Jewish history was such a declaration deemed particularly necessary?

The correct answer is given by Professor Ludwig Blau [7] that it was in view of the Persian dualism, against which Deutero-Isaiah entered his emphatic protest [8] while hailing Cyrus as God's anointed that this proclamation of God's unity every morning and evening was introduced. However, Professor Blau, in making the Mishnaic description of the Shema recital in the Hall of the Hewn Stones at the Temple, the Seat of the Sanhedrin, [9] the starting point, failed to consider that neither the place nor the time of the priestly morning service could have given the impulse to such a solemn confession of the Jewish faith in opposition to the Persian dualism, nor, in fact, would such an origin account for the dating of this institution back to Mosaic times. Least of all should the priests of the Temple, whom Dr. Blau, following Dr. Buechler, identifies with the *Vatikim*, [10] be credited with the introduction of this most important element of the Synagogal liturgy. The very fact that the Decalogue preceded the Shema in the priestly service [11] is sufficient evidence that they laid more stress on the Torah to be read, in accordance with Deut. 6:6, than on the confession of the faith; and indeed it seems that the second of the two Benedictions preceding the Shema, which dwells on the value of the Torah, was the product of the priestly Soferim, as it fitted in with the priestly morning service at the Temple; whereas the first Benediction, praising God in Isaianic terms as the Creator of light, would have been hardly in place if recited in the Temple at a rather late hour.

Let us see, then, whether we cannot trace the whole practice to a more ancient time than is assumed in the

Talmudic sources. We have first of all Josephus' description of the Essene practice: [12] "Before the rising of the sun they speak of no profane matters, but send up towards it certain prayers that have come down to them from their forefathers, as if they were praying for its rising." This was identified already by Rappaport in his biography of Kalir [13] with the practice of the Watikim, "the Strongminded," the preservers of ancient traditions, of whom we are told that they started their prayers at dawn and managed to conclude them with the recital of the Shema at the time of the Radiation of the Sun. Similarly are the Therapeutes, an Egyptian branch of the Essenes, described by Philo [14] as "praying twice a day, at dawn and in the evening," "standing up with their faces and their whole bodies turned towards the dawn" and "lifting their hands towards heaven when they see the sun rise, praying for a happy day and for the light of truth and penetrating wisdom." Here we have a direct allusion even to the two Benedictions preceding the Shema, the one thanking for the light of day, the other for the light of the Torah. According to R. Zera, the Watikim followed the Psalmist's injunction in Ps. 72:5, which they interpreted: "They worship Thee with the sun and before the gleam of the moon throughout all generations." That neither the Essenes nor the Therapeutes had anything to do with the Persian sun-worship, as so many Christian writers maintain, needs no argument. Other references to the same practice we have in the Wisdom of Solomon 16:28, where, speaking of the Manna which "melted as the sun grew hot," it says: "This is to teach us that we should anticipate the sun in offering thanksgiving to Thee and pray unto Thee at the rising of the light of day." Likewise, in the third Book of the Sibyllines 591f. we read: "They lift up to heaven their purified hands, rising early from their bed in the morning, having their hands cleansed in water." Evidently the class of Hasidim spoken of under various names, assembled in the open field where they could watch the sun rise from daybreak on and, beginning with their benedictions, they greeted the sun, as it appeared in full radiance over the hills, with uplifted hands, while solemnly reciting the Shema. It is easy to see that, being meant to be a demonstrative proclamation of the Unity and the Uniqueness of Israel's God, in opposition to the Zoroastrian dualism, the practice originated neither in the Temple nor in the Synagogue, but in the open under the free heaven and before the very eyes of the surrounding Mazdean priests. In all likelihood the Mazdean worshipers themselves gave the impulse to the Jewish practice, as we learn from the Avesta [15] that every morning they hailed the rising sun, the god Mithras, with the sacred prayer, *Asheu Vohu,* and likewise the setting sun with the same prayer. What a strong incentive that must have been for the pious Jews to adopt the same impressive ceremony in honor of their One and holy God, the Maker of the sun, and at the same time to find in the Deuteronomic words: "And thou shalt speak of them . . . when thou liest down and when thou risest up," the very Shema recital prescribed twice a day!

But there is another important point which induces us to ascribe the practice to those ancient Hasidim. It is the response: "Blessed be the Name of His glorious Kingdom for ever and aye," which has been taken from the closing verse of Ps. 72 and from Neh. 9:5. The fact that this response was regarded as important enough to interrupt the Biblical verses 4 and 5 of the Shema, can only be explained by the assumption that the leader of the service pronounced the sacred Name as was done by the priests in the Temple and loud enough to make the assembly respond aloud forthwith, as was done on the Day of Atonement after the high priest's pronunciation of the Name.[16] Only when the substitute Adonai took the place of J H V H, the response was to be said in a whisper. Only the men of Jericho would not pause after the first verse of the Shema, but had it so closely connected with the following, that is, "had it folded up with the rest," that there was no room left for the response.[17]

And here we come to another feature of the Shema recital strangely misinterpreted by Elbogen.[18] The name *Pores Al Shema* can have only one meaning, "the lifting up of the hands toward heaven at the recital of the Shema," which was done by some chosen member of the assembly of worshipers in continuation of the ancient practice of the Hasidim. The term corresponds with the one used for the priests' blessing, *Nesiat Kappayim*.[19]

The function of the recital of the Shema included also that of the Benedictions preceding and following the Shema proper.[20] Apparently the first Benediction introducing the Shema, which directly refers to the Deutero-Isaianic verse: "the Former of light and Creator of darkness, the Maker of peace and the Creator of all things"—the term *Ra,* "evil," being intentionally changed, in order not to have evil ascribed to God—was brief, as the Shema itself was originally brief and only gradually extended, as were also the Benedictions.

A glance at Enoch 83:11 to 84:3, and the Syr. Baruch Apocalypse 21, shows how the sight of the rising sun induced the ancient mystics to offer solemn praise to the Ruler of heaven and earth whose throne is surrounded by the angelic hosts and the holy living creatures, the

Hayyot of the Merkabah. Accordingly the *Yozer Or* Benediction was enlarged by a dramatic presentation of the angelic praise after Isa. 6:2-3 and Ezek. 3:12. It seems that the older Hasidean practice of facing the rising sun at the Shema recital gave offense to the Pharisean teachers, it being regarded as a rather pagan practice,[21] and it was accordingly no longer recited in the open and at the time of the sunrise, but in the Synagogue or the Temple. Only the few, anxious to preserve the Hasidean practice, such as were the Watikim, recited the Shema morning and evening exactly at the time when "the sky was reddened by the rising or setting sun." Thus the saintly Jose ben Halafta said: "May my portion be with those who pray when the sun reddens the sky." [22]

The next step taken by the Hasidim was to affirm in the strongest possible language the acceptance of the monotheistic truth, "the yoke of God's sovereignty," and this they did in the half-Hebrew, half-Aramaic form: *Emet We-yazib*—"True and firm, established and enduring . . . is this word to us forever"—closing with the words: "There is no God beside Thee." This affirmation, as a confession of faith, formed part of the Shema recital in the Temple and was urged as a Biblical command with the view to Deut. 16:3, by the Tanna Judah ben Ilai.[23]

The second Benediction preceding the Shema, also called "the Benediction of the Torah," which voices in most exquisite language God's love for Israel as manifested by the Torah, is by no means older than the first, as Elbogen asserts.[24] It refers rather to the second and third verses of the Shema and represents a later stage, when the original connection with the sunrise was altogether forgotten and the emphasis was laid upon the Torah. This accounts also for the fact that in the priestly service at the Temple the Decalogue was placed before the Shema and the second Benediction took the place of the first.

The chapter concerning the Zizit [25] was added to the Shema and its supplement, Deut. 11:13-21, in order to give the monotheistic faith its historical setting by reference to Israel's deliverance from Egypt.[26] Elsewhere [27] it is taken for granted that the Zizit chapter represents "the acceptance of the yoke of the ceremonial laws" in addition to the yoke of God's sovereignty. In accordance, however, with the former view, the Benediction following the Shema dwells on Israel's redemption from Egypt, ending up in a dramatic presentation of the Song on the Red Sea, a favorite passage of the ancient saints, as is shown also by Philo's description of the divine service of the Therapeutes.

The Benedictions preceding and following the Shema at the evening service, while corresponding to those of the morning, are certainly later compositions, as they contain no reference to the setting sun and indicate the influence of Hellenic thought when alluding to the creative "Word" or "Wisdom" and "Understanding." Of course, the Benediction: "Make us lie down in peace," is a night prayer added much later.[28] The dispute between the Shammaites and Hillelites, whether the Biblical words speaking of "the lying down" in the evening and "the rising up" in the morning should be taken literally or not,[29] shows how the Shema recital took on a legal character in the Pharisean school, though all stress was at the same time laid on the devotion with which the Shema should be recited.[30]

CHAPTER XIII

THE TEFILLIN (PHYLACTERIES) AND THE ZIZIT (FRINGES)

I

It was quite logical to connect the wearing of the Tefillin and the Tallit, the fringed four-cornered shawl, with the Shema recital, since both ordinances are, according to the traditional interpretation, contained in the Shema chapters. Thus Ulla, a third-century Amora, says: "He who recites the Shema without the Tefillin is like one who contradicts his own testimony"; and his teacher, R. Johanan, compares him to one who brings an altar-offering without the libation.[1] True, the scriptural precept: "Thou shalt bind them for a sign upon thy hand and they shall be for frontlets between thine eyes,"[2] has, together with the following verse, only a figurative meaning, like Prov. 3:3; 4:21,[3] or is at best to be taken literally. In fact, the Samaritans did not accept the words as a law. But already Josephus[4] refers the passage to the signs worn on the arms and the forehead, and placed on the door; and so does the Letter of Aristeas[5] tell us that the seventy-two Elders who translated the Pentateuch for Ptolemy Philadelphus wore, following the Jewish custom, "the signs upon their hand."

However, the very name Phylacteries given them by the Hellenists,[6] as well as their mention side by side with the amulets (*Kemiot*) in Shab. 6, 2; Shek. 3, 2 and else-

61

where, indicates their original talismanic character.[7]
Also the name Tefillin has nothing to do with *Tefillah,*
prayer, as Luther's *Gebetriehmen* would suggest, but it
denotes, like *Kemiah,* a "pendant," a charm attached to
the body.[8] Very significant is the fact that neither on
the Sabbath nor on Holydays were the Tefillin to be
worn, for the reason that these days are themselves pro-
tective "signs";[9] nor were they to be worn during the
worship at the Temple.[10] They were worn during the
whole day in Talmudic and Geonic times, but not at
night,[11] and therefore not at the evening service either,
while the common people, the *Am Ha-arez,* did not wear
them at all.[12] Their whole construction and mode of
wearing, however, from the leather cases with their
parchment scrolls containing Ex. 13:1-10, 11-16; Deut.
6:4-9 and 11:13-21, to the leather straps with which
they were attached to the forehead and the arm, were
ascribed to a tradition from Moses on Sinai.[13] Special
importance was given to the knot (Kesher) on the back
of the head on which the two letters SH and D of the
name *Shaddai* stood out, and the knot on the arm on
which the letter Yod was prominent. Eliezer ben
Hyrcanus, of the first century, referred the verse Deut.
28:10: "And all the peoples of the earth shall see that
the Name of the Lord is called upon thee; and they shall
be afraid of thee," to the Tefillin on the forehead.[14]
Moreover, we are told by Simeon the Hasid [15] that God
Himself showed the knot of the Tefillin He wore to
Moses when allowing him to see His back (Ex. 33, 23).
Strange as this anthropomorphic notion of the Deity
appears to us, it receives some light from the sacred girdle
of the Parsees with which each person from his fifteenth
year on was to be provided, with the admonition not to
walk three or four steps without it, lest he be guilty

of sin.[16]   And with the selfsame sacred girdle Ahura
Mazda is said to defeat the fiends Angrimainyus and
Az.[17]   It was regarded as a sign of covenant between
Ahuramazda and his followers.

It seems, then, that under Persian influence the Hasidim introduced the wearing of the Tefillin, which had
been used before as amulets, as a religious practice based
upon the scriptural passage, and also made it a rule not
to walk four ells without wearing them.[18]   While women
are not enjoined to observe the rite, we learn that
Michal, the daughter of King Saul, wore them;[19] but
they were apparently used as amulets.   It is instructive
to notice that the Samaritans, instead of referring Ex. 13 :
9 and 16 to the Tefillin, as the Rabbis do, smeared the
blood of the Passover lamb on the arms and temples of
their children as a charm.

II

The Zizit ritual seems to have gone through a similar
process of transformation.   The older law in Deut.
22:12: "Thou shalt make thee twisted cords upon the
four corners of thy covering, wherewith thou coverest
thyself," was apparently a police ordinance intended to
prevent the exposure of the pudenda in walking, exactly
as was the one for the priest [20] to guard against having
his nakedness uncovered when ascending the altar, as
was David's when dancing.[21]   The Priest Code, under
altogether different conditions, gave the old practice a
higher meaning when ordaining,[22] that upon the fringes
of the four corners of the garment a blue or violet tassel
should be put to serve "as a *Show-piece,*" to gaze upon,
that the people "may look upon it, and remember all the
commandments of the Lord, and observe them; that they
go not astray following their own hearts and their own

eyes." Possibly the violet tassel had a talismanic character originally, as our modern exegetes think and as
was actually assumed later on, as we shall see.

The violet dye was obtained from the blood of the
purple snail found on the Phœnician coast;[23] and when,
owing to the disappearance of the snail, the dye became
scarce and subsequently also its imitation, a white fringe
took the place of the violet tassel,[24] though the stress was
always laid on the color which, according to R. Meir,
was to remind the people of the sky and the divine Presence.[25] However, the Shammaites and Hillelites already
made the number of the threads of the fringes a matter
of dispute [26] and later schools enlarged on all this, pointing to an original talismanic character of the practice.
A legend telling of the saving power exerted by the Zizit
on a scholar who came near committing a sin with a
beautiful woman he had heard of living in a far-off land [27]
seems to show that the talismanic character was given
a more spiritual meaning in Rabbinic circles.

Like the Tefillin, the fringed Tallit was worn in Talmudic and Geonic times during the whole day. When,
however, this square-shaped garment went out of use,
it was reserved for the morning service, while for all-day
use a substitute was introduced to be worn under the
upper garment. But especial stress was laid upon one's
enwrapping oneself with it. Accordingly, the Benediction formulated for it reads: "Blessed art Thou, O
Lord . . . who commanded us to enwrap ourselves with
the Zizit." [28] God Himself is said to have appeared to
Moses enwrapt like a leader in prayer when revealing to
him His thirteen Attributes.[29] Still, the talismanic character of the Zizit, shown in the number of knots, remained
in the popular mind, as we learn from Isaac Luria.[30]

CHAPTER XIV

THE DAILY PRAYERS
OR
THE EIGHTEEN, RESPECTIVELY SEVEN, BENEDICTIONS

The need of communing with God in prayer has at all times been felt by man, and no special command to that effect was required by Law. But our Rabbis found it implied in the Deuteronomic words: "To love the Lord your God, and to serve Him with all your heart and with all your soul,"[1] inasmuch as prayer is, in contradistinction to sacrifice, "a service of the heart." Still, this does not comprise any regular service and is at best an appeal to the pious individual. It is of Daniel, presented as a type of the Hasidim at the Maccabean time, that we learn for the first time of praying three times a day—if this is not already anticipated by the Psalmist in Ps. 55:18, who speaks of his prayer "at evening, morning and at noonday." This practice apparently led R. Jose ben Hanina, or, according to the Jerusalem Talmud, R. Joshua ben Levi, to the statement that the three Patriarchs introduced the three prayers of the day.[2] With better reason Samuel ben Nahmani[3] declared that the three periods of the day prompted the three prayers, and he gave brief and appropriate forms for them.

No doubt the three Hasidean prayers were originally simple and brief. As Dr. De Sola Pool, in his little work on the Kaddish[4] suggests, the prayers in Dan. 2:20-23; 9:4-19; 1 Chron. 29:10-13; 2 Chron. 20:5ff. and Neh.

1:5, offered the type for the Synagogal Prayers. The statement of R. Joshua ben Levi [5] that the prayers were instituted to take the place of the daily burnt-offerings fails to account for the evening prayer. Whether this evening prayer was obligatory or voluntary is discussed in Ber. 27b. As a matter of fact, all these prayers, being Hasidean in origin, have no reference to the daily offerings nor to the priesthood and the sacrificial cult in general. The institution of the three daily prayers is ascribed in Mid. Teh. on Ps. 17,[6] to the ancient Hasidim —for which Sifrè, Deut. 343, has the ancient Hakamim, and Mid. Sh'muel [7] the ancient Nebiim; but, as the passage refers to the Prayer for the rebuilding of Jerusalem, we can scarcely see in it an old tradition.

At any rate, the old Synagogue practice kept the Shema recital apart from the daily Prayer. The former was the function assigned to someone from amidst the Congregation, called *Pores of Sh'ma*—"he who lifts up his hands while reciting the Shema." He started at the proper time, calling upon the assembly to "bless the Lord," and after hearing their response began with the Benediction *Yozer Or* in the morning, without asking the people to stand up for the Shema recital. On the other hand, he who offered the Prayer was summoned to do so by the Archi-synagogue in the term applied to sacrifice, namely, *Kareb* "offer up";[8] and, taking his place before the ark containing the scroll of Law, he offered the Prayer on behalf of the Congregation, which was to stand up—hence the name *Amidah* given to the Prayer—and to respond to each Benediction with Amen.[9]

Coming to speak now of the Eighteen or Seven Benedictions on weekdays and, respectively, on Sabbath and Holydays, we may find it strange that what was to be the Prayer should have passed down in the form of Benedictions, and we can only assume that the Synagogue adopted this form from the Temple liturgy of old. As Zunz states,[10] the three first and the three last Benedictions are of a higher antiquity than the rest, since they formed part also of the Sabbath and Holyday service called *Birkat Sheba*, "the Sevenfold Benedictions," fixed as early as the schools of Shammai and Hillel,[11] and the Mishnah R. H. 4, 5 knows them by their specific names: *Birkat Abot, B. Geburot* and *B. Kedushat Ha-Shem; B. Abodah, B. Hodayah* and *B. Kohanim*—the "Benediction concerning the Forefathers, the B. concerning the Divine Power, the B. concerning the Sanctification of God's Name, the B. concerning the Temple Service, the B. concerning Thanksgiving to God and the B. concerning the Priestly Blessing." Zunz also distinguishes those which were composed before the destruction of the Temple and those which, in the present form, could only have been written after the destruction. But these differentiations fail to solve the problem. Still less light is obtained from the statement of R. Johanan b. Nappaha, the Palestinian authority on Rabbinic tradition at the close of the third century,[12] that "the men of the Great Synagogue instituted the prayers, the Benedictions and Sanctifications," for which another statement of his [13] has "One hundred and twenty elders, among them many prophets, have instituted the Eighteen Benedictions in their definite order," as the whole existence of this organized body of Synagogal leaders since Ezra, based on Neh. c.10, is mythical rather than historical.[14]

The Eighteen Benedictions, including the three first and the three last ones, are neither the work of one body nor of one age. They are all the product of gradual growth and development, constituting various groups which were combined in the course of time, and not always systematically. For the Seven Benedictions we are fortunate in having an exact Greek parallel product, only more elaborate, which goes back to the time of the Temple and has undergone slight alterations at the hand of the Judeo-Christians.[15] As to the original of the Eighteen Benedictions, we may point to the Temple Psalm in the Hebrew Ben Sira 51, 12f., which, modeled after Ps. 136, has thirteen verses each beginning with *Hodu,* "Give thanks to God," and closing with the response, "For His mercy endureth forever." The order of the verses is rather confused: (1) Give thanks to the God of praises; (2) to the Keeper of Israel: (3) to the Creator of all things; (4) to the Redeemer of Israel; (5) to Him who gathereth the dispersed ones of Israel; (6) to Him who built His city and His Sanctuary; (7) to Him who causeth the horn of the house of David to sprout forth; (8) to Him who hath chosen *The Sons of Zadok* for the priesthood; (9) to the Shield of Abraham; (10) to the Rock of Isaac; (11) to the Strong One of Jacob; (12) to Him who hath chosen Zion; (13) to the King of Kings." These Benedictions correspond to the eight Benedictions recited by the high priest on the Day of Atonement in connection with his reading from the Torah,[16] the concluding sentences of which have been preserved in Jer. Yoma 7, 44b; and similar Benedictions are recited according to our ritual on each Sabbath and Holyday in connection with the Scripture reading. The Eighteen Weekday Benedictions, as was suggested first by Herzfeld [17] and then by Elbogen,[18] probably had the Fastdays and Maamadot Service,[19] which were laic and of Hasidean origin, as basis. To judge, however, from the Mishnah, the Tosefta Taan. 1, 9, the Baraita in Taan. 27a and Mas. Soferim 17, 5, it would appear that the authentic records of these services have not been preserved, leaving us in the dark as to their original character.

That the original number of the Weekday Benedictions was *eighteen,* and not seventeen or nineteen, is evidenced by the Mishnah Ber. 4, 3, in which R. Joshua and R. Akiba, as well as R. Gamaliel, speak of them as of a long-established institution, differing only in regard to the form of their recital in private. In fact, the Palestinians endeavored to maintain this number by combining the prayer against the heretics with Benediction XI, and other prayers with Benedictions XII and XIV.[20] Later on they were less particular and increased the number to nineteen [21] or decreased it for some unexplained reason to seventeen.[22] The omission of Benediction XV concerning the Messiah, the "sprout of David," by the Palestinians must have had its reason in the political situation.

Regarding the form of the Eighteen Benedictions, it must be stated that, while the rhythmic tripartite form prevails in the twelve middle Benedictions, we can by no means take the Yemen version and similar ones which present this form throughout these Benedictions as the original one, as is the opinion of Dernbourg [23] and Dalman.[24] It is far more correct to assume with Elbogen,[25] that, not being written down at first, the Benedictions had no stereotyped form and that only later on, when they were put down in writing, was uniformity aimed at. This accounts, also, for the many divergences between the Palestinian and the later Babylonian versions which show the process of gradual growth.

Taking up the contents of the Eighteen Benedictions briefly, we find the stamp of Hasidean conception imprinted upon all and nowhere the least allusion to the priesthood and the sacrificial cult, except in those Phar-

isean alterations of the time after the destruction of the
Temple.

Benediction I

The Benediction concerning the Forefathers, *Birkat
Abot,* which beginning with "Blessed art Thou . . . the
God of our fathers Abraham, Isaac, and Jacob, the great,
the mighty and fearful God" [26] and concluding with
"Blessed art Thou, Shield of Abraham," [27] expresses as
the main idea that "the pious deeds of the forefathers
are remembered by God" as merits by which "their children are redeemed." It expresses the *Hasidean* doctrine
of *Zekut Abot*—"the merits of the fathers."

Benediction II

The Benediction concerning the divine Powers, *Birkat
Geburot,* dwelt originally, as the name indicates, on God's
power as manifested in Creation and His sustenance of
the world, and in this form had its right place in the
Temple liturgy; but it was so altered by the Hasidim as
to lay special stress, in the words of Dan. 12:2, on the
belief in Resurrection which the Sadducean priesthood
denied; and, accordingly, the closing eulogy was formulated: "Blessed art Thou, O Lord, who quickeneth the
dead."

Benediction III

The Benediction of the Sanctification of the Name,
Birkat Kedushat Ha-Shem, has a peculiar history. While
the first of the three Benedictions was to offer praise to
the God of history and the second to the God of the
creational powers, the third was to praise the God of
the heavenly theophany with its Thrice Holy as proclaimed by the angelic choir, called "the holy ones," [28] its

essential part having been the Isaianic verse 6:3 to which Ez. 3:12 was added as the antiphonal response, and the whole was offered in dithyrambic form. The Benediction goes back to the pre-Christian time and became an essential part of the Church liturgy, in which the Cherubim, the Ofanim and the Hayyot ha-Kodesh [29] were especially mentioned, as was also done in the Talmudic and Geonic times. For the Congregation, however, the Benediction was given a more sober form, and the theophany, with its dramatic presentation by the Hasidean mystics, was omitted, and the term "the holy ones" transferred to the people of Israel. Only for the Sabbath and Holydays the more elaborate and solemn recitative of the Kedushah was reserved, part of the older form being embodied in the *Yozer Or* Benediction.

Benediction IV

The first of the twelve Benedictions forming the middle contains the prayer for knowledge, so characteristic, as Israel Abrahams says,[30] of Israel's idealism. Possibly it was first offered by the judges who began the weekday's work at the Court session, and when the original purpose was forgotten it was made a Congregational prayer.

Benedictions V and VI

The next two prayers, the one voicing the people's longing for a return to God, His Law and His worship, the other imploring God's forgiveness for their sins, belong together, as they are similar in their construction and in addressing God as our Father and King. They probably formed part of the Fast-day and Maamadot prayer. Landshut's suggestion that they may have been composed after the victory of Judas Maccabeus deserves consideration.

Benediction VII.

Regarding this prayer for Israel's redemption from
trouble and strife, Zunz [31] says that it is partly super-
fluous and partly misplaced. It certainly contrasts with
the serene and calm spirit pervading the other Benedictions, and may have had its place originally in the Fast-
day prayer, as suggested by Elbogen. Sifrè Deut. 343
has here a different Benediction preceding B. VIII.

Benediction VIII

The prayer for the sick, formulated after Jer. 7:14,
closes in the Palestinian version [32] with the eulogy:
"Blessed art Thou, O Lord, who healeth the sick"; the
Babylonian version [33] has "the sick of His people," as
adopted in our prayerbooks. Its proper place is also in
the Maamadot and Fast-day service, whence it was probably also taken over into our daily prayer.

Benediction IX

Most peculiar is this prayer for a year of prosperity—
of course, with a view to Palestine. Both its initial words
and its closing eulogy indicate clearly that it was originally a new year's prayer; whether offered by the high
priest on the Atonement Day, [34] or at the Water-libation
on Sukkot, or in Spring, or the real New Year's Day, [35] is
hard to tell. At any rate, it at last found its place in
the daily prayer. Altogether Benedictions IV to IX have
little connection with each other, except insofar as they
are of a more social character.

Quite different is the relation of Benedictions X to XIV
to each other, and Elbogen [36] well characterizes them as
eschatological. Their arrangement corresponds with the
Hasidean system which is of Apocalyptical origin.

Benediction X

The prayer for the regathering of the exiled, which forms the first stage of the Messianic era.

Benediction XI

The prayer for the divine Judgment, as Elbogen has ingeniously shown,[37] has undergone a radical transformation so that its original character would hardly be recognized but for the words: "And do Thou alone reign over us," which refer to the Messianic time. This meaning is brought out especially in the Baraita,[38] which says: "When the exiled have been gathered, judgment is held, and the wicked are humbled, and the righteous are made to rejoice." Similarly has the compendiary prayer *Habinenu*, both in the Palestinian and the Babylonian version,[39] after the words: "Thou wilt gather our dispersed ones from the four corners of the Earth," the sentence: "And Thou shalt judge those that have gone astray from acknowledging Thee, and then wilt Thou sway Thy punitive hand over the wicked, and the righteous will be made to rejoice."

Benediction XII

After what has just been stated, there can hardly be any doubt that the two Benedictions, which have the doom of the evil-doers and the salvation of the righteous for their subject, also in their original composition referred to the Messianic future. The severe language in which God is asked "to uproot, to crush, to hurl down and to humble speedily the Kingdom of Arrogance," and the corresponding closing eulogy: "Who breakest the enemies and humblest the arrogant," can refer only to the World Kingdom of either Syria or Rome, and not to the handful of Christian maligners, the so-called heretics.

If these, having become a menace to the Jewish people
at the time of R. Gamaliel, were included in the great
malediction in some demonstrative form by Samuel
ha-Katan, at the instigation of R. Gamaliel, the main
prayer remained the same, and it is preposterous to
assume that this Benediction, which is better called Malediction, is the product of R. Gamaliel's time.

Benediction XIII

The Benediction concerning the righteous ones has
likewise undergone a radical alteration. It no longer
refers to the Messianic future, offering a logical contrast
to the punishment of the wicked in the last Judgment, as
the words in Meg. 17b, speaking of "the raising of the
horn of the righteous," still do, and instead mentions the
Zaddikim, the *Hasidim,* the *"Elders,"* by which term
the Sanhedrin are named, and the *remnant of the Soferim,*
the parties and ruling authorities of Pharisaic Judaism
as they existed when the Temple and the State were still
unimpaired, and finally the Proselytes, which still occupied a prominent place at Jerusalem, as was the case with
Queen Helena of Adibene and her family.

Benedictions XIV and XV

The group of eschatological prayers is concluded by
Benediction XIV, the prayer for "the return of God's
majesty (the Shekinah) to Jerusalem," and Benediction XV, containing the prayer for the advent of the
Messiah from the house of David. The former has
been reconstructed after the destruction of the Temple,
but was originally a prayer for the still existing Temple
and had its place as early as Ben Sira among the prayers
for the people of Israel.[40] It must, however, be noted
that no allusion is here made to the Messiah, whereas in

the hymn 51, 12, the praises for "the Gatherer of Israel's dispersed" and for "Him who builded His city and His sanctuary" are followed by the one "for Him that maketh the horn of David to sprout forth." On the other hand the high priests' prayer on the Day of Atonement[41] omits the reference to the Messiah, the sprout of David.

Of course, after the destruction of the Temple, the prayer in Benediction XIV had to be changed into one for the rebuilding of Jerusalem and the Temple, and similarly the closing eulogy. Obviously the sentence: "And let our eyes behold Thy return in mercy to Zion," with the corresponding closing eulogy in Benediction XV, belong to Benediction XIV; whereas the words: "And set up speedily the throne of David," anticipate Benediction XV. This confusion can be explained only as having been due to a combination of the two Benedictions proposed for the purpose of maintaining the number eighteen.[42] Instead of "the throne of David to be set up in Jerusalem," the words apparently read originally: "and establish Thy sanctuary therein speedily" as the compendiary prayer, Habinenu, still has it.[43] The prayer for the Messiah, the sprout of David, is decidedly old, as it is attested by the Ben Sira Hymn, and its omission in all the Palestinian versions down to the eighth century must be accounted for in some way or other. The closing eulogy proposed for the combination of Benedictions XIV and XV: "Blessed be the God of David and the Builder of Jerusalem," is too awkward and artificial to be regarded as original, as Elbogen does.[44]

Benediction XVI

The prayer for the divine acceptance of all the prayers offered, with the closing eulogy: "Thou who hearest prayer," already formed part of the group of prayers offered by the high priest in the Temple on the Day of Atonement, and undoubtedly belonged from the very beginning to the Eighteen Benedictions, like the three first and the three last Benedictions. But the second and the fourth sentences hardly belonged to the original Benediction; the second, particularly, adds a new petition of a special character, while the fourth, as Elbogen rightly suggests, seems prompted by the private prayers inserted here.

There is reason to believe · that, like the second sentence of this Benediction taken over from the Palestinian version, the entire Benediction VII containing the prayer for Israel's speedy redemption from affliction and adversity, which is so different from the rest of the prayers, and, as Zunz [45] remarks, appears to be altogether out of place and to have been prompted by some temporary calamity, was originally an additional prayer offered on fast days and did not belong to the Eighteen Benedictions. This assumption would best solve the problem concerning the number *eighteen,* now increased to nineteen.

Benedictions XVII-XIX

The three last Benedictions have emanated from the Temple, but were partly altered after its destruction to suit the new conditions. The second and fourth sentences of Benediction XVII containing the petition to God "to receive the fire-offering of Israel with favor" and that "the worship of the people of Israel be ever acceptable to Him" could only have been recited in the Temple, and so the first sentence may have formed the original beginning of the prayer, whereas the words: "and restore the worship to the sanctuary of Thy house," were inserted after the destruction of the Temple. The closing eulogy of the original Benediction has been preserved in Jer. Yoma 7, 44b; Jer. Sotah 7, 22a, and in the Palestinian version, and reads: "Blessed art Thou whom alone we worship in reverence," if it was not rather, as Rashi to Ber. 11b, following Taan. 27b has it: "Blessed be He who receiveth the worship of His people Israel with favor."

Benediction XVIII

This is a thanksgiving prayer formulated after 1 Chron. 29:13. Considering the fact that after the offering of the sacrifice the people, at the blast of the trumpets by the priests, fell upon their faces in adoration of God, offering their thanksgiving, which was followed by the priests' Blessing, as the Mishnah Tamid 7, 3 and Ben Sira 50, 16-21 show, we find here the explanation for the thanksgiving following the prayer for the acceptance of the sacrifice offered at the Temple; this thanksgiving being offered in the form of prostration in adoration of God, as the term *Modim,* according to the commentators, implied.[46] When the prayer took the place of the sacrifice, the formal act of adoration by the people falling on their faces was, as Elbogen [47] wisely suggests, transferred to the time after the recital of the Eighteen Benedictions, and hence the *Tahanun,* the free outpouring of prayer with this formal act of adoration by the people, became part of the weekday liturgy.

The main part of the Benediction is old, as is shown by the high priests' Benediction in the Temple [48] and the closing eulogy: "He to whom it is proper to offer thanksgiving." In the course of time the Benediction was greatly amplified.[49]

Benediction XIX

The last Benediction, called *Birkat Kohanim*—the Priestly Benediction—immediately followed after the Priests' Blessing at the Temple, where it was offered daily in accordance with Num. 6, 22-27, with the pronunciation of the sacred Name, whereas outside of the Temple the substitute name Adonai was used. It is noteworthy, however, that the priests are not even mentioned in this Benediction and instead God is asked to "grant peace, welfare and blessing to Israel His people," and correspondingly the closing eulogy reads: "Blessed art Thou, O Lord, who blessest Thy people Israel with peace." We easily recognize here the hands of the Hasidim who would not countenance the mediatorship of the priesthood.[50] There is indeed throughout the Eighteen Benedictions a noticeable tendency to ignore the priesthood and its functions and instead to bring God's majesty nigh to the people, in conformity with the democratic spirit of the Synagogue.

CHAPTER XV

THE SEVEN BENEDICTIONS FOR THE SABBATH AND HOLYDAYS

Instead of the *twelve* middle Benedictions which follow the first three and precede the last three in the weekday prayer, the Sabbath and Holyday prayer has only *one* middle Benediction, the *Birkat K'dushat Ha-Yom*,[1] the one concerning the Holiness of the Day. As Elbogen suggests,[2] originally the Sabbath and the Holyday prayers probably had the same construction, both beginning with the words: "Thou hast chosen us from all the peoples," and so forth, and closing with the sentence: "Sanctify us by Thy commandments," and so forth, and the corresponding eulogy.[3] Nowhere in these prayers is there an allusion to the sacrificial cult of the Temple, and this spiritual character indicates their Hasidean composition. The Musaf prayer, however, with its direct reference to the sacrifice at the Temple and its supplication for its speedy restoration, by its very diction shows its late Pharisaic origin.

As to the three different prayers for the Sabbath, one for the evening, the other for the morning and the third for the afternoon, they are, as Zunz[4] assumes, the product of the Babylonian Amoraim. Originally there was no Sabbath Eve celebration at the Synagogue, just as there was none at the Temple. "The hallowing of the Sabbath Eve" was introduced by the Hasidim as they sat around the festive board, blessing the Sabbath over the cup of wine.[5] Apparently in connection therewith R. Zadok, who lived in the closing period of the Temple, introduced a short prayer beginning: "In Thy love for Israel Thy people didst Thou give us the seventh day," [6] which was also used in Geonic times, as shown in Amram's Prayerbook, but was afterwards replaced by our Sabbath eve prayer, already mentioned in Shab. 119b.

The Sabbath morning prayer refers to the precious gift of the Sabbath through Moses when "he brought down the two tables of stone upon which the observance of the Sabbath was written"; but, strange to say, the fourth of the Ten Commandments alluded to has for some reason or other given way to the verses in Ex. 31:10-17. Still later, probably for polemical purposes, sentences were added which emphasized the idea expressed in Ex. R. 25, 12 [7] that the Sabbath was an exclusive gift to Israel, not to be shared by other nations or creeds.

The Sabbath afternoon prayer also accentuates the uniqueness of Israel as God's people, with especial allusion to the patriarchs as having already celebrated the Sabbath, and may belong to a still later period. In all these prayers the spiritual character is emphasized in contrast to the priestly Temple service. The same also holds good of the Holyday prayer which refers to the blessing of these festivals.

Regarding the additional prayers on the New Year and the Day of Atonement see the next chapter.

CHAPTER XVI

THE SABBATH AND HOLYDAYS AS DEVELOPED BY THE HASIDIM

The Sabbath and the Holydays of the Pharisean law and practice differed widely from those of the Mosaic Code, and these great changes, dating from the Babylonian Exile, can be ascribed only to the Hasidim, the pious men among the laity who were the real creators of Pharisaism. The Sabbath in pre-exilic time played an inferior rôle to the New Moon, which is always mentioned first,[1] and wàs, like the ancient Babylonian Sabbath, celebrated on the 7th, the 14th, the 21st and the 28th of the month, while the 29th and 30th days formed the New Moon festival, as may be learned from 1 Sam. 20:5, 19, 27, the 30th being counted either as the last day of the old month or the first of the new, according to the appearance of the new moon. After the Babylonian week of seven days had been established, however, and the Sabbath had become the closing day of the week independently of the four lunar phases, the Sabbath assumed a higher character for Jewish life in the Mosaic Law, and the New Moon fell into abeyance, retaining only the character of a sacrificial day in the Temple, without holiness. Henceforth the Sabbath as the Day of the Lord became the distinguishing "sign" between Israel and his God,[2] and ever new restrictions were made for its sanctification both in the Mosaic Code and afterwards. Whether instituted for the redemption of man

81

from continuous labor and as a reminder of Israel's redemption from Egypt, as the Deuteronomic Decalogue has it, or as a testimony to God as the world's Creator who rested on the seventh day after the completion of His work, as the Exodus Decalogue has it, following Gen. 2:2-3, the Sabbath became for all time the most significant characteristic of Judaism. Especially when the priestly sacrifice, which could not be brought in the land of the Exile, was replaced by common prayer and public instruction in the Law, the Sabbath was transformed into a day of spiritual elevation and delight, hallowed even at the meals by blessing and praise of God.

Like the Sabbath, the three pilgrimage festivals, which were in ancient Israel adopted from the Canaanites as agricultural feasts, became historical festivals. The Passover festival, originally celebrated on the New Moon of the month of the ripening of the fruits as the pastoral Spring festival with its ancient rites, became the memorial feast of the Exodus and was transferred to the eve of the full-moon day, all the rites receiving a historical meaning. But the Hasidim gave the Passover eve a higher spiritual character, stressing the scriptural words: "And thou shalt *tell* thy son on that day," [3] and combining them with the name "The night of watching," [4] thus making it a night for *telling* all about the events of the Exodus, the *Hag'gadah* night. Moreover, calling the Passover the season of deliverance, the Hasidim referred not merely to the past redemption, but, pointing to the future, made it the season of the eventual redemption of Israel in all lands. [5]

The Feast of Weeks, also called the Feast of the First-lings of the Fruitage, was actually the closing day of the seven harvest weeks of the field, on which two loaves of bread made of the new wheat flour were offered on the altar as a thanksgiving sacrifice, after the first sheaf of the new barley had been offered at the beginning of the seven weeks, "on the morrow of the Sabbath." An especial date, however, could not be assigned to the festival, as it all depended on the ripening of the harvest each year. Quite different was it during the Exile and afterwards, when the people living far from the holy land required a special day on which to celebrate the Biblical festival. Hence it was connected with the great event of the giving of the Law on Sinai, which, according to Ex. 19:1, took place in the first week of the third month, and accordingly the words "on the morrow of the Sabbath" (Lev. 23:11, 15) were interpreted to mean "the morrow of the first day of Passover," so that the Feast of Weeks could be fixed to be the sixth (or the seventh)⁶ day of Sivan and called the season of the Giving of the Law. This was probably the work of the *Soferim* who, in striking contrast to the Sadducees who celebrated the festival in strict conformity with the letter of the Law, as did their successors the Boethusians,⁷ made of the "counting of the seven weeks,"⁸ from the second day of Passover until Shabuot, an *actual* command. The Book of Jubilees 15:1, places the festival on the fifteenth of Sivan, apparently giving to the name *Shabuot* the meaning of "Feast of Oaths," and taking it to be the feast of the Covenant of God, first with Abraham and then with Israel.

The Feast of Tabernacles or Booths, called in the older Covenant Code "the feast of ingathering at the end of the year," was in ancient Israel *the* pilgrimage feast (*Hag*) of the year, and in all likelihood its name refers to the tents of pilgrimage set up around the sanctuary, whether at Shilo or Jerusalem, to accommodate all the people that gathered there for the festival; but it afterwards received a historical meaning in Lev. 23:42f., which probably refers to the city of Sukkot— "the city of tents"—the rallying point of Israel at the Exodus. According to Neh. 8:15, these booths were made of branches of the olive tree, the myrtle, the palm and the thick-leaved tree, whereas the Priest Code, in its additional portion 23:40, ordains these plants together with the fruit of the beautiful tree (citron?) to be used for the solemn procession in honor of the feast of rejoicing.[8]   To the Mosaic celebration were added later on the popular festivities of the Water-libation, symbolizing the prayer for rain for the winter season,[9] which took place outside of the sanctuary proper amidst great illuminations, with singing and dancing, in which the Hasidim and wonder-workers, that is, the prayer heroes of the people, took a prominent part.   In the seventy bullocks that were offered during the seven festive days, the Rabbis, as early as Philo's time, found a symbolic prayer for the seventy nations of the Biblical world, while the one bullock for the eighth day symbolized for them Israel's special relation to God, the Only One.

The two great Holydays of the year, the New Year's Day and the Day of Atonement, were not known before the Exile, being neither mentioned in 1 Kings 8:65 nor in Neh. 8:1-18.   The former, according to the Mosaic system, was to be celebrated as the New Moon of the seventh or Sabbatical month of the year by a specific trumpet blast, to distinguish it from the blowing of the trumpet with which every New Moon was promulgated.[10]   Owing, however, to the Babylonian or Syrian calendar which began the year with the autumnal month Tishri, the tenth day of that month, with a view to the solar year, became the New Year's Day,[11] and afterwards the first day of Tishri was made the New Year's Day.   Subsequently the Hasidean leaders rendered the day, apparently adopting the idea from the Babylonian New Year's day of the gods, the day of divine Judgment for the year, on which God's "Book of Life" was opened to have his destiny assigned for the year to every mortal, either for good or for evil, in conformity with his merits or demerits. Moreover, under the name or according to the tradition, of the so-called *Watikim*, "the firm-minded," [12] they instituted, in connection with the trumpet blasts, the recital of three series of ten Biblical passages taken from the Pentateuch, the Psalms and the Prophets in which the three fundamental principles are expressed—to wit, that God is the world's Ruler, *Malkiot*, that He is the world's all-remembering Judge—*Zikronot*, and *Shofrot*, that He is the God of History who revealed Himself amidst the sounds of the Shofar at Sinai and will again reveal Himself in the same manner at the end of days. [13] Together with these Biblical verses, there were introduced certain sublime prayers, which bear the stamp of ancient composition, originally meant to be recited in the morning prayer, but afterwards transferred to the Musaf prayer [14] and called "the Tekiot prayers of the Schoolhouse." They invested the day with an eminently lofty character, especially when the so-called Adoration prayer, the *Alenu*, [15] at a later time made the concluding prayer of each divine service at the Synagogue, was placed at the head of the *Malkiot* section.

As to the Day of Atonement, we find the first mention of it in Ezek. 45, 18f. as the day of expiation for the sanctuary and the people, but assigned to the first and seventh day of the first month. Possibly the Holiness Code, which shows great similarity to Ezekiel, had the same date fixed for the day originally, as the verses

Lev. 16:29-31 are obviously a later insertion. Only the Priest Code, like Num. 29:7, has the day fixed on the tenth of the seventh month, possibly with a view to the solar year, which was supposed to have *ten* days more than the lunar year. At any rate, this was rendered in the Mosaic system the great day of the sanctuary, on which the high priest was to function as the mediator between God and His people, while making atonement for them as well as for the sanctuary and the priesthood by the various sacrifices of the day. Inasmuch as the sacrificial cult could not be observed outside of the Temple, however, the great day assumed a different character in the Diaspora, and it became the day of prayer, of fasting and repentance for the entire community of Israel. Thus we learn from Philo [16] that "the day was spent by the people in prayer and fervent supplications for God's forgiveness for their sins committed wittingly or unwittingly." The same we find among the Samaritans also.[17] And it is especially to be noticed that the function of achieving atonement for the people assigned to the high priest in Lev. 16:30 was transferred to the day itself.[18] True to the Hasidean principle of religious democracy, the people were themselves to obtain pardon and forgiveness from God on high by appealing to His grace and mercy. Well does Dr. Elbogen in his *Studies* [19] point to the remarkable words of Philo dwelling on "the wondrous power of sanctification and moral elevation exerted by the unique fast day upon the life not only of those especially imbued with zeal for their ancestral faith, but also of the less religious portion of the people who on this day vie with the better ones in striving for virtue and self-control."

While the scriptural words: "Ye shall afflict your souls on that day," have been interpreted by the Rabbis, by way of analogy, to mean not only abstinence from food and drink, but also from bathing and anointing, from wearing shoes and from connubial intercourse, the prominent feature of the day is the Confession of Sins (*Widduy*). In the Temple such confession was made by the high priest on behalf of the whole congregation of Israel.[20] Later on it was elaborated into three solemn formulas of confession, each ending with the pronunciation of the verse: "Before the Lord shall ye be pure." When the sacred Name was uttered by the high priest, the people responded with the familiar "Blessed be His glorious Name" as they fell upon their faces. In the Synagogue the Confession of Sins was made a prominent part of each of the five services of the day, the one on the eve of the Day, the other four on the day itself, the last being at the close, *Neilah*—literally, the closing of the Temple gates—as on all public fastdays. These Confessions of Sins were expanded even more and arranged in alphabetic order at an early period, as is evidenced by its Judeo-Christian adaptation in the Didache, and they were further developed by the Babylonian Amoraim Rab and Samuel.

Another element of the liturgy of the day was the *Selihah*,[21] the litany pleading for God's forgiveness by an especial appeal to His attributes of mercy, as revealed to Moses in Ex. 34:6-7, called the Thirteen Attributes. Talmudic tradition has it that it was exactly on the tenth of Tishri that God granted pardon to the people of Israel for the sin of the Golden Calf, after having revealed to Moses these thirteen attributes of His, and it also ascribes to their very recital an unfailing efficacy.[22] Hence they found a place in the liturgy of the fastdays and on the penitential days between the Day of the New Year and the Day of Atonement.

The Concluding, or Neilah, service, forming the climax of the day's worship, voices particularly the most sublime and broadly humane views concerning the relation of man to his Maker, and though we find reference to the liturgy in the discussion of the Babylonian Amoraim Rab and Samuel only,[23] we may well assume that it originated among the old Hasidean circles.

CHAPTER XVII

THE MUSAF PRAYER

As the Morning and Afternoon Prayers correspond to the Morning and Afternoon sacrifices offered in the Temple—the name of the latter being Minhah or Minhat Ereb [1]—so does the Musaf Prayer, offered before noon, correspond to the Musaf or additional sacrifice offered in the Temple on Sabbath and Holydays, including the New Moon. [2] R. Joshua ben Hananiah, who participated in the Levite choir at the Temple, speaks of having also attended the Musaf service at the Temple, held before the Musaf sacrifice. [3] Outside of the Temple the Musaf service was to be held only where there was an organized community of Hasidim—*Heber Ir.* [4] It is possible, however, that this refers to the Musaf or additional service of the Maamadot, [5] as Elbogen suggests. [6] Our Musaf Prayer was composed after the destruction of the Temple and is the product of the time of the (Babylonian) Amaraim, [7] its late origin being betrayed by its Rabbinic Aramean language. Only the Musaf of the Atonement Day, containing the description of the Temple service of that day and of the New Year's day, is of an older date, and it originally formed part of the morning service.

CHAPTER XVIII

THE HALLEL AND OTHER PSALMS IN THE LITURGY

Unique as is the position of the Psalms in the religious literature of the world, their all-surpassing significance lies in their having become the hymnbook of the Temple, of the Synagogue, and of the Church. No matter what historical value may be ascribed either to the Books of Chronicles, which represent David and his guilds of singers as the founders of the Temple liturgy, or to the Psalm headings, based partly on the Chronicles, certain it is that the Levitical singers invested the whole worship at the Temple with a spiritual character unknown before as they accompanied the sacrificial cult with their hymnal song and their elevating music. Not to speak of such Psalms as were chanted on every weekday by the Levites, according to Tamid 7, 4, it was above all the Hallel-psalms that gave solemnity to the festal days, whether the Biblical or the post-biblical ones,[1] or some day of rejoicing over the fertilizing rain after a season of drought.[2] In all of these Psalms the multitudes chimed in with their *Halleluyah* or *Hodu*.

The name Hallel was given especially to Pss. 113, 118, called, on account of Ps. 114, the Egyptian Hallel.[3] They were to be chanted on the Passover eve,[4] on the eight days of Sukkot, on the first day of Passover and on Shabuot, and likewise on the eight days of Hanukkah.[5] On the later Passover days Ps. 115:1-11 and Ps. 116:1-11 are omitted, as they have no special festive character,

such as the eight Sukkot days have.[6]   No Hallel is to
be recited on the New Year's and Atonement Day, as
they are not for joy but for the earnest contemplation
of life.   The Levites at the Temple chanted Ps. 24 on
the first day of the week, Ps. 48 on the second, Ps. 82
on the third, Ps. 94 on the fourth, Ps. 81 on the fifth,
Ps. 93 on the sixth day, and Ps. 92 on the Sabbath day,[7]
as is shown also by the heading of the last-named Psalm
in the Massoretic text and of the rest in the Septuagint.
As reason for this selection the Baraita [8] tells us that
they refer to the creation of each of the six days, while
the Sabbath Psalm is referred by R. Akiba to the seventh
Millennium, the cosmic Sabbath.   The idea probably
emanated from the Hasidim in connection with the
Maamadot.[9]   That the Hasidim extended the use of the
Psalms in the Synagogue may be learned from the introductory and concluding prayers to the Hallel and other
Psalm groups, in which the Hasidim are especially mentioned in connection with certain characteristic terms
used in the glorification of God.

Especially the fifth book of the Psalms appears to
have been recited by some of the Hasidim every morning, to judge from the remark of R. Jose ben Halafta; [10]
and so King David himself is represented as a type of
the Hasidim in chanting God's praise from midnight
until dawn.[11]   At a later time only the last five Psalms
were daily recited in the early morning, and, in addition
to these, other Psalms or "Psalm-verses," called *P'suke
De-Zimra,* were recited in the early service previous to
the Shema Benedictions, as a substitute for the whole
Psalter.   As to the Psalms selected for the various festivals both at the Temple and in the Synagogue, see
Mas. Soferim, 18, 2f., and Müller's notes.[12]

CHAPTER XIX

The Reading from Scripture

The reading from the Law on the Sabbath, the Holydays, and certain other days for the instruction of the people, is an institution which goes back to the very beginning of exilic Judaism and became fixed since Ezra's time, though it underwent many changes in its development through the ages. Its origin is ascribed to Moses by Josephus,[1] by Philo,[2] in Acts 15:21, and in the Talmud.[3] Deut. 31:10-12 already prescribes the reading of the Law to all Israel on the feast of Sukkot every seventh year; according to Josephus[4] this was done by the high priest; according to the Mishnah[5] by the King.[6] At what time began the regular reading from the Law on the Sabbath in the successive order of the five books of Moses, and whether the Deuteronomic interval of seven years was of some influence upon the triennial cycle observed in Palestine and on the conclusion of the annual cycle on the last day of Sukkot, is difficult to say, in spite of all that has been written about the subject, especially by Büchler.[7]

It was, above all, the democratic spirit which actually made the Torah "the inheritance of the Congregation of Jacob," wresting it from the monopoly of the priesthood, that created its reading in the Synagogue on each Sabbath morning and, later on, also on Sabbath afternoons as well as on the two market days of the week, Monday and Thursday, and at any other time when there was a large gathering of the people ready to hear the word of God. The mere legal concept which was to have the commandments concerning the various festival seasons of the year brought home in time to the people [8] cannot have been the impetus or initiative to such a mighty institution as Büchler maintains, seconded by Elbogen.[9] Most significant is the fact that the reading from the Law which was originally assigned to *one* priest or elder [10] was afterwards handed over to a select number, on the Sabbath morning to *seven* members of the Congregation, probably at first to the seven elders who sat on the platform; on the Day of Atonement to six; on the other Holydays to five; on half-holydays to four; and on Sabbath afternoons and weekdays to three members with special reference to the three classes: the priests, the Levites, and the ordinary Israelites, the underlying idea being that all alike have a share in the Torah. It was natural that all the memorial events of the year should find expression in the selection of the reading for the day. Nor must we be led to overestimate the importance of the four Sabbaths previous to Passover, as does the Talmudic law; during the Temple time they had a special function to fulfil in preparation for the pilgrims coming to Jerusalem for the festival, and afterwards they were retained in remembrance of the old custom and in view of the future when the Temple was to be rebuilt anew.[11]

Regarding the reading from the Prophets, the opinion has already been expressed above that as long as the prophets themselves or their disciples lived their words were spoken or read to the people either for admonition or consolation; and they occupied the foremost place at the devotional assemblies of the Exile. But when the book of the Law became the religious center and focus of the Synagogue, the Prophets were given a secondary place and the time or origin of their introduction was forgotten. But the Hasidean leaders stepped forth at "the dismissal of the worshipers"—the *Haftarah*— and rendered the Prophetic reading a source of comfort and hope to the people. While the *Soferim,* probably the very ones who occupied the "chair of Moses" on the platform, the seven who read from the Law, developed the Torah as *Halakah*—the legal part of Judaism, in accordance with the spirit and requirements of the time—these Hasidean leaders developed the Haggadah, the philosophical and ethical part of Judaism, appealing particularly to the sentiment of the people.

In the course of time the so-called "five scrolls" found a place in the liturgy; among these the book of Esther was first introduced as the reading for Purim, Lamentations probably next on the Ninth of Ab, and the other three on the three festivals, Pesah, Shabuot, and Sukkot.

CHAPTER XX

The Benedictions in the Synagogal Liturgy

Like the Prayer of the Eighteen and Seven Benedictions, so were all the Benedictions ascribed by Talmudic tradition, as handed down by R. Johanan, the Palestinian Amora, to the Men of the Great Synagogue,[1] in whose place we have put above the early Hasidim. Ever since Ezra's time, and that of Nehemiah and the Psalmists, the term Berakah and the formula "Baruk Y H V H" were made parts of the service, and so we find *Seder Ha-B'rakot*, "order of the Benedictions," as the name for the entire service.[2] As at the Atonement Day service the high priest at the Temple recited eight Benedictions in connection with his reading from Scripture,[3] so were also similar ones recited on Sabbath and Holydays in the Synagogue. In fact, it became the rule ever since Ezra[4] to recite a Benediction before the reading from the Law, with the introductory summons: "Bless ye the Lord!" and to close with the Benediction.[5] Likewise, the reading from the Prophets, the Haftarah, was preceded by one Benediction and followed by three or four others, formulated after those recited at the Temple.[6] To the same category belong also the Benedictions before and after the Hallel and the Psalms, and others.

Of a more ancient origin, as well as of a different character, are the Benedictions to be recited before and after the *meal* in accordance with Deut. 8:10.[7] Whenever three men partook of a meal together, Grace was

95

said in common,[8] consisting of three Benedictions or
thanksgivings, for the meal, for the land, and for Jerusalem, to which a fourth one was added after the Bar
Kokba war.[9] Especially did the drinking of wine as
a social element give rise to Benedictions before and
after. And this happened particularly when "the hallowing of Sabbath and Festival," Kiddush, made the
Hasidean brotherhood, or afterwards the members of
the family, sit around the festive board, or when there
was the "leave-taking," Habdalah, of the Sabbath and
the Holydays;[10] also on the Passover Eve;[11] formerly,
also, at the New Moon meals of the Hasidean brotherhood;[12] likewise, at the marriage festivities;[13] the
mourners' meal,[14] and the Circumcision rite.[15] Special
Benedictions were formulated, also, for the various kinds
of fruit, or food and perfumes.[16] Moreover, it was
declared to be almost a sacrilegious theft committed
against God to eat or drink or enjoy any pleasure without offering a Benediction.[17] It also became a Hasidean
custom, as may be learned from Enoch 22:14; 25:7;
36:4, and elsewhere, to bless God at the sight of Nature's
great phenomena, such as the rainbow, thunder and light-
ning, lofty mountains and the ocean, beautiful trees, animals and persons, the first blossoms of Spring, giants and
dwarfs, elephants and apes, earthquakes and hurricanes;
also on hearing good or evil tidings, on seeing a long-
missed friend, a sage of distinction or the ruler of a
country; and on the renewal of the season and the like.[18]
To these must be added Benedictions for personal bene-
fits, such as escape from danger, from prison or grave
disease, the perils of a sea voyage, or for any other
manifestation of God's protection.[19] The Benediction
was called Ha-Gomel, "Thanks to Him who conferred
a certain benefit upon the individual." Besides these,

there were instituted Benedictions for the performance of Biblical or Rabbinical commandments, this being viewed as a sacred privilege.[20]

It is difficult to ascertain how far the Parsee custom influenced the numerous Jewish Benedictions, as has been pointed out by J. H. Schorr.[21] Certain it is that the Benediction at the appearance of the New Moon was instituted in view of the Parsee prayer in the worship of the moon.[22] Likewise, the Benediction at the cock's crow every morning[23] can be ascribed only to Persian influence.[24] Especially interesting are also the three Benedictions: "Who hast not made me a heathen, a bondman, and a woman,"[25] which have their parallels in those recorded of Plato or Socrates,[26] and which were discovered by Darmstetter in a similar Persian formula, thus pointing to a Persian original, while adapted to the Jewish faith.[27] Similarly, the various Benedictions to be said privately, from the moment of awakening to the putting on of the different parts of one's dress, formulated by the Tannaim more or less after Scriptural expressions[28] and now placed at the beginning of the Prayerbook, have their parallels in Parsee custom.

The transfer of the individual Benedictions from the home to the Synagogue, for the convenience of the people, caused the change of the last of these from the singular to the plural with the corresponding close. At the same time the singular form was retained in the prayer that follows.

The Benedictions preceding the reading from the Law given in several formulas after the Talmud,[29] which in our Prayerbook precede the just-mentioned private Benedictions of the home, were no doubt intended for the early risers eager to begin the morning with the Torah reading, and accordingly a proper selection of passages from the Torah and the Talmud was made.

A rather difficult problem is offered by the portion taken from Tanna deb-Eliahu Rabba (c. 19) at the close, which begins with the words:

> At all times let a man fear God in secret, confess the truth and speak the truth in his heart, and rise early every morning and say: "Sovereign of all worlds! Not because of our righteous deeds do we lay our supplications before Thee," and so forth.

A parallel to this is found in the one prayer suggested by the Palestinian R. Johanan for the Day of Atonement, and this is followed by one suggested by Samuel the Babylonian,[30] but the whole appears to be older than both, as the contrast to the vanities of the men of the world presented by the descendants of the patriarchs who recite the Shema twice each day is original here. However, the real climax of the prayer is not, as Elbogen and Baer think, the early Shema recital, as if this were its main object, but rather the solemn Benediction relating to Jewish martyrdom, the *Kiddush Ha-Shem*—the sanctification of God's name by those who in a time of persecution were ready to offer up their lives for the monotheistic truth. And we have the testimony of Zedekiah ben Abraham Anaw, the author of the *Shibbale ha-Leket,* and particularly of his brother Benjamin of the middle of the thirteenth century, that the prayer was composed in a time of persecution when the recital of the Shema was forbidden under the penalty of death.[31] This was done by the Persian King Isdagert II, about the middle of the fifth century, and it became the cause of having the Shema inserted in the Kedushah, instead of its recital in its ordinary place in the morning prayer.[32] But it is more probable that it was during a Byzantine persecution,[33] when the Shema recital was prohibited, that our prayer, with its Benediction concerning Israel's martyrdom, was composed. The initial words of the latter found a place in Jer. Ber. 9, 12d,[34] and are ascribed there to the angelic hosts praying to God to save the world, doomed by its pagan customs, for the sake of Israel's monotheistic faith, voiced in the Shema twice each day, and themselves joining in the Benediction: "Thou wast the same before the world was created, and Thou art the same since the world has been created," and so forth. The passage, in abbreviated form, is found also in Seder Eliahu Rabba, showing that it was already well known in the tenth century. This proves its composition in the early Geonic time, if not before, and it is embodied in the Siddur of the Gaon Rab Amram, where it is placed before the regular morning liturgy. At any rate, the words introducing the whole portion: "Always should man fear God *in secret,*" must be stressed. It was while *in hiding,* and before dawn, that the prayer, with the Benediction referring to acts of martyrdom, was to be recited.

While the Tanna R. Meir, of the second century, declares it to be the duty of everyone to recite a hundred Benedictions daily,[35] the Midrash[36] claims this recital of a hundred Benedictions each day for King David, as corresponding to the numerical meaning of AL (על) in 2 Sam. 23:1. And R. Jose, the contemporary of R. Meir, goes so far as to say that "he who changes the form of the Benedictions as fixed by the wise has failed to fulfil his obligations." [37]

CHAPTER XXI

PROSTRATION AND ADORATION

Throughout antiquity, and in the Orient today, we find in the main two modes of adoration, or attitudes of prayer; the one, standing erect with both hands stretched out and the eyes lifted up towards heaven, expressive of the soul's aspiration; the other, the whole body cast down with the face touching the ground, expressing submissive humility. Between the two there are middle forms, such as kneeling and bending the head.

All these occur also in the Scripture. At the Temple the priest prostrated himself frequently during the service, and particularly after each act of service.[1] The people outside of the Temple prostrated themselves when hearing the sacred Name pronounced by the high priest on the Day of Atonement, and likewise at each trumpet blast after the sacrifice and the priest's blessing.[2] So did the visitors, when approaching the Temple at its various gates, prostrate themselves—thirteen times according to Shekalim 6, 1-3. Elbogen[3] thinks that, when fallen on their faces, the people offered a silent prayer called *Tahanun*. In the Synagogue the regular prayer was offered standing, and this was originally followed by the prostration of the Congregation, during which the individuals, presumably the Hasidim, prayed in silence. On fast days it became customary to recite aloud words of contrition, such as penitential Psalms and confessions of sins, while the prostration gave way to

milder forms, such as bending of the head; and only
the name prostration, or the falling on their faces by the
people, was retained for these silent prayers. For the
non-Hasidic laymen collections of such silent prayers
arose.[4] Inasmuch as this part of the service assumed
more and more the character of the litany of fastdays,
it was dropped altogether on Sabbath and Holydays;
and also on days of joy or of extreme grief, and confined to the average weekdays.[5]

A peculiar position in our liturgy is occupied by the
prayer of Adoration called *Alenu,* after its initial word,
with which, since the fifteenth century, each Synagogue
service closes. It is mentioned neither by the Geonim
or Maimonides, nor by Abudarham, as a daily prayer,
but an old tradition, referred to by R. Eliezer (of
Worms) and others,[6] ascribes an ancient origin to it,
as if it had been composed by Joshua the son of Nun
upon his entrance into Canaan. Zunz[7] ascribes it to
Rab, the Babylonian Amora of the third century, taking
it for granted that it formed a part of the New Year's
liturgy, opening the Malkiot portion which received its
permanent form in the Babylonian school, and his view
is without criticism accepted by Elbogen.[8]

But on closer analysis this sublime prayer stands in
no organic connection with the Malkiot portion of the
New Year's liturgy and differs from it widely in diction
and character. It is a unique glorification of God's
unity, in opposition to the polytheism and idolatry of
the surrounding nations, expressing the hope for the
speedy coming of the time when heathenism would cease
forever and the world would be regenerated by "the
Kingdom of the Almighty," to whom homage shall be
given by all the families of men on earth. In contrast
to all the nations who prostrate themselves before vanity

and folly, praying to a god who cannot help, "do we"—
it says in the prayer—"bend the knee and prostrate ourselves and bow down before the King of kings, the Holy
One, blessed be He." This was obviously written, as
Moses Mendelssohn [9] rightly states, when the Jews still
lived in their own land, as there is no allusion made to
the restoration of the Temple and the State, nor to a
personal Messiah. The very name "King of kings"
points to Persian times when the rulers bore the title
of King of kings. Hence Manasseh ben Israel [10] was
inclined to ascribe the prayer to the Men of the Great
Synagogue. In fact, no more appropriate conclusion of
the service could have been found than this magnificent
form of adoration which the Middle Ages, in view of the
Christian persecutions, invested with special solemnity.[11]

Possibly the prayer fell out of use when the admission
of proselytes, which had been a solemn public affair of
the Synagogue as it afterwards became of the Church,
had become rare and dangerous. The very custom of
forswearing heathenism with forms of the utmost contempt, and then turning around in prostration before
God the Most High, appears originally to have been
Jewish, before it was adopted by the Church and made
part of the admission of converts at the close of a
service.[12]

CHAPTER XXII

THE KEDUSHAH OF THE SCHOOLHOUSE, AND THE KADDISH

Besides the Kedushah which forms part of the first three of the Eighteen or Seven Benedictions on Week- and Holydays, and the one which was embodied in the Yozer or Benediction, there is one placed at the close of the morning service of the weekdays in which the two passages, one from Isa. 6:3 and the other from Ezek. 3:12, are recited both in Hebrew and Aramaic, together with other Biblical verses. It is referred to in the Talmud as the Kedushah de-Sidra, "the Kedushah of the Schoolhouse," and is estimated so high by Raba, the Babylonian Amora of the fourth century, as to make him declare: "The world so replete with strife is maintained by the spiritual power of the *Kedushah* of the schoolhouse and of the *Kaddish* (the exclamation: 'Let the great Name of God be praised') with which each school lesson closes." [1] To the former, two prayers are attached, one expressing thanks for the law of truth given to Israel in distinction to the heathen and pleading that "God may open our hearts unto His Law and put His love and fear into our hearts to enable us to serve Him with a willing soul"; [2] the other praying that "we may observe His statutes in this world and be worthy to inherit His bliss in the Messianic days and in the world to come."

Obviously the underlying idea is to give the house of

learning the same value as is claimed by the house of
worship in regard to certain prayers. And it is mainly
the Messianic hope that finds expression in both the
Kedushah of the schoolhouse and the Kaddish. The
prevailing opinion was that the Haggadist, the public
preacher, should always end his address with the hope-
ful outlook into the Messianic future. Consequently,
the lessons following the prayers at the Synagogue, given
for the convenience of the people there instead of at
the schoolhouse, closed with the Kedushah, the beginning and end of which referred to the Messianic hope.

But the Messianic hope found its solemn expression
at the close of the Haggadic discourse, whether in the
schoolhouse or before any large assembly, in the form
of the *Kaddish,* the Aramaic prayer which had for its
main subject the speedy advent of the Kingdom of
heaven, exactly like the so-called Lord's Prayer which,
as we learn from Luke 11:1, arose in the Essene circles
to which John the Baptist belonged. It grew out of
Ezekiel's eschatological vision, which closes with the
words: "Thus will I magnify Myself, and sanctify
Myself, and I will make Myself known in the eyes of
many nations; and they shall know that I am the Lord." [3]
In literally following these words, the preacher would
close his address, saying: "Magnified and sanctified be
His great Name in the world which He hath created
according to His will, and may He establish His Kingdom in your lifetime . . . speedily and at a near time";
whereupon the assembly responded: "His great Name be
praised for ever and aye!"

The great importance attached to this doxology of
the Haggadah and its response is shown in many passages of the Talmud and Midrash, as shown by Dr.
David De Sola Pool's instructive work on the Kaddish. [4]

The omission of the personal Messiah in the original form of the Kaddish, as Dr. Pool [5] rightly maintains, proves its origin in the pre-Christian era. Once transferred to the Synagogue, it was frequently repeated at the various parts of the service and with ever new additions adapted to its various uses. [6]

CHAPTER XXIII

THE MAAMADOT SERVICE

Concerning the Maamadot Service we possess no clear information, as our sources in the Mishnah, Tosefta of Taanit 4, and the Gemara are of a rather late date, and Josephus, the former priest, does not even mention it. The institution of having *Bystanders* from among the laic men attend the daily sacrifices at the Temple alternately every second week was based on the same democratic principle that prevailed when it was decided that the two daily burnt-offerings, ordained in Num. 28:1-4, should no longer be supplied from private or the high priest's treasury but from that of the people.[1] Inasmuch as the people were to offer these daily sacrifices, they were expected to attend them.[2] The underlying idea is that the priests should no longer be regarded as the mediators between God and the people, but the people themselves should offer the sacrifices out of their own treasury.

Thus it came about that, corresponding to the twenty-four divisions of the priesthood and the twenty-four divisions of the Levites,[3] the whole community of Israel was also divided into twenty-four sections, out of which the men were selected to serve as bystanders at the daily sacrifices (*Anshe Maamadot*) for one week each half-year, with the view that while the divisions of the priests and Levites were to function alternately at Jerusalem— unless they stayed over in Jericho for the support of the rest—the Israelitish division was represented by a certain portion of delegates at the Temple, and the rest of the division remained at home, spending the week, that is, from Monday to Thursday, in fasting and holding service four times a day. Each day they read a part of the Creation chapter in Genesis, which was followed by prayers in conformity with each day's lesson; for the seafarers on Monday, for the travelers on land on Tuesday, on Wednesday for the children that they may not be afflicted with skin diseases, on Thursday for women in the state of pregnancy or suckling their babes. On account of the Sabbath, no service was held from Friday to Sunday.[4] As a matter of course, the men selected for these functions were especially pious and competent men, and it is safe to assume, as does Elbogen,[5] that parts of the Synagogal liturgy were adapted for the Eighteen Benedictions. How far the Maamadot service was indebted to the older Fastday Service, as described in Taan, c. 2, is open to conjecture. As to the six Benedictions that were added to both, there is no unanimity among the Tannaitic records. How great an importance was attached to the Maamadot service, even after the destruction of the Temple, may be learned from the remarkable dictum of Rab Assi,[6] of the third century: "Were it not for the Maamadot, heaven and earth would not be sustained; and since the sacrifices are no longer offered, the reading of the laws concerning them serves as a substitute." Subsequently the Maamadot services were not only retained by the later Hasidim, but were ever more enlarged, as may be learned from the Geonic rituals. Likewise were the fastdays observed on Monday and Thursday each week, possibly as a survival of the Maamadot fasts.[7] The Synagogal liturgy also, at a later time, invested Monday and Thursday with something of the character of fast and penitential days by the addition of appropriate Biblical verses and devotional prayers.

CHAPTER XXIV

The Hasidim and the Pharisees

The Hasidean movement, in opposition to the Sadducean priesthood with its claims of a religious monopoly based on the Mosaic Law and the Temple, was undoubtedly started by pious individuals among the laity who formed the nucleus of the Synagogue. Only when, under the Syrian reign, the Sadducean high priests degenerated into a perilous force threatening to undermine the very foundations of Judaism, did the Hasidim, in conjunction with the Scribes, organize themselves into a separate group, "the Assembly (Synagogue) of the Asideans," as we find them called in 2 Macc. 7:13.[1] They inspired and aided the Maccabean heroes in their battle against the Syrian army, which was ten times as large as their own, and led them to lasting victory over the heathen power, having, as the last but one Psalm depicts them, "the high praises of God in their mouth, and a two-edged sword in their hand, to execute vengeance upon the nations, and chastisements upon the peoples." [2] Still they cared only for the triumph of their religious cause, obtained by the recapture of the Temple, and withdrew when the Hasmonean rulers made the acquisition of political power their aim. In negotiating with Alcimus, however, the treacherous high priest of Sadducean descent, many fell into a trap, and among the sixty that were slain was the leader of the scribes, one of the Elders revered as "the Father of the Jews,"

Jose ben Joezer, as the corrupt name Razis in 2 Macc.
14:38 ³ must be read. The Mishnah, Hagigah 2, 7,
calls him the Hasid among the priesthood, and in
Eduyot 8, 4 we find him to be the foremost teacher of
the Halakah, and in Aboth 1, 4 he is named as the
first of the Duumviri (Zugot). Most tragic as was his
end, it is illumined by the watchword given out by him
which gave first to the Hasidim, and afterwards to the
whole party of the Pharisees, its name *Perishut, Amixia*
—"Separation from the Gentile world," contrasting with
the slogan of the Sadducees ⁴ *Epimixia,* "Assimilation
with the rest." There ought to be no dispute among
scholars that the name Pharisees, *Perishata,* Hebraized
Perushim, is derived from *Perishut,* and denotes *Separatists,* a name probably given them by the ruling Sadducees and then proudly adopted by the Hasidim, whose
principal endeavor was to keep away from all who con-
nived with the Hellenists. Later on the name Pharisees
—the Separatists—denoted the keeping away from the
non-observing Jewish masses, the *Am Ha-arez* and the
sinners in the community.

Naturally the Hasidim would not call each other Hasidim, "the pious or saintly ones," nor would the Pharisees
call each other Pharisees, "the Separatists." Of the
latter we know, and this had possibly been done previously by the former, that they called each other
Haberim, Brothers, Comrades, as members of their
Haburah, Brotherhood, Company, Society. Into this
brotherhood they would admit only such as pledged
themselves, in the presence of three fellow-members, to
live in accordance with their fixed rules of piety, avoiding
contact with the *Am Ha-arez* and sinners, and especially
to observe the Levitical laws of purity at their meals.
The prevailing idea of the Hasidim was to emulate the

priests at the Temple in observing Levitical purity and sanctity; and in their austerity they went so far as not to allow a woman in her monthly period to come near her husband and sit with him at table. The Pharisees, on the other hand, representing the bulk of the law-observing Jews, were more anxious to pay regard to the dignity of woman in the household and to social welfare in general.[5] So, among other things, they assigned to the mistress of the house the honor of kindling the Sabbath eve light and thus hallowing the Sabbath. Altogether Pharisaism stood for progress and religious democracy, and, wherein the Hasidean brotherhood was wanting, for the hallowing of the home.

Especial notice must also be taken of the fact that in the so-called Psalms of Solomon (a collection of Pharisaic prayers written between 80 to 40 B.C.E., in which the impiety and cruelty of the Sadducean rulers, especially of Alexander Jannaeus, are vividly described, and Pompey's invasion of Judea represented as divine vengeance) the bulk of the law-observing Jews who suffer from the oppression of the Sadducean rulers appear under the name of *the righteous* instead of Pharisees, while the other class are called the saints, or the saints of the Lord—the Hasidim. They are the leaders of the religious assemblies more closely connected with the Synagogue.[6]

The Pharisees as a party first came in conflict with the Sadducees under John Hyrcanus.[7] Whether legendary or not, the story is told that it was owing to a personal insult he received from a Pharisean leader who cast doubt on his legitimacy as high priest that John left the Pharisean party and joined the Sadducees. It is more likely, however, that his great political success, owing to his conquest of the Idumean and Iturean countries, filled the successors of the Hasidim with dismay. Certainly this wearing of both the tiara of the high priest and the crown of the national head could do anything but please those who only cared for the maintenance of the people's religion and not for the political ambition of its rulers, however much the nation enjoyed a prosperity suggesting the days of David and Solomon. The long reign of Alexander Jannaeus, his successor, brought matters to a crisis. The people were massacred by the thousands while siding with the Pharisees, and the dying tyrant warned his widow, saying: "Fear not the Pharisees nor the non-Pharisees, but those who commit crimes like Zimri and expect a reward like Phineas." Since as a woman she could not succeed her husband in the high priesthood, Alexandra Salome was wise enough to give in to the Pharisees, whose leader, Simeon ben Shetah, happened to be her brother. Under her, then, the Pharisean party grew in power politically as well as religiously, and the priests at the Temple were forced to accept the Pharisean teaching given out as "the Traditions of the Fathers." The social state of woman also was greatly improved by Simeon ben Shetah. Thus Pharisaism became too deeply rooted in the hearts of the people to be endangered by the civil war carried on by the two heirs to the throne with their embattled armies, the one besieging the capital from without, the other defending it from within. They only brought about the intervention of Rome and the loss of independence, until subsequently the reign of the Idumean Herod glorified Judea with her magnificence in the eyes of Rome, while at the same time it sapped her strength and so prepared her ultimate end.

But, as the destruction of State and Temple in the pre-exilic period, so was the destruction of the second commonwealth and its Temple by the Roman conqueror, though a great national disaster, the means of a religious revival. The Sadducean priesthood, and its successors the Boethusians, ceased to exist, and Pharisaism became the soul and salvation of Judaism. The Torah, as interpreted by them, claiming for the Oral Law the same divine origin as for the Written Law, became "the inheritance of the whole Congregation of Jacob," and the Synagogue became the great factor of education of the people. The aristocracy of blood and of wealth represented by the upper classes, the ancient priesthood and the patrician families associated with it, were swept aside by the aristocracy of learning which henceforth fashioned Judaism. Pharisaism received more and more of an ethical meaning, and the great Mosaic principle of ethics: "Ye shall be holy, for I the Lord your God am holy" [8] was boldly interpreted in Sifra: "Be *Perushim,* for the Lord your God is a *Parush,*" which means: "Keep aloof from whatsoever is profane and unclean, as God himself is aloof from all that is impure and unholy." Of course, there were also eccentric types of Pharisees who made themselves conspicuous by their vainglorious display of excessive piety, so as to be singled out as "fools," as "plagues of society" and confounders of the world. [9] Moreover, the Talmud enumerates frequently seven classes of Pharisees, only *two* of whom are looked upon favorably, namely, those who are moved by real love of God, and those who act more from fear of God. But against these are *five* classes who are more or less under the suspicion of hypocrisy [10] and accordingly are treated with disdain, as they are treated by Jesus in Matt. 6:15; 12:34 and parallels.

While priestly consecration of life is the main motive of Pharisaism, there is also another side to it. In accordance with the rule laid down by the Men of the Great Synagogue: "Make a fence around the Law" (Abot I, I), an endless line of restrictions was introduced by it in order to prevent people from trespassing against any of the Mosaic commandments, and thus statutes were piled upon statutes to such a degree as almost to obscure the real purpose of the law. Thus we find, for instance, the drinking of wine and the partaking of a meal with the heathen prohibited, lest it lead to intermarriage and idolatry.[11] The Sabbath particularly was hedged in by ever new prohibitions, so as to incrust the kernel with an almost impenetrable shell hiding the very spirit that made the day one of elevation and sanctification. The redeeming feature of this minute legalism was that it also extended to the moral laws, warning people against any unfair dealing with one another, as for instance, by gambling and betting or keeping animals that fed on alien property, and likewise against what appeared as usury, or slander and deceit.[12]

Two leading ideas the Pharisees took over from the Hasidim: the one was what they called the *Kabbalat Ol Malkut Shamayim,* "the Acceptance of the yoke of God's sovereignty," that is, the realization of man's responsibility to God as Ruler of life. Of course, this implies the doctrine of man's freedom of action, upon which Josephus lays special stress:[13] "Everything is foreseen (by God), yet freedom is given to man." But it goes deeper and demands the consecration of the whole life to God's service, the surrender to Him of every desire and, when He requires it, of one's position or even life itself. But this also implies the recognition of His goodness in all vicissitudes of life, in adversity as well as in prosperity.[14] Like the priest, every member of Israel, the priest-nation, was so to live and act as to hallow and glorify God's name and shun everything that may cause its desecration.[15] Also fundamentally Pharisaic, based on the Prophets and the Psalms, is the doctrine of God's fatherhood, representing Him as having the same relation to all men without exception as His children, all depending on His grace and all-forgiving mercy, since all are alike fallible and none altogether free from sin or fault, as is especially accentuated in the liturgy for the Day of Atonement. The Thirteen Attributes, with which God revealed Himself to Moses,[16] therefore play a prominent part in this liturgy. However, God is above all the Judge of the World who demands justice in all men's doings; but He is at the same time the God of loving mercy, ready to pardon the sinner who turns to Him in sincere repentance, and there is no need of any mediatorship, whether human or divine. The most distinctive doctrine of Pharisaism, in contrast to the Sadducees who in their worldliness denied this hope for the future, is the belief in the universal recognition of God's Kingship at the Messianic time, which formed a prominent feature in the liturgy of the New Year's Day.

The other leading thought of Pharisaism is the *Ol Ha-Mizwot,* the acceptance of the yoke of God's commandments, whether the ceremonial ones, which, like the Zizit, are intended to render life holy with duty and chiefly to prevent the yielding to the passions of the heart and the desires of the eyes,[17] or the moral laws which are the essentials of religion. The basic principle of the entire Law is expressed in the words: "Ye shall be holy; for I the Lord your God am holy," which is understood to mean: Strive to imitate God. As He is merciful and gracious, so be thou merciful and gracious; as He is righteous and true, so be thou righteous and true. As He clothes the naked, attends to the sick and comforts the sorrowing, so do thou clothe the naked, attend to the sick and comfort the sorrowing.[18] Justice, mercy and humility, as required by Micah 6:8, are declared to be fundamental principles of human conduct in the ethical treatise of the Mishnah.[19] But all stress is laid on honesty and uprightness in intention as well as in mien.[20] Hence we are told: Let your yea be yea, and your nay, nay.[21] Particular emphasis is placed upon social justice, which seeks to establish human welfare and demands the readjustment of the unequal social conditions. Accordingly, organized and unorganized charity and philanthropy were included in the name of *Zedakah*, "righteousness," which asserts the claim of the poor upon the rich, of the helpless upon him who possesses the means to help.[22] But just as divine justice, being too severe for mortal man to be dealt with, is supplemented by redeeming love, so are love and kindness the corollaries of human justice. Far, then, from declaring love to be the exclusive principle of ethics, Pharisaism takes the sober view that the Golden Rule: "Love thy neighbor as thyself,"[23] cannot be taken in the *absolute* sense, it being impossible for us to love all men alike, and must be understood in the negative sense: "Do not unto others what thou dost not wish to be done unto thee." Thus it is taught in the Talmud by Hillel.[24] Yet in this sense the Biblical command includes all men made in God's image,[25] the proof being given, according to Ben Azzai in Gen. 5:1: "In the day that God created man, in the likeness of God made He him."

As virtues characterizing the true Pharisee are singled out meekness, modesty, and peaceableness.[26] Nor does Pharisean ethics stop with one's fellow-man. Kindness for the dumb animal and due care for its life are also demanded in the name of the Law.[27] Above all does

Pharisaism insist on purity and holiness of life, in contrast to the heathen world which indulged in lewdness, incest and sexual depravity. "Nothing is so loathsome to God," we are told in Sifrè,[28] "as sexual depravity." Every unchaste look, thought, or act is condemned by the Rabbis as approaching incest.[29]

The very acme of ethical teaching is reached when Antigonos of Soko, of the second pre-Christian century, said: "Be not like slaves who minister to their master with a view to receiving recompense; but serve him without a view to recompense, and let the fear of God be upon you."[30] · In other words, do the good for its own sake and shun evil because it is evil.[31] Similarly, did Ben Azzai teach: "The reward of the good deed is the good deed, and the reward of the sinful deed is the sinful deed,"[32] which is as much as to say: The bliss of heaven and the woe of hell are to be sought *within* you, not in places outside of you.

Considering the high ethical standard of Pharisaic Judaism, it is all the more deplorable that it fell short of the ancient prophetic and the early Hasidean teaching in clinging to the belief in the sacrificial cult of the Mosaic Law and waiting for its restoration in the future. Only the Haggadist R. Levi, in the third century, looked upon the sacrifices as a concession made to the people who were disposed to idolatry and were meant to be won thereby for the pure monotheistic ideal.[33] This was also the view of Maimonides[34] and other medieval writers; whereas Philo[35] and Jehuda Ha-Levi[36] assigned a symbolic meaning to the sacrifices.

CHAPTER XXV

THE ESSENES

The Essenes are the enigma of history. The Talmudic sources fail to mention them expressly, but allude to them either as Zenuim, Hashaim, or Hasidim,[1] and what Philo and Josephus wrote about them has all the fascination of a romance. Consequently, most Christian writers see in them a mixture of Jews and non-Jews, at least as regards their customs. Jewish scholars, for the most part, classify them with the Hasidim, but, accepting Josephus' description of their lives and views, they are puzzled by certain strange characteristics, as well as by their names. It is generally acknowledged that Josephus, in order to impress his Roman readers favorably, represented the three Jewish sects, the Sadducees, the Pharisees, and the Essenes as equal to the three philosophical schools of Greece, the Epicureans, the Stoics, and the Pythagoreans; but it has escaped our historians that he followed the same method in ascribing to the Essenes the Greek view of the hereafter, instead of the *Jewish* one, which was a belief in the resurrection of the dead. However, we actually possess a description of the Essenes, which, while otherwise identical with that of Josephus, has preserved the Jewish character, as we shall see.

Let us first consider the name, about the meaning and etymology of which there is dispute among scholars. Philo regularly names them *Essaioi*, which corresponds to the Talmudic *Hashaim*, "the silent" or "reticent" ones, while Josephus uses mostly the name *Essenoi*, which corresponds to the Talmudic *Z'nuim*—"the modest" or "humble" ones, the class of men to whom special mysteries were entrusted, according to Talmudic sources. Other etymologies, suggested by non-Jewish writers, may be passed by as valueless.

Taking up the few single Essenes mentioned by the historian Josephus as having appeared in the character of prophets, we find one Judah, who influenced the life of Aristobulus, the son of John Hyrcanus [2] and who had a regular school at the Temple. Another, Menahem, predicted to Herod his rise to royalty; [3] he was the predecessor of Shammai as head of one of the Academies, according to Hag. 2:2 and other Talmudic passages. A third one is Simon. [4] During the Roman war a general by the name of John the Essene is mentioned by Josephus in *J. W.* II, 20, 4; III, 2, 1. Evidently, then, some of the Essenes were patriotic enthusiasts and occasionally took part in public life. Their original history, however, is obscure. In all likelihood they withdrew from the Hasidean circle soon after the Temple had been recaptured from the Syrians because of their disapproval of the political ambition of the Hasmonean rulers, and retreated into separate little colonies in the neighborhood of the cities, as, for instance, the name of the gate of Jerusalem named after them suggests; [5] while others settled down in the outskirts of Judea at En Gedi near the Dead Sea, as described by Pliny. [6] These seem to have been an object of marvel to the surrounding nations in view of their living without wives and children and without money, deriving their support from the palm trees that grew there and keeping up their

ranks by the multitude of newcomers who resorted to
them from contempt of the world. Thus they exist
there, says Pliny, through thousands of ages.

Of course, we get more sober views of them as we
read Philo. He tells us in his juvenile work on *The
Virtuous Being Free* that they numbered over four thousand, living in villages, cultivating the soil and other arts
of peace, but avoiding all such industries as are connected
with war and tend to covetousness. They strive for a
life of holiness, but different from the priests at the
Temple who sacrifice animals; they invest their own
meals with the character of holiness. They never violate
the principle of equality, having everything in common
and practicing mutual love to be admired even by the
most ferocious tyrants—which probably refers to King
Herod. Their philosophy concerns itself only with the
existence of God and the creation of the world—probably a reference to the Maaseh Merkabah and Maaseh
Bereshit mysteries—but chiefly with ethics. They are
principally taught the love of God—whom they believe
to be the source of all good and of no evil—the love of
virtue, and the love of mankind. On the Sabbath day
they assemble in the Synagogue to listen to the reading
of the holy books, which is done by one of them, and
their interpretation, which is done by another. In his
later work, *The Apology of the Jews,* which has been
preserved only in part by the Church—father Eusebius,
Philo speaks rather strongly of the myriads of the disciples of Moses who live in the Essene colonies, being
drawn there by their zeal for philanthropy as full-grown
men and declining toward old age when sensuous passion
no longer moves them, and where they are undisturbed
by the attractions of a selfish wife and the burden of

children. They are happy in their life of mutual help-
fulness and brotherly affection, and cared for as if by
their own children.

Coming now to Josephus' description of the Essenes
in *J. W.* II, 8, 2-13, we note the fact that we have
another text of the same description preserved in Hippolytus' *Refutation of all Heresies,* discovered at Mount
Athos in 1842, and edited by Schneidewin and Dunker
in 1859.[7] Careful comparison of the text proves it to
be, not, as is assumed by many, a copy of Josephus, but
rather one derived from another source and of a more
genuinely Jewish character. Leaving aside the question
where Hippolytus obtained his version, we present it here
in preference to that of Josephus, pointing out, now and
then, the essential differences. It is significant that the
three Jewish sects are not represented as philosophical
sects, as is done by Josephus, but simply as divisions.
After the Sadducees and the Pharisees have been mentioned, the Essenes are made the main object of the
treatise, as follows:

XVIII. They practice a holier life, exhibiting mutual
love and exercising self-control (*Z'niut*). They abstain
from every act of inordinate desire, being averse even
to listening to such things. They renounce marriage, but
adopt foreign boys as children and train them to observe
their own habits, thus educating them and impelling them
to accept their teachings, but they do not forbid them
to marry, though they themselves refrain from marry-
ing. Women, however, though they might be willing
to follow the same mode of life, they do not admit, as
they place no confidence whatsoever in women. (This
by no means refers to conjugal infidelity, as Josephus
the Romanizer puts it, but they doubt the trustworthi-
ness of woman in all that pertains to their religious prac-

tices and their mysteries, just as the Rabbis would not accept woman's testimony.)⁸

XIX. They despise wealth, and they do not merely shirk sharing what they have with those in need, but none among them is richer than the other. For the law with them is that anyone who joins their order must sell his possessions and hand over the proceeds to the common stock, and the one at the head distributes it to all according to their need. The overseers who take care of the common goods are elected by vote.

They do not use oil, as they regard ointment to be a defilement. They are always clad in white garments.⁹

XX. They have no special city of their own, but live together in large numbers in each city. But if any of the adherents of their sect arrives from a strange place, they take it for granted that all things they have in common belong also to him, and those whom they had not known previously they receive as kindred and friends.

They traverse their native land, and whenever they go on a journey they carry nothing except arms (of course, for protection). Accordingly, in each city they have a presiding officer who disposes of what is collected there for that purpose, providing them with clothing and nourishment.

Their dress and general appearance are modest. They neither possess two cloaks nor two pairs of shoes, and when those they use are worn out, they receive new ones. They neither sell nor buy anything at all, but whatever anyone has he gives to him who has not, and what he has not he receives.

XXI. From early dawn they keep in fine order and in continuous devotion while offering their prayer, not talking until they have praised God in their hymns. (At this point Josephus has a sentence referring to their facing the sun in their morning prayer, which is omitted here.)

Thus they go forth each to do the work they are engaged in, and after having worked until the fifth hour they stop. Thereupon they assemble again in one place, and, after having put linen girdles around themselves to cover their pudenda, they thus bathe in cold water, and, having thus purified themselves, they assemble in a special house, allowing none who differs from them in their views to enter the house with them, and then they proceed to take their meal. (Here Josephus has the sentence: "They enter in purity the dining hall as if it were a holy temple.")

And when they have taken their seats according to their order amidst silence, they partake of the bread and then of some sort of additional food, of which each receives a sufficient portion. No one, however, tastes these before the priest has offered a prayer of thanksgiving. And after the meal he again offers a prayer, for both at the beginning and at the conclusion they praise God in hymns.

After this they lay aside as sacred the linen garments in which they were clothed while taking their meals together within the house and put on again the garments they had left in the vestibule, and then hasten to take up their cherished occupations until evening. Then they partake of supper, doing all things in the same manner as mentioned before.

No one will at any time cry aloud, nor will any other tumultuous voice be heard, but they all speak gently and with becoming dignity they give each other leave to hold conversation, so that the stillness within appears to outsiders like some mystery. They always observe sobriety, as both when eating and drinking they do everything in measure.

XXII. All pay due attention to the presiding officer, and whatever he orders they obey as law. But—the word "for" is scarcely correct, see especially Josephus— they are especially zealous in showing compassion and offering help to those that are in distress.

Above all they abstain from wrath and passion, regarding them as conducive to mischief. No one among them swears, but what anyone says they consider as more binding than an oath. If, however, one does swear, he is condemned as a person who cannot be trusted.

They manifest special zeal in the reading of the Law and the Prophets and of whatever scroll of the *faithful* they have besides.[10] Especially do they study diligently the curative powers of plants and stones, asserting that they have not been created without a purpose.[11] To those who desire to become disciples of the sect they do not immediately deliver their traditions, unless they have previously tried them. Therefore they would, for a space of a year, sit before them outside of their own assembly in a different house, after they had provided them with a small hatchet, a linen girdle and a white robe.[12] When, at the expiration of this period, one has given proof of his self-control, he draws nearer to their mode of life, and he bathes in purer water than before; but he cannot yet take part in their common meal. After having given evidence that he is able to exercise self-control, the conduct of the person is still tried for two years more, and when he is thus found worthy he is considered fit for admission into their midst.

Before he is permitted, however, to partake of their common meal, rigid oaths are administered: First, that he will show reverence to whatever concerns the

Deity; that he will observe righteousness toward men and in no way injure anyone, and that he will not hate anyone who is unjust to him *nor even his enemy, but rather pray for them*, and forever aid the righteous in their battle, and keep faith to all men, particularly to those in authority, for no one is given authority to rule except through God. And if he himself be made ruler, that he will in no way be arrogant in the exercise of his power, nor indulge in luxury and use any ornament beyond the custom; furthermore, that he will be a lover of truth and reprove him who is guilty of falsehood; that he will neither steal, nor ever pollute his conscience by setting his mind on iniquitous gain, nor conceal anything from his fellow-members, nor divulge anything to others, even though he should be tortured to death. Besides these, he swears that he will not impart to anyone the knowledge of their doctrines differently from the way he received it himself.—Here our version differs strangely in one point from that of Josephus. The latter has: that he will always *hate* the unjust, while our version has, on the contrary, that he will *not* hate anyone who is *unjust* to him, nor his *enemy*, but rather pray for them. As we cannot impute to a Christian copyist the change of the text so as to bring the Essenes nearer to the Christian doctrine,[13] we must surmise that a Christian copyist changed Josephus' text. In the last period our text seems to have omitted two sentences which Josephus contains: to abstain from robbing—possibly from misappropriating the secrets of the order—and equally to watch over the writings of the society and the names of the angels.

XXIV. With such oaths they bind those that come to join them. If, however, any of them be condemned for any transgression—Josephus adds, "heinous"—he is expelled, and sometimes perishes by an awful death. For inasmuch as he is bound by the oath taken and by the rites adopted, he is not at liberty to partake of the food in use among others; so at times when they thus destroy the body by starvation, they pity many at the last when they are in a state of dissolution, considering such punishment to the brink of death sufficient.

XXV. As regards their judicial decisions, they are most accurate and just. They do not pass sentence by less than one hundred persons, but then what has been decided by them is unalterable.

They honor the legislator (Moses) next after God, and if anyone be guilty of blasphemy against him, he is punished (Josephus has it, "with death"). They are taught to obey their rulers and elders (Josephus has it, "the majority," instead of rulers). While ten sit together for the same object, one does not speak unless it be approved by the other nine.

They take care not to spit into their midst, nor toward the right.

In regard to abstaining from work on the Sabbath—Josephus has it "on the seventh day"—they are more scrupulous than all other Jews. For not only do they prepare their meals one day previously so as not to touch the fire, but they would not even move a utensil from one place to the other, nor turn aside to ease nature. Some would not even move from their place, interpreting the passage Ex. 16:29 in a literal sense.

On other days when they wish to ease nature, they choose an isolated spot, dig a hole a foot deep with a paddle—for of this description is the hatchet which they hand first to those who join them as disciples—and, covering themselves on all sides with their garment, they sit down, saying it is not right to affront the rays of the Shekinah.¹⁴ Then they throw back the upturned soil into the pit; and after they have done so, at once undergo ablution, as they consider the excrement to be defiling.[15]

XXVI.   They divide themselves according to the time and do not observe their discipline alike, being separated into four classes. Here belongs the later sentence, just as Josephus has it: And those of a later period of discipline are so inferior to the seniors that if the latter should be touched by the former, they must undergo ablution as if they had been touched by a foreigner. This corresponds to the four degrees of holiness spoken of in Mishnah Hag. 2, 7.

Altogether omitted by Josephus are the following paragraphs which were probably inserted later, causing the confusion in our text, owing to the fact that the writer mistook the *four degrees* of purity observed by the order for the *four classes* of Essenes he had in view: "For others observe a still more rigid practice in not even handling a coin, saying that they ought neither to *carry nor look at nor fashion an image*.[16] Wherefore none of them goes into a city, lest he should enter a gate on which statues are erected, regarding it as unlawful to pass beneath images.[17] Others again, when they hear a discussion about God and His Law, by one who happens to be uncircumcised, they watch him closely, and when they meet him at any place alone, they threaten to slay him if he does not undergo circumcision; and if he refuses to comply with their demand he will not be spared.[18] And it is from such occurrences that they received from some the name of *Zealots*, from others, of *Sikarii*. Others again call *no one Lord except God*,[19] even though one should put them to torture or kill them.

Most of them enjoy longevity, so that some live more than a hundred years. And this *they say*—Josephus, "I believe"—is due to their extreme fear of God and to their condemnation of all excessive passion, which makes them keep self-control and free from anger.

They despise death, rejoicing in that they can finish their course with a good conscience. If, however, anyone would put these men to torture in order to blaspheme the Law or to eat offerings of idols, he would resist, enduring death and torment in order not to violate his conscience.—Here Josephus adds from his own experience, telling how during the war with the Romans, "those superb souls" underwent with scorn and smiles the most cruel sufferings and modes of death which their tormentors inflicted upon them; closing with the sentence: "They surrender their souls cheerfully, as being sure of receiving them again."

XXVII. The doctrine of *Resurrection*, however, is very firm among them, for they teach both that the *flesh* will rise again, and that it will become immortal in the same manner as the *soul* is *already* immortal. This, they say, when departing hence will enter into one place of fragrant air and radiant light, there to enjoy rest until Judgment Day, a locality which the Greeks who heard of it call the "Isles of the Blessed."—Contrary to this view Josephus states that, while the bodies are to fall into decay, and the matter they are made of is not permanent, the *souls* are immortal and continue forever. Emanating from the most subtle ether, they are enveloped by their bodies with which they are united or imprisoned as if by certain physical attachment; but when they are set free from their bonds of flesh, they rejoice in being released from a long bondage and soar up to higher realms.— Further elaborating upon the view of the Isles of the Blessed, allotted by the Greeks to their heroes and demigods, as a place of reward for the good, and in contrast to this assigning a gloomy and icy den for the chastisement of the wicked, Josephus thinks that in these notions the Greeks, with their mythological figures of Hades, have followed the more ancient teachings of the Essenes.

But there are other doctrines of theirs which many Greeks have appropriated and given out as their own. For the disciplinary system these have with regard to the Divinity is of greater antiquity than that of all nations, so that it can be shown that all those who ventured to speak about God or about the creation of the world derived these principles from no other source than the Jewish legislation. Among them it was especially Pythagoras and the Stoics, who were living among the Egyptians, that learned their views from them (the Essenes); they also affirm that there will be a judgment and a conflagration of the universe, and that the wicked will be punished.

And among them is also practiced the art of prophecy and the prediction of future events.—Here Josephus adds: "For this purpose they are trained in the use of holy books and of various rites of purification and of utterances of prophets, and it is but seldom that they fail in their predictions."

XXVIII. Then there is another order of the Essenes who avail themselves of the same customs and mode of life, but differ from them in one respect, and that is in marriage; for they say that those who reject marriage commit an awful crime, as this leads to the destruction of life and they have no right to cut off the succession of children; for if all would entertain this view, the entire race of men would soon be exterminated.

However, they put their prospective spouses to a test for three years, and if after they had their natural purgations thrice they have given proof of their power of child-bearing, they marry them. When they are in a state of pregnancy they have no intercourse with them, thus showing that they do not marry for sexual pleasure but for the sake of having offspring.—The women undergo ablution while arrayed in linen garments in similar manner as are the men in their girdles. These are the things concerning the Essenes.

In speaking of the Pharisees afterwards the Hyppolytus version correctly states that they teach the resurrection of the flesh and the immortality of the soul, and that in the future judgment the righteous never die, but the unjust are consumed in the eternal fire; whereas Josephus ignores their belief in resurrection, stating only that the soul is immortal, and that the soul of the good enters a new body, whereas that of the bad ones suffers everlasting punishment.—This certainly is another proof of the unreliability of Josephus.

Attempting after all this to give a final characterization of the Essenes, we cannot but see in them an integral part of the Jewish community down to the time of the destruction of the State and the Temple, though they lived apart and had peculiar customs distinguishing them from the rest. By no means did they form an order of monks, but, as may be learned from Philo, they joined the order in an advanced age, having probably married before, thus leaving their wives and children and going in quest of a more holy life. This they attained by giving their common meals an especially sacred character, as if they were emulating the priests in the Temple—R. Tarfon especially taught that the eating of Terumah is similar to priestly service [20]—though there is no indication of a *sacramental* character, as some writers assume. As to their claim of still possessing the power of prophecy which, according to the Pharisees, ceased with Haggai, Zechariah and Malachi,[21] this seems to have been connected with their waiting for the advent of the Messianic Kingdom which is spoken of also as "the consolation of Israel" or "the redemption of Jerusalem." [22]   Such prophesying we found practiced by Menahem and Judah, the Essenes, as told by Josephus. In fact, the mysteries of the highest antiquity of which they also claimed to be the keepers were connected with their Messianic calculations based on the old prophecies. Besides this, they were believed to be endowed with the Holy Spirit which enabled them to perform miraculous cures. But their abstinence from marriage, which is so contrary to the Jewish Law and the Jewish conception of life, is itself to be explained only as intrinsically connected with their eagerness to attain that state of consecration which would enable them to receive prophetic messages from heaven. Only when separated from his wife could Enoch learn the mysteries of God, just as the people of Israel and Moses had to be when receiving the Law from God. [23] When Zipporah, the wife of Moses, learned of Eldad and Medad having become prophets, says the Midrash, [24] she cried out: "Woe to the wives of these men, for this means cessation of connubial intercourse."

Another point left unexplained by the writers on the Essenes is their frequent, if not constant, journeying through the land and finding in every city some storehouse in charge of an administrator to provide them with food and clothing, while they were not allowed to carry a large supply of either. Obviously they went from place to place as *Sheluhe Mizwah,* "Apostles of Benevolence," to ransom the captives, release the enslaved and offer aid and comfort to the distressed, as we see many of the Hasidim in Talmudic literature engaged in such activities, and we can well understand that they had to use caution and secrecy, so as to deserve the name *Hashaim,* "the Silent Ones."

Far, however, from being detached from the world as a class of quietists, they watched the events of the day, waiting for the Kingdom of God which was to make an end to the tyranny of Rome and her allies, and they formed rather an element of restlessness amidst the Pharisean community, whether sympathizing with the Zealots or not. In fact, the Apocalyptic books, having the Messianic hope as their main object and presenting their predictions as divine mysteries, did in all likelihood emanate from them, whereas the Pharisees failed to recognize those works, with the exception of Daniel. Also, the angelological and demonological systems were mainly products of theirs; they made special use of them in their miraculous cures. Likewise did they make use of the ineffable Name to make their prayers more effective.[25]

When Philo calls them in particular "disciples of Moses," we are reminded of those select men singled out in Ex. 18:20-21, as commented on by the Mekilta Yithro 2 [26] and the Talmud B.M. 30b. So we are told by Josephus [27] that the name of Moses the lawgiver was regarded by them as inviolably sacred, next to God. In fact, we learn from numerous Talmudic passages that some Palestinian Amoraim, such as R. Haggai and R. Safra, swore by Moses.[28]

The Essenes of the En Gedi Colony, near Jericho, seem to have traced their origin back to the Rechabites, the kinsmen of Jethro.[29] At any rate, the claim of the Essenes to a high antiquity for their traditions is not a mere invention of late writers.

Down to the second century there existed in Jerusalem an organization by the name of *Kehala Kadisha* or *Edah Kedoshah,* "the holy Congregation," which made it

a rule for its members to spend one-third of the day in
the study of the Torah, another third on their work, and
the last third on religious devotion,[30] which was probably a survival of an Essene community. So were the
Morning Bathers or *Hemero Baptists,* spoken of in the
third century as a class of pious ones,[31] undoubtedly followers of the Essene practice. The same must be said of
those who dispossessed themselves of their property in
order to have it devoted to God, to charity, or to have it
declared to be "common to all" (*Makdish* or *Mafkir
Nekasav*), as was frequently done in the Tannaitic time.

Under the name of *Habaraya,* "the Brethren," members of the *Haburah,* "Brotherhood," there existed down
to the Amoraic period·an organization for charity work,
especially bent upon visiting the sick or comforting the
sorrowing.[32]   At any rate, the Essenes seem to have
existed under different names such as *Watikim,* "the
strongminded," *Kedoshim,* "the saintly ones," and
Nemukim, "the meek ones." [33]

The miraculous cures performed by the Essenes, which
consisted in the driving out of the evil spirits obsessing
the diseased (exorcism), were ascribed already to King
Solomon, whose book, called "A Book on Modes of
Healing," is referred tò in the Mishna or Baraita Pesa-
him 56a as having been "hidden away" by King Hezekiah
in order to prevent people from trusting in magical
powers instead of God.[34]   In all probability it is the
Testament of Solomon,[35] in which Solomon is described
as having, by the help of magic seals or rings in the form
of *Pentalpha,* forced the chief demons, such as Beelzebub
and Lilit, to reveal their secrets to him, that connected
with these objects of King Solomon the magic lore of the
Essenes and their cures. This seems to be confirmed
by the remarkable story of Josephus,[36] that he knew a

certain Eleazar who in the presence of the Emperors Vespasian and Titus had drawn an evil spirit out of the nostrils of a demoniac by the help of a magic ring of Solomon. To this very day the magic seal of King Solomon plays a great rôle among the Mohammedans in Egypt.

In regard to the daily ablution of the Essenes before their meals, as described by Josephus or his source, Graetz is certainly right in calling attention to the controversy between the Morning Bathers (*Toble Shaharit*) and the Pharisees recorded in the Tosefta Yadayim c.2 at the close, the former saying: "We blame you for pronouncing the name of God in the morning without due ablution"; whereupon the other ironically answer: "We blame you that you pronounce God's name with a body that is not clean of sin." These so-called Hemero Baptists were certainly closely related, if not identical, with the Essenes, and they continued under this name down to the third century when the reason of their practice was no longer known.[37] With the extinction of the order, the individual members did not give up the Essene practice, and numerous pious men observed the rule not to eat their meals unless they were handled with the same purity as the priestly meals were handled. In fact, we already find the rule observed by the Hasidim of the Maccabean time.[38] The line between the Essenes, the Hasidim, and the Pharisees was probably never sharply drawn, the name *Pharishaia*—"Separatists"—covering all three in various degrees.

That the Essenes are nowhere mentioned in the New Testament is perhaps the best proof of their having been merged in the early Church, which alone preserved for us the Apocalyptic books written after Daniel.

CHAPTER XXVI

Pharisaism as a System

Pharisaism had its beginning with the introduction of the Book of Law of Moses by Ezra the Scribe who read from it and expounded it to the people gathered at the water-gate in Jerusalem, assisted by the Levites around him.[1] Henceforth the practice of reading the Scripture and expounding it to the people was continued by his successors, the Scribes. Inasmuch, however, as this *reading* of the Written Law and its interpretation implied also its application to the requirements of the time and its ever changing conditions, there arose gradually what was afterwards called the *Oral Law* alongside of the *Written Law;* that is to say, the latter was so modified and expanded in the course of time by the Soferic interpretation that it assumed a different character from what it was at the beginning, and the simple letter received a different meaning. Thus, for instance, the law prohibiting the doing of any work on the Sabbath was so extended as to have thirty-nine kinds of work with all their derivatives specified, with a particular view to the work done for the Tabernacle, referred to in Ex. 35 :1-3; or the law forbidding the eating of the flesh of a torn or fallen animal was expanded to include eighteen or more fatal injuries. Again, when the Law says at three different places: "Thou shalt not seethe a kid in its mother's milk," it was declared to mean that meat and milk should not be eaten, cooked or used together; the original intent of the Law being no longer understood. Far, however, from beholding in these interpretations of the Scripture the product of the human mind, "the *tradition* of the fathers" rendered them the direct accompaniments of the Written Law, as having been received by Moses on Mount Sinai, and equally divine in character and origin.

At what time this Soferic interpretation of the Oral Law was accepted cannot be ascertained, but as this became the issue between the Pharisees and the Sadducees we may assume it to have occurred in the *pre-Maccabean period*. Nor must we overlook the fact that before the rise of Pharisaism, the priests, the keepers and executors of the Law, possessed the exclusive authority to decide what was enjoined, permitted or forbidden, what was clean or unclean, profane or holy, or what was juridically right or wrong; and that all that concerned the agricultural, the social and juridical life, as well as the things pertaining to the sanctuary and to Levitical purity, was under their control. Hence, their practice determined the rule and measure of things where the Written Law was not explicit or sufficient for guidance. Consequently, large sections of the *Mishnaic* Code in possession of the Pharisees emanated from the priesthood and could actually be traced back to ancient times, whether given originally in the form of interpretation, *Midrash,* or in the form of legal decision, *Halakah.* Only the disputes of the schools belong to a later period.

But the Pharisean leaders, "the Wise," were not satisfied with merely following the Soferic interpretations of the various laws of the Torah. Following the maxim of the Men of the Great Synagogue, whoever they were, "Make a fence around the Law," they added numerous provisions of a palliative nature lest the Law itself might be transgressed, or prohibitions of their own along the line of the Mosaic ones, as they did, for instance, in connection with forbidden marriages. Whatever in single instances induced them to increase the yoke of the Law, their only motive was to enhance the power of the Torah as the guardian and sanctifying guide of life. What the Hasidim in their narrower circle attempted to do, Pharisaism made its main aim and purpose, the realization of the Scriptural, and may we not say *Prophetical,* ideal to render the whole people of Israel a "kingdom of priests and a holy nation."

As long as the Jewish people formed a nation fighting for political independence, its religion was naturally bound up more or less with the state and its political interests, and many of its leaders were fervent patriots as well as religious teachers. With the fall of the nation and its final defeat in the Bar-Kokba war the Torah remained its all, and Pharisaism, with its eagerness for peace, became the determining factor of Jewish life. It was the marvelous decree of Providence that Rabbi Akiba, the most fiery patriot who had proclaimed Bar-Kokba as the Messiah and ended life as the great martyr, should also have been the foremost master of the Law who, with his great disciples, was to work out the comprehensive plan for the *Mishnah,* with its six sections comprising all the departments of the Law, performing the mighty task which two generations afterwards enabled Judah the Prince, the great-grandson of Hillel, to undertake the edition of the complete Mishnaic code bearing his name. An exquisite Talmudic legend tells that Moses, while on Mount Sinai, in a vision beheld a venerable sage, surrounded by hundreds of pupils, expounding the Book of Law and drawing wondrous lessons from every letter and dot. Struck by this sight, he inquired who this sage was, and he was informed that it was Akiba who was destined to eclipse the fame of all scholars before and after him. Thus the *Mishnah,* "the Learning," corresponding to the *Mikra,* "the Scriptural Reading," in its branching out became the *Second* Torah, the center and focus of the Pharisaic lore which finally grew into the gigantic *Talmud.*

CHAPTER XXVII

The Three Cardinal Principles of Judaism Distinctive of the Synagogue

I

The first of the three cardinal principles, as fixed by the Synagogue, is the absolute Unity of God. Throughout the entire history and literature of Judaism there runs but one leading thought: God is One. He has nothing in common with the numerous gods of the nations who rule over special lands or parts of the universe. He is not a tribal deity, a national God confined to a certain territory, as Yahweh was at the beginning of Jewish history. He is the God of heaven and earth, the omnipotent and omnipresent, the omniscient, the *all*-encompassing and *all*-pervading God of life, without beginning and without end, the Maker and Ruler of the world, the Source of all existence, the Father of mankind, just, benign, and holy beyond comparison, the One God beside whom all other gods are naught. He has neither a counterpart in the power of evil, as the Persian dualism maintained, nor does any being share in His divine nature. There is no multiplicity nor division in Him, whether as to powers and persons or attributes. He is *above* the world which is His creation. He directs it according to His supreme plans and purposes. All beings, from the highest to the lowest, are governed by His eternal laws. This pure monotheism, proclaimed by the Law and the Prophets, the Psalmists and the sages, the Talmud, the liturgy, and the philosophers of the various generations, constitutes the unique faith of the Jew voiced by him in the Synagogue every morning and evening, from the cradle to the grave, as his creed, in opposition to polytheism, pantheism, and tritheism.

Moreover, the Synagogue gave this monotheistic faith its broad, universalist character, particularly by setting aside as *ineffable* the name *Yahweh* (falsely pronounced Jehovah), the *proper name* of Israel's God throughout the ages past, which made Him appear as *a* God among many gods, and substituting for it the name *Adonai,* "The Lord," thus placing Him above all the gods as the world's only God and Lord. Nor is this God a mere philosophical abstraction arrived at by reflection and grasped by the thinking mind as the result of research for the highest truth. He appeared to the Jewish people as the living power of history, the Maker of the nation, and evolved through the wisdom of its seers into an ethical God, the God of humanity manifesting Himself in the human soul as the object of its highest longing and aspiration so as to shape man's conduct and render his life ever more godlike by striving for goodness and righteousness. For this purpose He revealed Himself first to Israel, singling this nation out as His witness and herald among the nations, to lead them all to His recognition and worship at the end of time.

Still the name *Adonai,* "Lord," kept God rather at a distance. To bring the human heart into a personal relation to Him, a more endearing term by which to communicate with Him in prayer was to be created by the devout worshipers, and thus He became "Father," "our Father" and "our Father in heaven." But here again it was only the people of Israel who in Biblical times were called the children of God and were expected to invoke Him as their Father.[1] It must be noticed, however, that R. Akiba, who claims the privilege of being called "the children of God" for Israel only and declares, in opposition to the newly risen Church and the Paulinian dogma, that it is God, their Father in heaven, that cleanses them from sin, at the same time emphasizes the divine dignity of man as having been created in God's image and of being conscious of this dignity.[2] The next step was to claim God's Fatherhood for all the children of men, all of whom depend on His all-forgiving mercy; and this, already implied in the teaching of the Book of Jonah, has found expression in our Atonement Day service.

It is significant that the Rabbis insist that every bene-diction should have the words "King of the Universe" added to "Lord our God." Even the name *Adonai*, in reverence for the Deity, was to be avoided in common usage and was to be replaced by other appellations, such as "Master of the Universe," "the Holy One, blessed be He," "the Merciful One," and others.

The absolute Unity of God, the fundamental and cen-tral belief of Judaism, became the question of life or death for the Synagogue from the time when the Chris-tian Church placed Jesus, her Messiah, upon the throne of God, either as His son or His equal, thus turning Israel's Only One God into a triune God, and only the thousand-fold martyrdom of the Jew during the terrible conflict of the last eighteen hundred years preserved pure monotheism for the world. True, the Mohammedan faith, taken over from the Jew, aided him in the battle; but, after all, that was soon made a national religion which conquered half of the world by its military might and numerical force; whereas the Jew was destined to continue only by his unconquerable spirit, ever waiting and waiting, now in bright days confronting the *credo quia absurdum* of the Church with his powers of reason and science, and then, in dark periods, indulging in mysticism and visions of false Messiahs, but always waiting and hoping for the time when all men will "take hold of him that is a Jew, saying: We will go with you, for we have heard that God is with you." [3]

II

The second all-penetrating principle of the Synagogue is the observance of and loyalty to the *Torah*, "the Law which Moses commanded us to be the inheritance of the Congregation of Jacob." The word Torah has a double meaning. It connotes, on the one hand, the LAW which, while extending over all the spheres and conditions of Israel's national life, was to regulate and fashion its conduct by its social and ritualistic, its juridical and moral precepts. On the other hand, it means "Instruction" or "Doctrine" comprising the eternal verities of the Jewish faith concerning God and the world, man and the duties of life, the elements of religion in general as presented directly or implicitly. Aside, then, from the historical portion which, beginning with the Creation and leading up to the Revelation on Sinai, occupies the first and part of the second book of Moses, the Law forms the principal part of the five books. It deals at length, first with the sanctuary and the sacrificial cult in charge of the priesthood, and then presents in various codes, belonging to the different epochs, the divine ordinances concerning the people, whether in mandatory or prohibitory form. All of these, centered in the Ten Commandments, have for their purpose the creation of a God-fearing and man-loving holy and priestlike people amidst an idolatrous world steeped by its very worship in vice and crime and indulging in sexual impurity and cruelty. Accordingly, some of these ordinances are merely restrictive, others of a ceremonial character to counteract heathenish propensities, while most of them are positive moral commandments constituting the permanent laws of humanity. Well could the Deuteronomist, in surveying them all, exclaim in the name of Moses: "This is your wisdom and your understanding in the sight of the peoples, that, when they hear all these statutes, shall say: 'Surely this great nation is a wise and understanding people.' For what great nation is there that hath God so nigh unto them, as the Lord our God is whenever we call upon Him? And what great nation is there, that hath statutes and ordinances so righteous as all this Law, which I set before you this day?" [4] For we must not forget that even such precepts as the dietary laws are declared to have been given for the sanctification of the people, to render them a priestly people. Nor was the Law, when Ezra made the Mosaic Code the foundation of the new commonwealth in Judea, immovable like the rock of Sinai, as it is depicted by Sargent in the well-known picture of Moses. Its very interpretation, embodied in the Oral Law, pointed forward to continued progress according to the needs of time and environment. It was Israel's "life and length of days." Even while it served as a wall of seclusion from the world without, it was Israel's bulwark and citadel during all the centuries of peril and persecution.

But the Torah is more than Law. It was Israel's source of light, even amidst greatest darkness. It made the Jews a people of thinkers in enjoining each father to teach his son and in rendering the Synagogue a house of instruction for all. It served to broaden the mind of the Jew by declaring wisdom to be the sister of his religion, as Miriam was the sister of Moses. [5] The books of Wisdom have their place alongside of the Prophets and the Law. The Torah comprises them all. On the one side was the *Halakah,* the codified Law, which invested the Jewish people with the wondrous power of endurance and that keen sense of duty which impressed their whole life with the ideal of holiness; and on the other side the Hagadah, the "discursive," that is, the ethical and more expansive, treatment of the Torah which brought the larger view of life into relation with religion and gave it a more philosophical tendency. The Halakah was the study for the school, the Haggadah prescribed for the masses. The one gave the more national aspect, the other the universal aspect of the Torah, man and humanity being the goal of religion.

III

And here we have already touched upon the third leading thought of the Synagogue: the Kingdom of God, the world-wide Messianic outlook. The great future of Israel was first predicted in the glowing description in Isaiah of the reign of an ideal king who was to rise from the house of David and whose scepter would encompass the whole earth in righteousness and peace. But as such a ruler failed to appear and the small Judean monarchy ended in disappointment, a prey to the Babylonian conquest, the Messianic hope, frustrated also after the Exile, under the influence of Persian ideas assumed a more spiritual character in the form of the "Kingdom of God" which was to make an end to the more or less tyrannical world kingdoms. As the Judean commonwealth became a hierarchical state in accordance with the Mosaic system, which places the high priest at the helm and knows of no King, so the personality of the Messiah, "the anointed king," even if such a one was still looked for

by the Hasidim, was not put into the foreground, the
Psalms of Solomon⁶ probably being the first to depict
his expected reign; and instead we find the prophet Elijah
to be looked for as the one to bring about the better
time.⁷ In fact, though the Messiah is mentioned in the
Eighteen Benedictions and in the Temple Benedictions
as well as in the Ben Sira hymns, he never occupied a
central position in the Synagogal liturgy. The final
redemption which would establish the Kingdom of God
over all the earth was never believed to be the sole work
of a human king. God remained forever Israel's
Redeemer. The words of Zech. 14:9: "The Lord shall
be King over the whole earth; in that day shall the Lord
be One, and His name One," voiced this ideal of the
future for all ages. The prayer for the speedy arrival
of the Kingdom of God regularly closed the Torah lesson
in the house of learning in the form of the *Kaddish,*
re-echoed in the so-called Lord's Prayer of the Church,
and so did the liturgy of the Synagogue on the great
New Year's Day in the solemn *Alenu,* the closing prayer
of each service in the Synagogue, culminate in the prayer
for the speedy advent of the Kingdom of God.

Yet who should bring this about? Not the individual
personality of the Messiah, and least of all one who
would point to heaven for the realization of man's hope
of bliss in the hereafter; but, as the great seer of the
Exile, the so-called Deutero-Isaiah, stated it for all time,
Israel, the servant of God, the Messiah of the nations
working amidst woe and suffering for the divine·kingdom
of righteousness and peace on *earth.* Well does the
Midrash tell that Israel is likened to one who wanders in
the dark night with a torch in his hand to light up his
path; but however often it is rekindled he finds it blown
out by the wind and the storm until he finally concludes

to wait patiently for the light of day. So does the Jewish people, having been disappointed ever anew by the misfortunes and fallacies of the times, wait for the great day of universal redemption. Ever looking confidently forward to the better day to come, trusting in his God who is, who was, and ever will be, the Jew waits for the salvation of the *world* which is sure to come at the end of time.

CHAPTER XXVIII

THE PHARISAIC ETHICS

As the word ethics, which denotes a system of morality, is Greek, so is systematic ethics mainly the product of Greek philosophy, and under its influence it found a place among the medieval Jewish philosophers. In Judaism proper it formed an essential part of religion from the time of the Mosaic Law and the Ten Commandments. Priest and Prophet, Psalmist and sage, apocalyptic and Rabbinic writer, all present their ethics in imperative and religious form, not in the abstract language of philosophy and science. God is the source and pattern of morality. In vain do we look in the Scriptures for a system. Only certain summaries of ethics do we find, for instance, in the familiar verse of Mic. 6:8: "Do justly, love mercy, and walk humbly with thy God," or in Isa. 33:15; in Pss. 15 and 24:3-4, or 34:12-15. Ben Sira presents a certain order in setting up the rules of conduct for the various members of society and the different stages of life. Tobit ch.4 gives his son a number of rules at the latter's departure, and the Testaments of the Twelve Patriarchs offer a compendiary of ethics in the form of an Ethical Will which is afterwards paralleled by others. Besides the form, there is also a deeper psychological view presented by these Testaments, and certain vices and virtues, illustrated by the lives of the sons of Jacob, are brought out as contrasting the Two Ways, the ways of life and death, itself a characteristic mode of teaching employed

146

by the early Rabbis. Likewise, the love of God and love of fellow-man are emphasized here, long before this found its way into the New Testament. Especially significant it is that the whole Treatise of Abot is devoted to the ethical maxims of the early "fathers" of the Mishnah, and subsequently was commented on and enlarged in the Abot de-R. Nathan; and this was followed up by a series of ethical treatises such as Derek Erez Rabba and Zuta, and others of a later date. Some of these have a specific Hasidean character, whereas the ethical maxims scattered throughout the Mishnah and Talmud represent more the Pharisaic ethics which discourages asceticism and rather pays attention to the social welfare and the dignity of man and woman. Labor is especially praised and idleness condemned, no matter what one's situation may be, for it says: "When thou eatest the labor of thy hands, happy shalt thou be—in this world—and it shall be well with thee—in the world to come." [1] More than anything, the unselfish motive in good deeds and sincerity of word or action are greatly stressed.

To single out certain points that are particularly characteristic of Jewish ethics, let me take up the words of Rabban Simon ben Gamaliel:[2] "On three things the world rests, on *justice,* on *truth,* and on *peace.*" The first question a man is asked at the last Judgment is whether he dealt justly with his neighbor.[3] It is forbidden to take advantage of the ignorance of any fellow-creature, even of the heathen.[4] "Every breach of promise in commerce provokes the punishment of Him who punished the generation of the flood." [2] "A good deed brought about by an evil deed is evil," that is, the end cannot justify the means.[6]

Like the Hasidim, the Rabbis made it a rule not to

insist rigorously on one's right, but to act kindly beyond the line of justice. So in a case where laborers had spoilt the goods of their employer, the latter was told not to insist upon compensation, and referred to Prov. 2:20: "That thou mayest walk in the way of good men, and keep the paths of the righteous." [7]

"Truth is the signet of God." [8] "He who prevaricates is like a worshiper of idols instead of a worshiper of God." [9] "God hates him who speaks with his tongue what he does not mean with his heart." [10] "Let thy yea be yea, and thy nay, nay." [11] Peace is everywhere recommended as man's highest boon, [12] while quarrelsomeness is condemned as leading to murder. [13] That the human body should be honored as the dwelling-place of God's image was the view of Hillel. [14]

The saneness of Pharisean ethics is especially manifested in its attitude toward *marriage*. The divine blessing of man at the opening of Scripture: "Be fruitful and multiply," [15] is taken as a command which no man should shirk. [16] "He who fails to perform his duty for the preservation of the race is like one shedding human blood." "He who lives without a wife is not a perfect man; he lives without joy, without protection against sin, and without peace."

It is not the formal observation of the Law, but the spirit, the right motive and good intention that is valued. "God wants the heart." [17] Nourishing sinful thoughts in one's heart is worse than the sinful act. [18] In opposition to asceticism it is said that "he who fasts to no purpose sins, for the Nazarite is ordained to bring a sin-offering at the close of his Nazareate." [19] "Man has to give account for every lawful enjoyment he refuses." [20] "Man is in duty bound to preserve his life and his health." [21] "In the same degree that man has compassion upon his neighbor the Lord has compassion on him." [22]

Insulting, nicknaming and putting one's fellow-men to shame is branded as murder; and the spreading of evil report, even when true, or listening to slanderous gossip, or provoking unfavorable remarks is condemned as calumny.[23]

At the very time when the Roman laws encouraged the exhibition of the pitiless inhumanity of man toward man and beast, Philo wrote his treatise on "Humanity," pointing out that kindness is the leading principle of the Jewish Law, demanding regard also for the slave as well as for the beast; and this was likewise the teaching of the Rabbis who included even the culprit in the commandment of love.[24]   So did Hillel teach: "Love thy fellow-creatures." [25]

And as to the beast, Lecky in his *History of European Morals* [26] points out that of all ethical systems, the Christian not excluded, the Jewish alone imposes on man the duty of compassion on dumb animals.   And while Paul, the despiser of the Law, makes the rather sneering remark on the law which prohibits the muzzling of the ox when threshing,[27] saying: "Is it for oxen that God cares?" [28] the Pharisees added new laws warning against cruelty to animals to those in Lev. 22:28,[29] teaching, for instance, that one should not sit down to the table before the domestic animal has received its food.[30]   And how remarkable is the story that R. Judah the Prince, the Redactor of the Mishnah, suffered great pain in his old age and beheld in it a divine punishment for once having with his feet repulsed a calf running to him bleating for protection.[31]

The most powerful incentive to the Jew's noble conduct is the thought that it is related to his God, whose

name is sanctified by the Jew's good acts, or else desecrated by his ignoble acts. The one is called *Kiddush
Ha-Shem,* the other *Hillul Ha-Shem.*[32] "Thou shalt love
the Lord thy God" is explained: Act in such a manner
as to make Him beloved by His creatures.[33] Fraud committed against a non-Israelite is therefore considered a
greater crime than if committed against a fellow-
Israelite.[34] The saying of Antigonos of Soko,[35] quoted
above, tells us to do the right and the good without
selfish interest.

As one of the fundamental ideas of Pharisean ethics
we may point out the remark in Sifra to Lev. 18:5:
"Ye shall keep My statutes, and Mine ordinances, which
if a man do, he shall live by them: I am the Lord." This
verse, we are reminded, speaks neither of priest and
Levite nor of the Israelite, but of *man,* which shows that
ethics comprises all humanity without distinction of race
or creed.

But the brightest part of Jewish ethics is its conception of *Zedakah,* "Charity," to the practice of which we
had better devote a special chapter.[36]

CHAPTER XXIX

The Philanthropic Activity of the Synagogue

It is unnecessary to dwell on the various precepts of the Mosaic Law and the admonitions of the Prophets and the Psalmists concerning the support of the helpless and fatherless. The principle that the strong must bear with the weak and he who has much must share with him who is in want was ingrained in the soul of the Jew from the very beginning, and in making provisions for the needy he changed the moral aspect of the world. This was already recognized by the Emperor Julian so as to induce him to establish similar institutions in his Empire.[1] Whatever the Church did in this regard in her larger field was simply adopted from the Synagogue, as will be shown later on.

As early as the third pre-Christian century Simon the Just declared: "On three things the world rests: On the Torah, on divine worship, and on the work of benevolence."[2] And in the second Christian century R. Eleazar of Modin construes the words of Jethro to Moses:[3] "Show them the way wherein they must walk, and the work that they must do," as referring to the synagogue where the poor are sheltered, to the visiting of the sick, to the burial of the dead, to the bestowal of charity to those in need and to the doing of more than the strict law requires.[4] Accordingly it is made an indispensable condition of each community to have a charity chest, that is, an organized charity;[5] and this included a

151

public kitchen for those in immediate want, and a charity box out of which the poor of the town and the transient ones were provided with money according to their need and their personal merit.[6] Only men of the highest respectability, such as belonged to the old patrician families, were selected for the delicate task of administration.[7]

Where Jews and non-Jews lived together in the same city, it was decreed by the Pharisean authorities that for the sake of peace, and in order to further relations of good will, the non-Jewish poor should be supported together with those of the Jews, the sick non-Jews be visited together with those of the Jews, and the dead non-Jews be buried and honored like chose of the Jews, and likewise comfort be offered to the sorrowing of either non-Jews or Jews; also that the collectors of alms on both sides should coöperate.[8]

CHAPTER XXX

THE HOLYDAYS OF THE SYNAGOGUE AND THEIR MEANING

The Synagogue is what the Temple never could be, the educator of the Jewish people. In this light the Sabbath and the festivals are best understood and valued. They express the leading ideas of Judaism in the most impressive and palpable form, interlinking Israel with its God ever anew. Foremost among them is the Sabbath, which no longer has a mere negative character, demanding cessation from all kinds of work, as stated by the Law, both Written and Oral, but has assumed a positive character, having been made the means of sanctification of life by its specific liturgy and by the expounding of the sacred Scripture for the enlightenment and elevation of the people. Notwithstanding the many restrictive statutes it imposes on the Jew, well could the Rabbis declare that it was the most precious gift of God to the people, as it filled the house of God with light and the home with joy such as no other nation or creed was privileged to obtain.

Next to the Sabbath in importance and rank, though not in the order of the Law, comes the Sabbath of Sabbaths, as the Day of Atonement is called,[1] which, from the high priest's great day, as it was in the Temple, has become the unique day of the people of God on which they were privileged as children to approach their heavenly Father and obtain His forgiveness of their sins by

153

true repentance and contrition. On this day the Jew learns ever anew through his Synagogal service that man is in no need of any mediatorship, human or divine, in order to be released from his burden of sins, if he only steps, in purity and sincerity of heart, before the Most High, who is nigh to all who call upon Him. For what is sin with all its crushing weight? Not an infection of the soul brought about by the venom injected into the first man or woman by the serpent in Paradise, or by the evil power which is ever eager to thwart God's plan of goodness, as those believe who take the parabolic story of Genesis as an actual occurrence. It is man's own action in abuse of the freedom to choose between good and evil with which God endowed him from the beginning. It is the more or less wilful straying away from the right path of life toward the one which leads to perdition. Yet God says: "Seek Me, and live." "Return to Me, ye wayward children, and find pardon for all your misdoings." This is the appeal of the great day whose like is not found in any other religion. Thus, the Confession of Sins, as prescribed in the Law for the high priest in the Temple, in touching notes is pronounced by the delegate of the Congregation on behalf of the worshiping assembly at the different parts of the day's service in the various traditional formulas, and, as if God Himself responded favorably, as He did to Moses when he pleaded for his sin-laden people, the thirteen attributes of Mercy with which God revealed Himself are recited, assuring the people of His forgiveness. Thus the day spent in the Synagogue ends in the message of peace from on high.

Nor should this day, the Tenth of the Month of Tishri, stand out alone. The Synagogue turned the first day of that month, the Biblical Day of the Blowing of the

Trumpet, into a day of corresponding significance, designating it as the Jewish New Year's Day, on which the world's great Ruler summons all the sons of men before His tribunal of Justice to give account of their doings and according to His record be placed either among the good who deserve life, or among the sinners who deserve death, or among the mediocre men whose good and evil deeds are balanced against each other. However naïve this conception of God may be, it tells mortal man not to wait till death overtakes him when he may be least prepared and the last Judgment condemns his life as a failure, but to enter forthwith into a careful self-examination before his inner judge and rouse his conscience to pursue the right and the good. Thus, the Jewish New Year's Day, unlike any other, is solemn as it echoes forth the voice of the world's sublime Master and *King,* the voice of life's duty to be *remembered* at every step, and the voice of human history with the *trumpet blasts* of its progressive march toward the great goal.

The Feast of Tabernacles, the oldest of the three agricultural festivals of ancient Israel, and a real Pilgrimage festival, retained in the Synagogue the character of the Palestinian harvest feast, and it was probably in memory thereof that it was called a season of gladness, just as the four plants carried in the festive procession were a survival of the past. Likewise, the prayer for the winter's rain, together with the references to the Water-libation in the Temple of yore, points to Palestine. Only by way of allegory the festival was given a broader meaning, inasmuch as the seventy bullocks offered during the seven days of the feast were taken to be propitiatory sacrifices for the seventy nations representing the Gentile world, while the one bullock offered on the eighth day was made to signify the proper offering of

Israel as the one people worshiping the One God. In the Geonic time there arose the Day of Rejoicing in the Law, in celebration of the completion of the annual Sabbatic reading of the Pentateuch. Possibly this celebration was prompted by the Deuteronomic ordinance of having the Law read to the entire people on the Sukkot feast of each seventh year.[2]

The Passover festival received in the Synagogue the name of the Feast of Redemption, and that in a twofold sense: as memorial of Israel's redemption from the bondage of Egypt, and also as the season of hope for the future redemption from all slavery.

The Feast of Weeks was transformed by the Synagogue into the celebration of the Giving of the Law on Mount Sinai, to which the early Haggadists gave a broader meaning by declaring that the divine voice proclaiming the Ten Commandments was echoed forth in the tongues of all nations, as they were intended for all mankind.

The most significant feature of the Jewish festivals is that they were not instituted in honor of any personality however prominent in history, as are all the festivals celebrated in the Gentile world, the Christian included. The figure of Moses, the lawgiver, plays no rôle in any. God alone, as Israel's Redeemer and the World's Master, is the object of all the praises and thanksgivings, and He is the center of all hope for the future. Also, the Maccabean festival instituted by the Synagogue is not called after the Maccabean heroes; it is simply the Feast of Dedication of the new altar erected after the glorious victory by Judas, the Hasmonean hero. Purim, based on the legendary story of Mordecai and Esther, cannot be called a festival of the Synagogue, as it is not even marked by the recital of the Hallel Psalms.

CHAPTER XXXI

THE IDOLATER, THE STRANGER, AND THE PROSELYTE

In primitive life man does not behold in his fellow-
man a brother or friend, but a foe; and hence *war* is the
natural status. Only the monotheistic view of Scripture
makes a unit of humanity. In history we see each nation
or tribe fighting with the other for its place on earth.
Israel, too, on entering upon the arena of history, had
foes to meet and conquer in order to take possession of
the land in which it was to dwell. In this light we must
read its early laws, which are harsh in the extreme. Aside
from the military measures which throughout antiquity
were relentless and cruel, there was an additional element in the case of Israel that made its attitude to the
inhabitants of the land it was to conquer fierce and intol-
erant. Whether carried out or merely theoretical, the
laws of extermination given in Exodus, and still more
stringently in Deuteronomy, written when they could
scarcely be executed any more, were aimed at the idolatrous inhabitants of Palestine who actually became a
moral snare to the people. In fact, during the whole
period of their first occupation of the land the Jews failed
to escape the danger of following the idolatrous practices
of their Canaanite predecessors or neighbors, until they
were driven out by the Assyrian, and later on by the
Babylonian, rulers. Those rigid Mosaic laws, given
mainly against the seven idolatrous Canaanite tribes
which were to be conquered, were at least theoretically

kept in force against all idolaters, the Greeks and Romans included, since the danger of seduction remained the same; and the Pharisean leaders added new prohibitions aiming at a complete separation of the Jew from the heathen world. Moreover, they declared idolatry, murder, and incest to be the three capital sins, and decreed that a Jew should rather die than commit any of them.

In striking contrast, however, to the spirit of intolerance which found its expression in Jewish codes of law, even in that of Maimonides,[1] we are again and again admonished in the Mosaic books of law to love the *stranger,* "for ye were strangers in the land of Egypt," as well as the neighbor, and taught that there should be one and the same law for the stranger and the homeborn.[2] The fact is, however, that the word "stranger" is a mistranslation of the Hebrew Ger, which denotes a guest or an alien *under the protection* of the law of the land. This protection was afforded to him, in Semitic circles, as soon as he had entered the tent of the Sheik of the clan, and in Aryan circles as he approached some family hearth which brought him into relation with the tutelary deity of the clan; but at the same time he also assumed a certain obligation toward that deity. Accordingly, the Jewish Ger was enjoined to observe certain laws in common with the Israelites. Thus, he was especially bound not to violate the Sabbath by doing work on that day, nor to provoke God's anger by idolatrous practice or blasphemy, and, according to the Priest's Code, to avoid eating blood and contracting incestuous marriages.[3] These are the conditions of his admission into the category of a *political Ger* or protected alien. In order to become a full citizen, however, he had to undergo the rite of circumcision.[4]

With the transformation of the Israelitish State into

a religious community after the Exile, the *Ger* became a *Proselyte,* that is "one who has come over" in abandoning his heathen belief, and, according as he accepted certain parts of the Mosaic Law or the entire Law, he was regarded either as a mere *Ger Toshab,* a sojourner, or a full-fledged member of the Jewish community called *Ger Zedek,* a Proselyte of Righteousness, that is, an adopted citizen of the city of Righteousness, as Jerusalem was called.[5] The real meaning is "One who has come under the protection of the holy city," in the same sense as the Rabbis term it, "one who has come under the wings of the Shekinah." To this end he has also to offer "a sacrifice of righteousness," [6] which was to atone for his former life of sinfulness.[7] The prerequisites, then, of the adoption of the full proselyte, as stated in Ker. *l.c.,* were: (1) circumcision; (2) bathing for Levitical purification, originally perhaps for spiritual regeneration, as the Rabbinical idea adopted by Paul in regard to baptism was "the bathing of the' Ger, renders him like a new-born child;" [8] (3) sprinkling of the sacrificial blood upon his body. This, of course, is the legal aspect of the Talmud as practiced in Palestine during the existence of the Temple, as also the names Ger Toshab and Ger Zedek were the technical terms of the Palestinian practice.

A far broader term for the Proselytes is found much earlier in the Psalms, where they are classed along with the house of Israel and the house of Aaron and Levi as "Worshipers of the Lord." [9] The name "Worshipers of God" occurs afterwards frequently in the Midrashic, and more so in the Hellenistic, literature, and in the New Testament in connection with Paul's preaching. The entire propaganda literature of Hellenism aimed at winning such Worshipers of God without urging their acceptance of the whole Mosaic Law.[10] All the more stress, it seems, they laid on the regenerative bath. Thus does the fourth Sibylline book [11] admonish these converts to Judaism to "wash off in living streams their whole body and lift up their hands to heaven to pray for forgiveness for their former godless life." Likewise do the Haggadists tell of Pharaoh's daughter, whom they call by the name of *Bath-Yah,* "Daughter of the Lord," that she went into the river to cleanse herself from her father's idolatry before she discovered the babe Moses there in the floating ark and became his foster-mother.[12] Also the Israelites had to undergo baptismal purification before they received the Law.[13]

But it was not merely the extensive Hellenistic propaganda that won for the monotheistic faith large numbers of converts from among the heathen living along the Mediterranean coast and attracted by Jewish commerce to these colonies. These was a time when the Pharisean authorities of Jerusalem also sent forth missionaries to distant lands to make converts, as we learn from Matt. 23:15, which astonishing fact is confirmed by the Rabbinical statement [14] that it was made a certain rule to make at least one proselyte each year, so that by awakening the hope for the final spiritual conquest of the entire heathen world he might become an atoning power for all, as the verse Zeph. 2:5, was interpreted. Of course, this can only have been practiced in an older period, about which a Mishnah has been handed down by Rabban Simon ben Gamaliel, containing the statement: "If a Ger desires to espouse the Jewish faith, we extend to him the hand of welcome in order to bring him under the wings of the Shekinah." [15] This was not embodied in our Mishnaic Code, however, and, under the influence of the Hadrianic persecution, proselytism was discouraged. Omitting the above statement of the earlier Mishnah, the Halakah states: "If in these times a person desires to join Judaism, let him first be informed of the sad lot of the Jewish people and their martyrdom, so as to be dissuaded from joining. If, however, he persists in his intention, let him be instructed in a number of laws, both prohibitory and mandatory, easy and hard to observe, and also about the punishment for disobedience and the reward for fulfilment. Then, after the promise of adhering to the Law, he must undergo the rite of circumcision, take the baptismal bath, and then he is fully admitted into the Jewish fold." [16] It is significant to note that, while this late Halakic rule emphasizes instruction in the legal ordinances of Judaism, the manual for Proselytes preserved by the Church under the name of The Two Ways, but undoubtedly of Jewish origin, lays all the stress on the ethics of Judaism, as did the entire propaganda literature. This was also the attitude of Hillel,[17] who obviously favored a universal ethical monotheism when he declared to the heathen who wanted to join the faith that the rule of fair dealing with one's neighbor forms the center of Judaism.[18]

As the power of the Church increased, proselytism became a peril to the Jew, and instead of taking pride in the prophetic promise that the Ger (Stranger) will join himself to Israel, and they shall cleave to the house of Jacob,[19] R. Helbo of the fourth century gave these words the meaning that the proselytes shall become a loathsome plague to Israel.[20]

In order to give to the God-worshiper, who would not accept the whole Law, a legal status, Pharisaism took up the Biblical name Ger Toshab, declaring that he must pledge himself to observe certain humanitarian laws called Noahidic Laws. These were seven in number, though at times we find only six, and then again ten or thirty laws mentioned as such.[21] The name Noahidic Laws is based on the Rabbinic interpretation of the Covenant God made with Noah and his sons.[22] These laws are (1) Execution of Justice; (2) Prohibition of Blasphemy; (3) of Idolatry; (4) of Incest; (5) of Murder; (6) of Theft; (7) of eating parts of a living animal (or as some have it, of Blood; others add the hamstringing of animals and witchcraft). According to Acts 15:20, idolatry, fornication, and animals that were strangled were forbidden to semi-proselytes.[23] The thirty laws of Noah are nowhere specified, and were probably based on Lev. c. 19, as are the verses of Pseudo-Phocylides.

While the Halakah remained antagonistic to Proselytism, the Haggadists were favorable to it in the prophetic spirit, waiting for the better day to come when all men will seek shelter under the wings of the One and Only God. The remarkable fact pointed out by Graetz,[24] that at the very time when, after the destruction of the Temple, Judaism was humiliated and threatened with extinction, it gained many proselytes from the highest social circles of Rome, which induced the Emperor Domitian to take rigid measures against "the Jewish atheism," seems to show that the high standard of morality of the Jewish people impressed the more intellectual class of the Romans who had outgrown the vulgar views and practices of their own religion. Of special attraction was also the Sabbath, day of rest and domestic joy, with its beautiful lights kindled on the evening before, as Josephus tells us of the women in Damascus, and as we gather from the Roman poets. It is interesting to find that already Abraham and Sarah are made types of such as were going about and bringing men and women under the wings of the Shekinah.[25]

Wherever the Mishnah and Talmud speak of the *Goy*, the one belonging to the Gentile world—and there is a special treatise devoted to the subject of dealing with him—it is always the *Idolater*, also called *Akkum*, that is, *Obed Kokabim U-Mazzalot*, "Worshipers of the Stars and Constellations," such as the Babylonian heathen known to the Jews living in Babylonia. The other kind of Gentiles were not known to the Talmudic Jews sufficiently to have a specific legislation concerning them. The Persian fire-worshipers were occasionally mentioned. The Christians are never included in the name *Goy* or *Akkum*. They are at times mentioned under the name of Minim, "Sectarians," but were looked upon as a rule by Jewish writers as *semi-proselytes*, as they are believers in Israel's God, though their triune God strongly conflicts with the pure monotheistic belief of the Jew.²⁶

CHAPTER XXXII

THE PHARISAIC ESCHATOLOGY

It is certainly amazing that neither the Five Books of Moses nor the Prophets, with the exception of verse 8 in the late chapter 25 of Isaiah, contain any allusion to the hereafter, although this doctrine plays such a prominent part in Egyptian lore. The netherworld, the land of the shades, forms the end of life as far down as the Book of Ben Sira, and apparently also in the Sadducean belief, though Jeremiah [1] and Job wrestled with the problem of life's inadequacy in dealing with the problem of justice. *When* and *where* will the righteous receive their due compensation and the wicked their punishment, if in their earthly life they fail to do so? This is the question which remained unanswered for the ancient Hebrews and Babylonians and their kindred. The Aryan nations, the Hindoos and Persians, however, besides the Egyptians, set up and fashioned the world of Retribution in the hereafter. The Hasidim, under the Persian régime, adopted it, seemingly as an Apocalyptic or secret lore, and from them it was transmitted to the Pharisees, and at first probably kept within a certain esoteric circle. Thus, the words of Jacob announcing to his sons "what should occur in the end of days" [2] were referred by the Haggadists to the very end of history and taken to have been a revelation of apocalyptic mysteries to the Patriarch, which, finding himself divested of the Holy Spirit at that very moment, he could not communicate to his

sons.[3]   As soon as the schools took possession of those
ideas, they became common property as the subject of
the Haggadah. At the same time the principal doctrines
concerning the future, such as the belief in Resurrection,
with its corollaries—the last Judgment and Retribution,
assumed, in contrast to the Sadducees, a dogmatic
character.

But while the entire eschatalogical system, with all its
details, emanated from Persia, it was invested with a
Jewish character, mainly by the application of Scriptural
passages, specifically from the Pentateuch—notice the
words *Min Ha-Torah* in Sanh. 10, 1. Thus, instead of
referring to Dan. 12:2 or Isa. 26:19, where the belief
in Resurrection is enunciated, the Mosaic words: "the
land which the Lord swore unto your fathers to give
them" [4] are taken as proof that the fathers still live and
possess the land, as otherwise it would read: "to give
to you." [5] Likewise are the words: "the humble shall
inherit the land," [6] referred to the world to come,[7] the
belief having been that only those who lived in the holy
land were to be roused to the new life. The words:
"Land of the living," [8] were interpreted to mean the
land where the dead are to live again,[9] wherefore those
buried outside of the holy land would have to creep
through subterranean holes in order to have a share in
the resurrection. It is with the help of the heavenly dew
that the dead are revived,[10] and the great trumpet blast
which gathers the tribes of Israel [11] is to rouse the dead.[12]

The resurrection of the body has always been viewed
as a miraculous act of God. According to R. Eliezer of
Modin, of the second century, God himself goes down
to the netherworld to rescue His people.[13] Whether the
righteous among the heathen have a share in the world
to come is a matter of dispute between the Shammaite

Eliezer ben Hyrcanus and the Hillelite Joshua ben Hananiah, both basing their views on the interpretation of Ps. 9:18,[14] and the latter's opinion that they do have such a share is the one generally accepted. In the course of time the national resurrection connected with the holy land made way for the universal resurrection, which belief is well-nigh inseparable from the doctrine of the Last Judgment.[15]

As a matter of fact, the doctrine of the Immortality of the Soul is widely different from the belief in Resurrection and was adopted only by the Hellenistic Jews who followed Plato's philosophy, as did the medieval Jewish philosophers. The Synagogal liturgy, however, retained the belief in the resurrection of the body until the Reform movement in modern times adopted the doctrine of Immortality instead.

The resurrection, the time of which is identical with "the world to come," is preceded by the Messianic era, the first stage of which in the eschatological drama is the so-called "Travail of the Messianic time," consisting of all sorts of distress, of disorder of nature and of moral decline pointing to the end of things. The idea, though originally Persian, found its support in prophetic passages, such as Hosea 13:13f.; Joel 2:10f.; Micah 7:1-6; Zech. 14:6; and Dan. 12:1. At times seven periods of tribulation, at times ten, are enumerated. The last great trouble is the war with Gog and Magog, the concentrated powers of heathendom, described in Ezek. cc. 38-39. This is followed by the gathering of the tribes of Israel.

About the length of the reign of the Messiah from the house of David there is a wide difference of opinion among the Rabbis.[16] But all assign to him the task of annihilating the powers of wickedness and idolatry, of cleansing the holy land and city of all elements of heathenism and building the house of the Lord upon the foundations of righteousness and holiness. Elijah, his forerunner, is at times spoken of as the one who gathers together the twelve tribes and leads the people to repentance which brings about the resurrection.

However high the attributes given by the Prophets, the Psalmists and the Talmudic sages to the expected Messiah, or the functions assigned to him, the fact was never overlooked in Jewish circles that he was to act only as God's servant and never as His equal in ruling the world or acting as its Judge. Nor did the belief in his coming always form an indispensable part of the Jewish faith. So Rabbi Hillel of the third century dared to declare that Isaiah's prophecy concerning the Messiah had been fulfilled in the person of King Hezekiah.[17] The foremost task assigned to him was that of a redeemer of his people from the yoke of the nations.[18] What occurred in the time of Moses, the first redeemer, will also occur in the last redemption.[19] It will also take place in Nisan.[20] The same number of plagues that came upon the Egyptians will then be sent upon Israel's foes.[21] The Messiah will teach the nations the *thirty* Noahian laws.[22] He is called *Hadrach,* which means the converter of the nations.[23]

Regarding the New or Upper Jerusalem, the views of the Apocalyptic and Rabbinical writers differ too widely to be recorded here. That the sacred vessels of the Tabernacle of Moses would reappear was an old and general belief.[24] Opinions also differed as to whether all the Mosaic laws were to be in force in the Messianic time. Nor shall we discuss here the meaning and extent of the regeneration of the world, the renewal of heaven and earth predicted by the prophets and expected to be brought about by the world-conflagration.[25]

Retribution is essential to every ethical or religious system, no matter where or when it is executed. Yet only God, who looks into the heart from which the motives of action spring forth, can judge a man's merits or demerits. Therefore God only can be arbiter at the Judgment of the soul. So the Last, or Great Judgment, is placed after the resurrection by Pharisaism. In connection, then, with Ps. 50:4 the parable of the lame and the blind in the royal garden from which the fruit was stolen was applied to the human body and soul, concluding that God would summon the soul from heaven and couple it again with the body on earth to bring man to judgment.[26] But since the Scriptures do not indicate a place of punishment for those found wicked in the divine judgment, or a place of reward for those found righteous, the Apocalyptic writers borrowed their ideas from the Persians. They selected the valley of Gehinnom, the ghastly fire-place, where under King Manasseh human sacrifices had been offered to Moloch, as the place of punishment for the souls of the sinners, who, according to the measure of their wickedness, were to undergo pain or annihilation under the direction of *Dumah*, the chieftain of the netherworld. The prevailing view of the Apocalyptists regarded fire as the means of punishment for sinners.[27] As to the expiation of lighter trespasses, the stern Shammaites teach that the guilty ones would undergo a process of *purgation* by fire during a whole year, whereas the milder Hillelites declare that He who is plenteous in mercy would incline the scales toward mercy.[28] According to R. Akiba, the punishment of the wicked lasts twelve months, and only those who committed severe sins, acting treacherously against the Law or seducing others to heresy, will have to endure everlasting punishment.[29]

As the place of *reward*, the Jewish Apocalyptists selected the Biblical *Garden of Eden*, the abode of the Deity with its tree of life, from which the first human pair was expelled on account of their sin, and into which they were again to be admitted when found free from sin. The words in Isa. 65:13: "Behold, My servants shall eat, but ye shall be hungry; My servants shall drink, but ye shall be thirsty," and so forth, being referred to the world to come, gave rise to the idea of a *banquet* prepared for the righteous.[30] The Rabbis gave it the specific name of "Banquet of Leviathan," in view of the fact that Behemoth and Leviathan in Job 40:15-41:26 were taken by the Apocalyptists[31] to be destined to serve as a meal for the righteous, the verse Job 40:30 being interpreted: "The Associates," that is, the pious, "shall hold their meal over it." There is no doubt that the idea was derived from the Persian food of immortality prepared from the primeval ox Hadhaios.[32] To the meal of the banquet belongs also the *wine* prepared from the beginning of the world[33] and the *Manna*, "the brew of the angels."[34] This sensual view of the future reward was disputed, however, by the Amoraim R. Johanan and Rab. The former says:[35] "All the bliss predicted by the prophets refers only to the Messianic time, whereas in regard to that prepared for the righteous in the future life it is said: 'No eye hath seen it besides Thee, O God.'"[36] The other declares: "In the world to come there is neither eating nor drinking, nor procreation, nor envy and strife, but the righteous sit with crowns on their heads enjoying the splendor of the divine majesty."[37] Still, the later Midrashim give elaborate descriptions of Paradise with its joys, and of Gehenna with its pains, such as emanated from the Apocalyptic sources.[38]

CHAPTER XXXIII

The Apocalyptic Literature

A.

Just as the Essenes occupy a peculiar place among the Jewish parties or sects of the pre-Christian time, being nowhere mentioned in the Talmudic sources, so the Jewish Apocalyptic writings of the same period form no integral part of the Rabbinic literature. This fact led Dr. Schechter, in his *Aspects of Rabbinic Theology*,[1] to deny to them any influence on Rabbinic thought and to identify them with the so-called "external," that is, heretical, books condemned by R. Akiba.[2] As was pointed out by me, however, in the article "The Essenes and the Apocalyptic Literature,"[3] he failed to take due cognizance of the extensive eschatological and cosmological material scattered throughout the Talmud and the medieval Jewish literature, which can only have emanated from the Apocalyptic circles. In contrast to the Halakah, taught in the schools and traced back to Moses on Sinai, the Apocalyptic lore was esoteric in character, and was believed to have come down from the progenitors of the human race, from Enoch, Noah, and Shem, or the Patriarchs and Job.[4] After the destruction of the second Temple, the popular heroes of the Babylonian captivity, Baruch and Ezra, took the place of the men of the hoary antiquity, and in the Geonic period the martyrs of the Bar-Kokba war became the bearers of the heavenly mysteries. Specified among those mysteries are those of the heavenly throne-chariot of Ezekiel, the *Maaseh Merkabah,* already referred to by Ben Sira 49, 8, and those of the Creation, the *Maase Bereshit,* also "the chambers of Behemoth and Leviathan," or of "Paradise," or those of "the Messianic End," spoken of as having been revealed amidst ecstatic visions to the few elect by R. Johanan ben Zakkai and his disciples.[5] Now there can hardly be any doubt that the mysteries referred to in Dan. 8:26; 11:35; 12:4-9; Enoch 58:5; 104:12; Slav. Enoch 24:3; Jubil. 7:38; 12:27; 45:16; 4 Ezra 12:37f.; 14:6-7; 45-47 were substantially identical with the contents of the sacred books of the order of the Essenes who were pledged by a fearful oath not to divulge or alter any.[6]

The characteristics of those Apocalyptic books are that they are pseudonymic, some saint or sage of antiquity being presented as the recipient of the "revelation," and that in prophesying "the end" they offer a perspective of the history of the world in a cosmic rather than a national spirit. The beginning of the Apocalyptic literature is made by the Book of Daniel, written mainly, as is shown by Beerman,[7] for the circle of the Hasidim or Essenes during the Maccabean war, in expectation of heavenly intervention. It found its place in the last collection of the canonical books, but not among the prophets, where Josephus[8] and the Church placed it. Differently from prophecy, the Apocalypse deals mainly with superhuman or cosmic forces working after the plan of heavenly predestination which rules history. Moreover, the prophets, having only this world in view, announced in a rather indefinite way "the day of Yahweh," when the God of Sinai, who manifested himself in all the terrors and devastating powers of nature, would appear as the mighty moral power to execute His judgment upon the wicked nations and establish right-eousness on earth, while the Apocalyptic seer, with his view extended over a world beyond this, points, amidst the great tribulation and anxiety caused by the wicked world-kingdom, with a reassuring definiteness to the approaching doom of this world and the rise of God's kingdom in all its miraculous power. Here the Messiah of the prophets is transformed from a national ruler into a cosmic power, a savior of the world, parallel to the Zoroastrian Soshiosh (Saoshyant).

We may state with certainty that only when the Jews came in touch with Persia, probably in the lowlands of Babylonia, the belief in a hereafter and in the Resurrec-tion—alike unknown to Ecclesiastes and Ben Sira—was adopted by them, that is, by the Hasidean leaders and their Pharisean followers. And accordingly the entire history of the world had to be reconstructed from a larger point of view and a wider outlook upon the future. In order to achieve this, new types of men arose, differ-ent from the schoolmen and scribes whose work was centred upon the Law, men of bold vision who dared to soar on the wings of fantastic speculation to the mystic realms of the great above and beyond, and to disclose, under the name of some remote sage or saint, the beginning and end of things, thus offering light and comfort to their anxious contemporaries. Such were the Apocalyptists who succeeded in enlarging the horizon and vista of life for the Hasidean circle, while announc-ing in a form more definite than that of the prophets the approaching end of this earthly world of sin and woe and the dawn of a better one which would readjust the inadequacies of the present life. In the course of time the dualism of time—the here and the hereafter—and of space—the celestial and infernal realm with their angelic or demoniacal beings—between which the earth, as the human habitation, is swayed, became dominant also in Pharisaism. At the same time the pessimistic aspect of life which found expression in the words: "It would have been better for man if he had not been born," [9] was rejected by the more sober and practical Hillelites and their followers, who would not endorse such other-worldliness.

B. 1

For a brief survey of the entire Apocalyptic literature, we have to begin with the book of Daniel, which was written for the circle of the Hasidim during the Maccabean war, but apparently before the Maccabean victory,[10] and, on account of its influence upon the war, found its place in the last collection of the Canonical books, though not among the Prophets, where the Church, following Josephus,[11] placed it. Stress is laid upon the predestined end of days,[12] the seventy years of Jeremiah [13] forming the basis of the calculation;[14] and this end is to come without human interference.[15] Its termination, however, at the lapse of three and a half years [16] or of 1290 days,[17] after the great trouble has reached its climax [18] in the erection of the pagan idol *Baal Shomem,* "the Abomination of Desolation," on God's altar, obviously rests upon the historical event. The historical or cosmic construction after the four world-kingdoms, Babylonia, Media, Persia, and Syria, symbolized by the four metals [19] or the four beasts,[20] indicates Babylonian influence; whereas the eschatological figure, "the man-like being coming down with the clouds" to whom "the kingdom and the dominion over the nations will be finally given for ever," [21] can be no other than the Messiah, but of a cosmic rather than of a human

and mere national character, such as is the Persian
Saoshyant. Also, the Resurrection to be brought about
by the archangel Michael as "the salvation of those
inscribed in the book" when "many of them that sleep
in the dust shall awake, some to everlasting life and
some to reproaches and everlasting abhorrence," [22] is
adopted from the Persian system, which alone has a
Judgment Day after death.

Who, then, was this Daniel who is represented here
as the type of a Hasid initiated into the divine mysteries,
while serving as the great sage at the courts of the Babylonian and Persian Kings, like Joseph at the court of
Pharaoh? We find him mentioned by Ezekiel together
with Noah and Job as the righteous men of yore,[23] and
again as the ancient sage "to whom no secret is
unknown." [24] In other words, he is a legendary figure
of antiquity whom the unknown author of the Maccabean time makes the bearer of his great message of
divine comfort and hope to his oppressed people, as
foreordained in the book of the world's destiny.

Similarly did the authors of the books of Enoch select
the more famous sage and saint of antiquity, Enoch, who,
after having walked in communion with God, was taken
up to heaven,[25] and whom legend made a companion
of the angels and the possessor of all knowledge and
wisdom, as the bearer of all the divine mysteries from
the world's beginning and the preacher of righteousness
to the generations of men. As we know now, he had
his prototype in *Emenduraki*, "the priestly possessor of
all the mysteries of heaven and earth," like Enoch the
seventh of the kings of the ten generations before the
flood and "the heavenly scribe." [26] But he was also
the hero of Palestinian or old Semitic folklore which connected him with Mount Hermon, originally, as the name

betokens, a rallying place of the gods, and later on made the locality of the mythical story told in Gen. 6:1-3 of the sons of God who by their intercourse with the daughters of men became the progenitors of the generations of giants. Cast down from heaven, these fallen angels asked Enoch to intercede for them with God, but without avail; and the celestial rebels were doomed to be imprisoned forever in the infernal regions. This mythological story was again linked with another, relating how the two leaders of these rebels *Shemai-achzai* (Greek, *Semiazas*) and *Azazel,* each at the head of a group of one hundred, seduced the human race, and especially the women, to commit all kinds of *witchcraft* and deceit in order to lure men to sin. Of those two Azazel, the demon of the wilderness, was believed to have been imprisoned beneath the ravines of the rock near Jerusalem where the scapegoat, according to Lev. 16:22, was to be cast down every year on the Atonement Day for the expiation of the people's sins.[27]   Hence the Gehinnom, the valley below Jerusalem, was also made the place of the punishment of sinners.[28]

As to Shemai-achzai, the following mythological story is told by Rab Joseph, an Amora at the close of the third century:[29] When the generation of the Flood provoked God by idolatrous practices, Shemai-achzai and Azazel claimed that they had wisely opposed the creation of man, but God said: "What would have become of the world without man?" and as they replied: "We would have taken care of it," God replied, "If you would live on earth, the Evil Desire would take hold of you and make you worse than mankind." Thereupon they said: "Give us permission to live with them and Thou shalt see how we would hallow Thy name." But no sooner was this permission granted than the Evil Desire made them fall in love with the daughters of men and they corrupted the world. Among these Shemai-achzai beheld Isthar and, captured by her beauty, tried to persuade her to yield to him; but she said: "First teach me the pronunciation of the ineffable Name which enables thee to soar up to heaven." As soon as she had learned it, however, she escaped, rising to heaven in purity, and in recompense for this God placed her among the seven Pleiades. In the meantime the rebel angels and their offspring continued their mischievous ways, devastating the earth, sparing neither beast nor man. So Enoch-Metatron sent word to Shemai-achzai announcing the impending destruction of the world by the Flood, and when his two sons beheld the latter in dreams he repented and hanged himself upon the roof of heaven, seizing it with his feet while his head remained suspended downwards to the earth." Here we have the real meaning of his name, Shemai-achzai—"Heaven-seizer." Azazel, however, remained the rebel-leader.

All these astrological myths had their home in Babylonia, and here we see some part of the angelological system, including the star-angels of the Enoch books. Of course, the Biblical story relating Enoch's translation to heaven gave rise to the description of his journeys through the heavens and of all he saw on the earth below, especially Paradise and Gehinnom, and to the treatise on Astronomy with especial reference to the lunar calendar. Most of these, as well as his visions and exhortations, are presented as addresses to his son Methuselah, while the so-called book of Similitudes,[30] written much later, is addressed to his grandson Noah.[31] The older portion,[32] which contains no allusion to the Maccabean war as do the Similitudes, and may therefore be older than the Book of Daniel, offers views of reward and punishment which bear still, as in the Prophetic literature, the terrestrial character. The righteous enjoy a long life, "blessed with a thousand children and a wondrous abundance of wine and oil," [33] and the place of punishment, Gehenna, is still the valley near Jerusalem,[34] as in Jer. 7:31, while Paradise, the Garden of Eden (misread "of Righteousness" in 29:2 and 32:3) is, with its tree of life, to be transplanted from the Erythraean sea to Jerusalem.[35] Only Ch. 22 forms part of a later vision, as it presents Gehenna as having different partitions for the souls of the various sinners.

Of a far more spiritual character are the so-called Beast-Visions [36] and the Weeks of Vision.[37] Both present the history of the world with a view to the Messianic future ushered in by the great Judgment Day. In the former the seventy nations of the world figure as wild beasts and birds of prey, the people of Israel as the sheep protected by God, the Lord of the sheep, as long as they live in Palestine, but handed over to the seventy guardian-angels of the nations when in their spiritual blindness, that is, on account of their sins, they had to leave the holy land. The seventy years of the diaspora, of which Jeremiah [38] speaks, appear in this Apocalypse as seventy periods divided after the four world-epochs, the first ending with Cyrus (536 B.C.E.), the second with Alexander the Great (338 B.C.E.), the third with the Egypto-Syrian Kingdom (about 200 B.C.E.), and the fourth, the time when "the white lambs are born of the sheep," that is, the Hasidean party who opposed the Hellenistic movement in Palestine which ended with the Maccabean victory under Judas "the great horn," after one white lamb—Jose ben Yoezer, the father of the Hasidim [39]—had been seized and torn to pieces by the ravens (the Syrians). This, according to the Apocalyptic seer, was to be the turning point leading to the great war with Gog and Magog for which the sheep receive "the great sword" to bring the final defeat upon the nations, as it has been written down by Michael, the archangel in the heavenly book known to Enoch. This great world-drama, of which Enoch and Elijah are to be the witnesses, is followed by the last Judgment brought upon "the stars," the fallen angels, the idolatrous nations and the Jewish apostates, all of whom will be cast into Gehenna near Jerusalem. Then the rest of mankind will be converted to the worship of the One God, and, in place of the old Temple, which, condemned as impure,[40] will be torn down together with the old city of Jerusalem, a new Jerusalem will arise, and therein the throne shall be reared upon which the Lord of the sheep will sit and reign forever with the Messiah, the buffalo (*Reem*)[41] at His side.

The other vision, the Apocalypse of the Ten Weeks presenting the process of the world's history in so many weeks, is too obscure and in such a state of confusion and defectiveness that we need not enlarge upon it.

As concerns the life of Enoch, great interest has always attached itself to the story of his rise to heaven on the celestial chariot, the Merkaba, accompanied by various archangels through the different apartments until he reached the uppermost, accessible only to the very highest angels, where, transformed into a throne-angel, he beholds God in all His glory.[42] This feature was seized upon by the mystics of the Talmudic and Geonic time who combined his name with the Persian Mithra (Metatron), the charioteer of Ahura Mazda, to have him named Enoch-Metatron.[43] The most important portion of the Ethiopic Enoch is the *Similitudes,* written under the misrule of the Maccabean kings, which not merely show the influence of the book of Daniel, especially in the use of the names applied to God, but also indicate a greater development of the angelogical and the Messianic views. Particularly is Daniel's "the Son of Man," with his Messianic kingdom, conceived as altogether spiritual. A preëxistent being, he sits on God's throne in the heavenly Jerusalem as the Judge of men, the avenger of the life of the victims of the tyrannous rulers, "slaying the wicked by the word of his mouth." [44] Hidden from the creation of the world, his *name* being called before the Lord of the spirits before sun and stars were made, [45] he lives forever among the elect under His wings to be revealed in time as the Anointed, the incarnation of all wisdom. And he will bring about the resurrection. [46]

It is remarkable, however, that the name Son of Man, which plays so prominent a rôle in the Synoptic gospels and, in fact, colored the whole history of Jesus there, occurs nowhere else, even in the Enoch books, nor in any of the Jewish sources, but seems to have been repudiated by the Pharisean schools. It is not necessary to dwell further on the contents of the Enoch books, many of which have disappeared altogether. As has been especially shown by Beer in his notes to Enoch, the eschatological material was for the most part derived from Persia, as were the mysteries of Leviathan and Behemoth, referred to first in the Noah books, which now form a part of Enoch, [47] and afterwards in the Apocalypse of Baruch and Ezra, as we shall see later on. The whole eschatological material found its way also into the Talmud. [48] But the books of Enoch (though they spread and were remolded into a Greek version in Egypt about the middle of the first pre-Christian century, the so-called Slavonic Enoch) [49] fell into disfavor

among the Pharisean schoolmen, as did the entire Apocalyptic and Apocryphal literature afterwards. Even
the person of Enoch himself, though called by Ben Sira
"a wonder of wisdom" [50] and represented also in both
the Testaments of the Twelve Patriarchs [51] and the Book
of Jubilees [52] as "the scribe of God" [53] to whom "the
heavenly tablets" (of the Law) were ascribed, was depre-
ciated by later Rabbis. [54]

B. 2

In Enoch's place Abraham arose as the prototype of
the bearer of the divine mysteries, and accordingly we
have two Apocalypses of Abraham. The one, entitled
"The Testament of Abraham," was written in Greek
probably at the close of the first century in Egypt. [55]
Older than this is the "Apocalypse of Abraham," preserved only in Slavonic and edited in translation with
valuable notes by Canon Box in 1919, but originally an
Aramaic product of the first century, written probably
soon after the destruction of the second Temple, and
later on intermingled with Gnostic elements. Its first
eight chapters tell in Midrashic style of Abraham's conversion from his father's idolatry to the belief in the
One God, as told by himself. He there describes how,
seeing Terah's wooden god being devoured by the fire-
god, and this one by water, the water by the earth, the
earth being dried up by the sun, and the sun obscured
by the night, and likewise the moon and stars by the
changes of season, he finally learned to recognize as the
Creator of all things the God of gods. God's voice,
then, saved him from the fire that burned up his father's
house, the name *Ur* of the Chaldeans being taken to
mean fire. [56] Here follows the main portion, Chs. 9 to 32,
the Apocalyptic part based on Gen. 15, 9f., the revelation

of God to Abraham between the divided animals, which in Rabbinic tradition became the symbols of the four world powers first referred to in Daniel.[57]

A very prominent rôle in this Apocalypse is played by the angel Jaoel (Yahoel), in whom, as we are especially told in accordance with Ex. 23:21, the ineffable Name dwells, investing him with the highest powers— so as to enable him to restrain even the four living animals (the Hayyot) that carry the throne-chariot of God, as well as the Leviathan, the king of the water animals, between whose fins the earth is held up—and who, as the heavenly choir-master, teaches the Hayyot and the Cherubim how to sing.[58] In the Talmud (Sanh. 38b) the words of Exodus, "For My name is in him"—that is, the angel whom God shall send before Israel to show them the way—are referred to *Metatron*—that is, the Metator, "the heavenly guide"—"whose name is identical with the one of his Master." Elsewhere we are told that God's finger or voice was the Metator who showed Israel the land of Canaan.[59] While afterwards, in connection with the Merkabah mystery, the Metator, or the guiding angel, was identified with the Persian Mithras, the charioteer of Ahura Mazda,[60] and combined with Enoch as Enoch-Metatron in the Geonic mysteries, we find in the Geonic writings the name *Yahoel*[61] among the names assigned to Metatron. In all probability, then, the real name given to the Metator or Metatron originally was *Yahoel,* and being considered too sacred for common use was dropped and replaced by Metatron, whom we find spoken of in the Book of Jubilees 1:29 simply as the angel of the divine Presence who walked before Israel. The other functions of Yahoel were assigned to the archangel Michael, who was especially fitted to figure also as the heavenly choirmaster, as his name "Who is like God" suggests the celestial song similar to the one Yahoel teaches Abraham.[62] Ibn Ezra refers the very verse, Ex. 23:21, to Michael, whereas Rashi, no doubt following other authorities, finds the letters of Metatron to be numerically the same as *Shaddai.* In the Testament of Abraham it is Michael who guides and instructs Abraham.

Now this angel Yahoel, of godlike appearance [63] and with Michael [64] appointed guardian over Israel, led Abraham at God's bidding to Mount Horeb, where he was to bring the four animals mentioned in Gen. 15:9, for the covenant sacrifice. He then makes him soar up on the wings of the dove toward the heights of heaven, where, like Enoch, he is shown all things in heaven, on earth and in the sea, and likewise in the netherworld, Gehenna, and the Garden of Eden. But an unclean bird descends upon the carcasses [65] and it is none other than *Azazel,* the spirit of uncleanness and deceit that dwells on earth, but is in reality the lord of hell.[66] Against him Yahoel warns Abraham, telling him that the former heavenly garment of this fallen angel had been set aside for himself and that his former immortality was to be transferred to him, whereas Azazel is doomed to go down to the lowest parts of the earth. In the heights of heaven Abraham beholds the uncreated light and the fire out of which ever new forms of angels stream forth, but God himself he can only hear in "a voice of many waters," [67] but not see. Following the example of Yahoel, he bows down and worships, singing the celestial song the angel has taught him.[68] Here follows a description of the throne-chariot carried by the four fiery Hayyot of Ezekiel and the Cherubim with six wings like the Seraphim of Isaiah, all of whom are singing the song of praise to the Eternal One.[69] God then shows Abraham, while he stands above the stars,[70] the seventh heaven and all the other heavens below, the earth with its animate beings, and finally men with their righteous and unrighteous ways, and then hell with its torments, the Leviathan in the great sea, and at last the Garden of Eden. There he sees mankind divided, one part on the right side, the other on the left, the former set apart for the battle with (the text is here corrupt) Azazel, the latter the heathen nations doomed to perdition.[71] In the Garden of Eden he was shown Adam with his high stature and awful aspect embracing Eve, both standing under the tree which bore grapes, some of which they were eating,[72] while behind the tree stood Azazel in the shape of the serpent with human hands and feet and six wings on each of his shoulders,[73] exactly as Samael is pictured.[74] About him Abraham saw together with Cain the various vices and crimes personified, all the offspring of Azazel, the arch-fiend. This gives rise to a dialogue between Abraham and God which, in its present form, neither correctly nor completely preserved, discusses the questions of sin and future compensation. First, why the Evil Desire emanating from Azazel had been given such power over man; and the answer implies a twofold dualism, inasmuch as the evil seed, represented by Cain and the idolatrous nations, is contrasted with the good seed, represented by Abraham. The same contrast prevails in the cosmic life, as this world of sin rules the earth through Azazel, while the world to come is the world of righteousness which falls to the dominion of the good ones; and that is at the end of the twelve periods.[75] Despite this predestinarian idea, man's freedom, however, is upheld.[76] The last two chapters deal with the end of times, brought about by ten plagues, followed by the punishment of the

heathen and the wicked by the worm and the fire of
Azazel, and the salvation of the righteous. The latter
part of the text is altogether unintelligible and mixed
up with Christian elements.

It may be noticed that Azazel, in Ch. 24, is also
called the Adversary—*Satan* and the "Lawless One,"
which corresponds to the Talmudic interpretation of
Belial—*Beli Ôl,* the one who does not submit to the yoke
of the Law.[77] We have here the same dualistic view
as is expressed in the Testaments of the Twelve Patriarchs and the Book of Jubilees, as we shall see in the
following section. We may also remark here that, differently from the Ethiopic Enoch and other Apocalyptic
books, our author believes in the sacrificial cult,[78] as does
the author of the Book of Jubilees; nor does he allude
to the belief in Resurrection.

B. 3

The Book of Jubilees, a Midrashic expansion of Genesis and Exodus, occasionally referring to the tablets of
Enoch as if these had preceded the Mosaic Law, and
rather Pharisaic in spirit and exceedingly hostile to
heathenism, is a product of the first pre-Christian century. It opposes the calendar system adopted by the
Pharisees and proposes instead one based on the Jubilees,
which would correspond more to a division of history
after certain millennia. It represents the view or interests of the priestly tribe instead of a Davidic Messiah,
and makes Levi the chief bearer of the esoteric lore,
which, coming down from Enoch to Noah and Shem,
was transmitted to Abraham and Levi. To Moses it
finally assigns an Apocalypse which, in 23:11-31, presents the history from the Maccabean time to the advent
of the Messianic era of bliss under the reign of the Law,

when the sanctuary of the Lord will be renewed in Jerusalem but without any Resurrection or any world to come.[79] Its conception of the highest angels is very crude, as, like the Israelites, they bear the sign of the covenant, that is circumcision, on their flesh,[80] while the uncircumcised men and nations are called "the sons of Belial," Beliar,[81] that is, of lawlessness (בְּלִי עֹל), who do not submit to the yoke of the Law.[82]

B. 4

Far more pronounced is the character of Belial as the arch-fiend in the Testaments of the Twelve Patriarchs. This work is also a product of the first pre-Christian century, favoring the Messianic hope of the priestly tribe in connection with the Maccabean dynasty before its degeneration; but it differs from the Book of Jubilees in its attitude toward the Gentile world, for which salvation is made possible through the Law. Its teaching is centred upon Love of God and love of fellow-man.[83] It is the first book to speak of the Two Ways, which played so prominent a rôle in the teaching of proselytes, both Jewish and Christian, contrasting the good and the evil desires, righteousness and wickedness, and it is especially emphatic, throughout its ethical monitions, in warning aginst the spirit of *Beliar*.[84] Beliar is, in fact, identical with Satan: he will "be bound by the Messiah"[85] and "cast into the fire forever."[86]

There are many Apocalyptic portions throughout the book put into the mouth of Jacob addressing his sons, and frequently reference is made by the author to the Enoch books,[87] but this by no means implies that the Enoch books actually contained these predictions, as Charles thinks.[88] "The heavenly stables"[89] also are simply imaginary, like Jubilees 3:31. Especially interesting is the description of the seven heavens as part of the Merkabah mystery given in Levi ch. 3, which has much in common with the Talmudic one [90] and other Apocalypses. Peculiar and somewhat primitive is the view of the Resurrection presented in Benjamin 10, 6ff. First the patriarchs, from Enoch to Jacob, shall rise to share in the Kingdom when the earth will undergo a transformation. Then the twelve sons of Jacob, each with his tribe; and, finally, all men, some unto glory and some unto shame.[91] Israel will be judged first, and then all the Gentiles; but those found righteous will share in the future salvation.

As has been well shown by Charles in his illuminating Introduction, the Testaments of the Twelve Patriarchs, next to the Enoch books, was the most popular work in Hasidean circles. It went through several phases of composition and transformation and exerted a potent influence upon the New Testament writers.

The Hebrew Testament of Naphtali and the fragment of the Testament of Levi [92] are translations made in post-Talmudic time and have no claim to originality, as Dr. Gaster maintains.[93]

B. 5

The next book to be considered is the Assumptio Mosis, an Apocalyptic work which came down to us in a late, incomplete and defective Latin translation, and would bear the title "Testament of Moses" more correctly; whereas the original part, or book, describing the ascension of Moses to heaven, referred to in the Epistle of Jude 9 and by the Church fathers, is missing. Among modern exegetes and critics there is a wide difference as to the date, the authorship and the real historic background of the book. Most of them agree, however, that it was written in Aramaic soon after Varus, the Roman governor of Syria, in order to suppress a rebellion, had invaded Palestine and his soldiers had set fire to the Temple, which was after the year 4 B.C.E.[94] The peculiar feature of the book is its unique estimate of Moses, which comes quite near to being an apotheosis. Thus, Moses is made to say: "God who created the world on behalf of His people proposed me from the foundation of the world that I should be the mediator of the covenant." [95] Moreover, against the plain statement of Scripture that he was buried in the valley in the land of Moab,[96] it is stated that no place was to receive his body, but that all the world from the rising to the setting sun, and from the south to the confines of the north, would be his sepulcher.[97] This view can scarcely be ascribed to a Pharisean author. According to Josephus,[98] who followed a special tradition, Moses, while conversing with Eleazar and Joshua, was suddenly covered by a cloud and disappeared in a certain valley, but fearing that the people would say that on account of his extraordinary virtue he was turned into a divine being, he himself wrote in his holy books that he died. Philo at the close of his *Life of Moses* also writes that he was turned into a spiritual being when he wrote about his death. In the Sifrè Deut. 357, we likewise find the opinion expressed that Moses did not really die, but still stands before God on high, as he did when on top of Mount Sinai; and before he was taken hence, God showed him the whole world, from creation until the time of the Resurrection. In the Pesikta Zutarta and in the Midrash we are told that the place of his burial was not to be known to any man, not even to Moses himself, so that people might not there build a sanctuary and sacrifice as if to Moses himself. All these views which led to the ideas expressed in our Apocalyptic book, "The Assumption of Moses," of which the Midrash Petirat Mosheh in Deut. Rabba is the last outcome, originated undoubtedly, as stated by Jellinek,[99] among the Essenes, who "regarded next to the name of God that of the legislator Moses as inviolably sacred and set the penalty of death (possibly only nominally while leaving it to God) upon the blasphemy of his name.[100] In Talmudic times and far down into the middle ages people swore by his name.[101]

Now, whether or no the Assumptio Mosis and the Testament of Moses once formed one and the same book, certain it is that the story of the struggle of Samael, "the devil," with Michael about the body of Moses, referred to in the Epistle of Jude 9 as a quotation from the Assumptio Mosis [102] and reappearing in the late Hebrew Midrash, is Essene in its character as well as origin; and all the arguments presented against this and favoring a so-called Pharisaic Quietist [103] are of no avail, resting as they do on a false conception of Essenism based on a misunderstanding of Josephus as well as of Ch. 7 of our Apocalypse. As Geiger has almost convincingly shown,[104] the impious, gluttonous men, devourers of the goods of the poor who claim to be just, that is *Zadikim,* are none other than the Sadducean rulers of the Maccabean dynasty, who are depicted in the same colors in the Psalms of Solomon, though at the same time they are also accused of the crimes of the Hellenists before and during the Maccabean war.[105] But strange to say, Ch. 9, referring to the Levite who with his seven sons, after having fasted with them for three and a half days, went into a cave only to meet death, saying, "It is better to die than to transgress the commands of the Lord," has been generally misunderstood, while the story of Josephus,[106] which clearly refers to the same incident, has escaped all the interpreters, even Charles, who in his felicitous explanation of the name *Taxo*, as being a scribal error for the Hebrew word *Ha-kanna*, "the Zealot,"[107] had come so near the real fact. The incident must have made a deep impression, and we can fully realize that it induced the Apocalyptic writer to make it the turning point in Jewish history in Ch. 10, where Michael, the guardian angel of Israel, is to avenge the wrong that had been brought upon the people. Accordingly, Moses is made the revealer of the Messianic or theocratic era which was believed to be nigh, and which Michael was to bring about, and *not* the *Messiah;* and the *twelve* tribes of Israel are to be translated into heaven, where they would see their enemies in Gehenna;[108] and Moses, their intercessor before God,[109] was believed to be with them as in his lifetime.[110] It is interesting to find that the predestined end of time, from creation to the last Judgment preceding the Messianic era, is 250 year-weeks or 85 Jubilees,[111] which correspond with the Baraita.[112]

B. 6 and 7
The Baruch and the Ezra Apocalypses
The destruction of the second Temple, and the tragic fate which befell the city and the nation under the relentless power of Rome, came as a far heavier blow to the people than the fall of Jerusalem under Nebuchadnezzar. It cast them into a state of bitter anguish and despair, which was all the more overwhelming as their faith in God and their obedience to the Law had inspired them with greater confidence in the future. And yet in this great need of consolation and of reassuring hope for their restoration they lacked the prophetic guidance

which sustained their fathers in Babylon and caused them
to look forward to a resurrection of the nation. Here,
then, was a renewed opportunity for the Apocalyptic
writers to take the place of the prophets in announcing
the coming of the great day of Judgment and the establishment of the Messianic Kingdom, as they did under
the Syrian persecution. But, instead of having the
ancient heroes, such as Daniel, Enoch, and Abraham,
deliver the message of hope to the depressed and
despondent amidst the great desolation, they wisely
selected Baruch, the co-worker of Jeremiah and witness
of the fall of the first Temple, or Ezra the Scribe. Nor
were they satisfied simply with disclosing the mysteries
concerning the future, including Gehenna and Paradise,
with their modes of punishment and of reward. Owing
to the deeper religious consciousness of the people, they
indulged also in theological speculations on sin and the
consequence of Adam's fall, which, according to the
Scripture, brought upon mankind death together with
all the evil powers of Satan, and likewise on the destiny
of Israel and man as affected by sin, and these subjects
give to the Apocalypses of Baruch and of Ezra their
peculiar character among the Apocalyptic writings.

Until recently the Ezra Apocalypse was regarded by
critical scholars as older and more original than the
Apocalypse of Baruch. But this opinion was changed
by the convincing arguments of Wellhausen, who was
followed by Ryssel and Schürer. In the Baruch Apocalypse there is, first of all, greater detail in the description of the destruction of the Temple and of the conditions that preceded it—parallels of which are found
in the Rabbinical sources, as pointed out by Dr. Ginzberg
in the *Jewish Encyclopedia* article on the "Baruch Apocalypse"—giving the impression that the writer had actu-

ally had similar experiences to those he ascribes to
Baruch. Then the name of Baruch—whom, by the way,
some of the Tannaim [113] counted among the prophets—
was far more befitting for the pseudonym than that of
Ezra who lived so long after the destruction of the
Temple. Besides, the various Baruch Apocalypses and
the Baruch Apocryphal book speak in favor of the priority of the Apocalypse of Baruch as preserved in the
Syrian version.

Without going into details as to the composition of
the book, it is sufficient for our purpose to state that its
phraseology shows it to have been orginally written in
Hebrew, nay, in a Hebrew that comes near to the one
used by the Rabbinical Haggadists, and partly in words
recurring in the Midrash, as Dr. Ginzberg has shown,
referring to Pesikta Rabbati Ch. 26.[114] Still more interesting is the fact that the view expressed throughout
the book, that the world was created for the sake of
Israel, or for the sake of the righteous who observe the
Law, or for man, is also frequently voiced in the Talmud
and Midrash,[115] and it forms the basis for the ever
reiterated plaintive cry that in this very world Israel
is the great sufferer under the cruel yoke of the nations,
while these proudly dominate in crude arrogance;
although the sins of the former cannot be compared
with the unrighteousness and sinfulness of the latter.
Similarly man, with his intelligence, is far more unfortu-
nate than the brute creatures about him; nor does the sin
committed by Adam sufficiently account for his fate of
mortality and the other evils he is heir to, and so "it
would be better for him had he never been born"—a
pessimistic view which has found expression also among
the school of Shammai [116] as well as in the Apocalypse
of Ezra. Now the divine answer to this twofold com-

plaint is that this world of corruption, of physical and moral evil, is followed by a better world free from all evil, which, after the great Judgment Day, will bring eternal bliss to the good and annihilation to the wicked. After this, or, according to other Apocalyptic portions of the book, previous to the Judgment day, the Messianic era will be ushered in, preceded by a certain series of calamities called by the Rabbis "the travails of the Messiah," [117] and likewise by the last war with Gog and Magog as described by Ezekiel.[118]

The Messianic era, however, has a double character, a national and a universal one. The former naturally stands in the foreground, and the whole of Israel, including the Proselytes "who have come under the wings of the divine majesty," [119] are to participate in it. The universal one is fashioned more after the prophetic pattern and instead of the Messiah "who will summon all nations to the Judgment" [120] and "slay the arch-enemy with the breath of his mouth," [121] God himself as Judge of the world stands in the center. It is difficult, however, to separate the national and the universal view, as the redactor of the book has frequently combined or mixed the various Apocalyptic traditions which go back to the time when Babylonia and Persia together influenced their formation.[122] Thus, for instance, the belief that the righteous would, in the Messianic time, have Behemoth and Leviathan prepared as food for them together with the heavenly manna, expressed alike in the Noahic, the Baruch and the Ezra Apocalypses and the Talmud and Midrash,[123] was derived from Persian mythology.[124]

The Baruch Apocalypse lays great stress upon the observance of the Law as a condition of salvation.[125] Abraham is declared to have been already the possessor of the unwritten Law,[126] as is assumed in the Book of

Jubilees and the Talmud, and Moses is made the first
recipient of the mysteries concerning the heaven and the
future, in place of Enoch.[127] A specially important
feature of our Apocalypse is the accentuation of the principle of man's freedom of will despite the predestination
idea and the consequences of Adam's fall: [128] "Each one
of us is the Adam of his own soul." This is exactly the
principle of the Pharisees as stated by Josephus [129] and
by R. Akiba.[130]

So are its eschatological views the same as those
expressed in the Talmud, as when we are told that the
Resurrection will take place only when the predetermined
number of mankind is fulfilled.[131] Many terms of the
Apocalypse are similar to those of the Mishnah; as,
for instance, the Amorites for the heathen,[132] or "by
Thy will we come into the world and we depart not by
our own will"; [133] which fact throws light also upon the
time and the atmosphere of the book.

An essential part of the Messianic hope of the Exilic
prophets, especially Ezek. 37:15ff., was the return of
the exiled nine and a half tribes representing the Israel-
itic Kingdom, and so those tribes, spoken of later as
the ten lost tribes, became a prominent topic of the
Apocalyptic writers as well as of the Taanaite and
Amoraic times. According to the legend given in the
Syrian Apocalypse,[134] Baruch sent a letter to these tribes
by an eagle who flew over the immense Euphrates River
to inform them who lived in a far distant land of what
had happened to their brethren since their separation, and
to admonish them to prepare worthily for the miraculous
return, as he likewise sent a letter of the same character
to the Jews living in Babylonia; which letter, however,
is missing in the Apocalypse. Somewhat different and
more elaborate is the legend given in the Ezra Apoca-

lypse.[135] According to this, the nine and a half tribes, in order not to live among the heathen, went beyond the narrow passages of the Euphrates, a journey of a year and a half, into a land called *Erez Aheret*— "Another land," [136] a land where no race of men had ever lived before. There they observed the Law, as they had not done formerly. Yet this was made possible only by a miracle, as God held back the sources of the Euphrates, similar to what happened at the Jordan,[137] and so God would again lead them back by the same miracle. Josephus [138] also speaks of the immense multitude of the ten tribes that lived in a distant land beyond the Euphrates, to whom Ezra sent the letter he received from King Xerxes. So we are told [139] that the ten tribes were exiled beyond the River Sambation, the Sabbath River, about which Josephus [140] also has a strange legend, though by him it is located in Syria. There is, however, a controversy recorded between R. Eliezer and R. Akiba whether the ten tribes "who were exiled in Media" will return in the Messianic future or not. In Sifra, Behukothai ch. 8, the dispute is whether the verse Lev. 26:38 is to be taken in the sense: "Ye shall perish among the heathen," as R. Akiba says, or in the sense: "Ye shall be lost among the heathen," but at the end return, as R. Eliezer says. In the Mishnah, Sanh. 10, 3, the controversy is based on Deut. 29:27: "And He cast them into another land as it is this day," the closing words of which verse are interpreted by R. Akiba to mean: "As the day goes but never returns, so will Northern Israel go into Exile and never return"; but R. Eliezer takes them to mean: "As the day is now dark but may be light again, so Northern Israel." Whether R. Akiba was influenced to take this pessimistic view by the defeat of Bar-Kokba, whom he had proclaimed as the Messiah, as A. Neubauer suggests,[141] or not, the Apocalyptic view was certainly generally prevalent.

As in the time preceding the second fall of Jerusalem a number of Apocryphal writings appeared under the name of Enoch, so around the pseudonym of Baruch there clustered writings of different authors with differing views, but only the Syrian one is complete in the main. The Greek Apocalypse is only a fragment and of not much value, containing chiefly visions of heaven and its future inhabitants, based on Enoch. The one entitled "The Rest of the Words of Baruch" contains material identical with parts of the Syrian one and is partly Christianized. The Apocryphal Baruch contains in some altered form the letter to the two and a half tribes, which originally formed part of the Syrian Apocalypse.

The Ezra Apocalypse

While the Baruch Apocalypse seems to have enjoyed great popularity in Jewish circles, the Ezra Apocalypse became very popular in the Church, obviously because it contained many views similar to those voiced by Paul. And so it came down to us with Christian additions; to wit: the two chapters preceding, and the last chapter following, the main book, in which, with the exception of the name of Jesus which copyists inserted in 7:28, where the Messiah (Christ) is spoken of as dying, nothing Christian occurs. In regard to the main problems discussed, the destiny of Israel and that of mankind as affected by sin and likewise the Day of Judgment for both the nations and for the individual at the Messianic end, the resemblance between the Baruch and the Ezra Apocalypse is often striking, so that critics have come to the common conclusion that one author used the other's work, and they differ only as to the priority of the one or the other. There is no denying the fact, however, that the Ezra Apocalypse is more elaborate and systematical, and far more poetical, which speaks in favor of a later composition. It is furthermore noteworthy that Ezra first dwells with especial emphasis on the destiny of man and the consequence of Adam's sin, before he enlarges on the sad destiny of Israel and on the Messianic hope,[142] which indicates the cool reflection of a writer who is no longer under the immediate impression of the great tragedy, as was the author of the Baruch Apocalypse. Also, the world-view of Ezra is more pessimistic than is that of Baruch. The latter's cry of despondency in 10:6: "Blessed is he who was not born," or in 11:7: "Blessed are ye, the dead, more than we who are living," which is an echo of Job 3:11f., is but an outburst of woe occasioned by the calamity of the time, whereas in Ezra 4:12; 7:66, 116f., it is, as Charles[143] rightly remarks, rather the expression of resignation, in view of the future Judgment, to the dire punishment of sin dating back to Adam. Accordingly, we find Ch. 7 chiefly devoted to the theological assumption that only few are saved, the argument being brought forth that throughout the whole world the precious things are few, whereas the things that exist in abundance are worthless.[144] This view found expression in "the wide and the narrow gate" through which after the last Judgment the souls have to go, according to their merits or demerits, spoken of in the Testament of Abraham and especially adopted in the New Testament.[145] Paradise which with its great delights is destined for man, accordingly, is not apportioned to the larger part of "the sin-stained race,"[146] and Ezra's appeal to God's seven Attributes of Mercy in Ex. 34:6-7 is answered in

7:132-8:6, with the parable of the dust and the gold, *this* world being for the many who stray away from the Law and despise the Most High; whereas the future world is for the few who will live to see the heavenly Jerusalem.—Very emphatic is the assertion that there is no intercession possible any longer on the Day of Judgment,[147] since repentance had been open to the sinner before.[148]

Of a real Midrashic character is Ezra's prayer in which Israel is compared to the vine which is chosen among all the trees, to Palestine among the lands, to the Jordan among the streams, the lily among the flowers, Zion among the cities, the dove among the birds, the lamb among the beasts.[149] Specifically Midrashic is the interpretation of the verse in Genesis 25:26: "And his (Jacob's) hand had hold on Esau's heel," which is taken as the prophecy that at the Messianic time Israel's power will make an end to the Roman Empire.[150] About the signs of the coming of the Messianic time, the so-called "birth-throes of the Messiah," [151] Ezra speaks,[152] and what he says about the End not being reached until the number of souls in the chambers had been fulfilled [153] has its parallels in the Talmud, Yebamot 62a.

Seven classes of sinners come at once to the place of torment after the Judgment Day, without the interim for those held in suspense,[154] and correspondingly there are seven classes of righteous for whom there are the treasures of merit.[155]

The visions concerning the Messiah were given to Ezra in a field where nothing grew but herbs or flowers called *Arpad* [156] (probably a corrupt name for *Horbah*, "desolate place").[157] And most likely the passage about the reign of the Messiah called by God, "My son," [158] belonged originally after 10:57, the Vision of Zion and her son. The thirty years in 7:28 recur in 10:45, where they are explained to mean three thousand years. Of course, the whole chronology is too mystical for the understanding of the average reader.

The lion that comes out of the woods roaring against the eagle (Rome), in 11:37, is of course the same as the Man who is brought up from the heart of the sea and who, as in Dan. 7:13, "came with the clouds of heaven."[159] He, the son of David, has been kept hidden for the consummation of days,[160] to be revealed in time, that is, to achieve the victory over the hosts of Gog and Magog.[161] Then he will gather the nine and a half tribes that have been led captive to "another land" (the *Erez Aheret* of Deut. 29:27), where they did observe the Law, miraculously kept beyond the narrow passages of the River Euphrates.[162] But strange is the statement in 7:26-30, that, "after having been revealed with his companions when the new Jerusalem appeared as his bride, he will die after a *four-hundred* years' reign together with all those in whom is human breath," a statement which has no parallel in the entire Apocalyptic literature, though we find such views held by the Tannaim of the second century.[163] The whole doctrine concerning the Messiah must have lost its hold upon the people, seeing R. Akiba maintains that the days of the Messiah shall last only forty years, corresponding to the forty years of the wilderness, in accord with Ps. 90:15; whereas R. Eliezer awards him four hundred years, after Gen. 15:13 and R. Joshua, or according to other versions, R. Eliezer or R. Jose Ha-Gelili, a thousand years, after Ps. 90:4.

At any rate, the Ezra Apocalypse refers directly to the vision of Dan. 7:7f. concerning the fourth world kingdom symbolized by the Eagle, in whom it beholds the Roman Empire,[164] and the Lion as the Messiah.[165]

But the novel feature in Ezra is the definite form in which the Roman Empire under its twelve rulers, and principally under the three great emperors, is described as bringing about, by its world-wide tyranny, the End.[166] In all probability, however, the original Apocalyptic tradition is older than the description of the wings given here.

It has been well said that the Ezra Apocalypse is a compendium of Apocalyptic views artificially combined by its last author. The main book seems to have closed with the praise of God for the revelation of all the eschatological mysteries.[167] The last chapter, containing the personal task entrusted to Ezra and his five companions and his miraculous restoration of the Scriptures, the twenty-four Canonical and the seventy Apocalyptic writings, was added at a later period, and it must have been written at a time when a supernatural origin was ascribed by the Essene mystics to this collection of Apocalyptic writings.[168]

BOOK· II

BOOK II

CHAPTER I

The Conditions of Jewry Before the Rise of Christianity

The Babylonian captivity was the crucible from which emerged the Synagogue, a house of God for the people, a religious democracy. The Maccabean war created a people of martyrs ready to die for their God and their faith. But at the same time the issue of the war divided the people into three parties. There were, first of all, the Hasidim, the spiritual leaders who rose to the front to champion the cause of Judaism when the Syrian culture threatened to rob the Jew of his treasure, the Torah; but no sooner was the Temple recaptured and religious independence secured than they withdrew from the battle, being concerned solely with the preservation of the faith. On the opposite side were the Sadducean rulers and their followers, who would not rest until their foes were subdued and their political freedom was obtained and, by the subjection of all the neighboring nations, firmly established. Between the two stood the bulk of the nation which rejoiced in the victory of the Maccabean dynasty as long as it did not interfere with the Law as interpreted by the Scribes.

No doubt, originally the watchword of the Hasidim was Perishut, as we learn from 2 Maccabees,[1] *Amixia,* "Separatism," while the Sadducees followed the principle of *Epimixia,* "Assimilation." [2] Out of this emanated the Pharisaic party which soon became the strong opponent of the Sadducees. What most likely offended the Pharisean teachers was the alliance with Rome made by John Hyrcanus, contrary to the Law, which expressly states: "Thou shalt not conclude a covenant with them" (the idolatrous nations),³ rather than the cause stated by Josephus and the Talmudic story concerning the captivity of his mother incapacitating him for the office of high priest.⁴ Then, too, the union of the priestly tiara with the royal crown by the Sadducean dynasty could only be a thorn in the flesh of the Pharisees.

Matters grew far worse under the savage tyranny of Alexander Jannaeus, who shed Jewish blood like water, and finally on his death-bed recommended to his wife Salome Alexandra (Shelom Zion) to endeavor to make peace with the Pharisees; and henceforth, owing to their leader Simeon ben Shetah, her brother, their influence became dominant. Still, Rome was lurking in the background, and no sooner had fraternal strife and civil war broken out under Salome's sons, in course of which the great Essene saint fell a victim to fanatic party hatred, than Pompey entered the land as conqueror and practically made an end to the Maccabean dynasty.

But greater than this calamity, described especially in the Psalms of Solomon, was the subsequent rule of the Idumean Antipater and his son Herod, the murderer of the Maccabean house. Herod was the incarnation of Rome, henceforth called *Edom* by the Jews. All over Judea and around it, he erected Roman statues and other structures which gave the land a pagan character. In order to dazzle the people he renovated the Temple and made it a monument of grandeur and beauty undreamt of before. At the same time he did not shrink from erecting an eagle over the portal of the Temple, as a sign of Roman dominion, thereby provoking the revolt of the Zealots, the sworn enemies of Rome, who adopted as their slogan: "There is no King but God on high," and also, walking about with concealed daggers, were ready to slay any apparent follower of Roman practice. The reign of the half-Judean Herodian house merely delayed the impending doom of Judea, brought ever nearer by the Roman prefects who had become the governors of the land, each more cruel and barbarous than the other, making the entire people realize that the end was nigh.

But as the Rabbis say, God never sends a plague but he has the remedy prepared beforehand. So in Herod's time there arose the great schools of Shammai and Hillel, the one rigorous, the other mild, which spread Jewish learning throughout the land, thus building the bulwark of Judaism for the future. Yet, while the Torah was fostered zealously by the Pharisean schools, there were those who hoped and prayed, under the great Roman oppression, for the speedy advent of the Messiah to bring about the redemption of Israel. Such were chiefly the Essenes, a side branch of the ancient Hasidim, who sent forth their so-called prophets from time to time, announcing the nearness of the looked-for Kingdom of God which was, according to Daniel, to follow the four world-kingdoms. Over against them stood the men of *action*, the Zealots, restless and unrelenting, who played the foremost rôle in the final war. We can understand better the personalities of John the Baptist and Jesus when we see them as members of the Essene party.

CHAPTER II

John the Baptist

All the Gospels agree that the Messianic movement, centered in the unique personality of Jesus the Christ (which is the Greek word for Messiah, "the Anointed"), was started by John the Baptist on the shores of the Jordan. Nothing in John's own words or attitude, however, speaks in favor of the view taken by the Gospels that he actually was the Elijah-like precursor of Jesus, heralding his advent as the Messiah. As a matter of fact, according to Josephus,[1] he must have made a far greater impression upon his contemporaries than did Jesus, judging from *Ant.* XVIII, 3, 3. This is what Josephus writes: "Some of the Jews thought that the destruction of Herod's army came from God, and that very justly, as a punishment for what he did against John, who was called the Baptist, for Herod slew him, who was a good man, and commanded the Jews to exercise virtue, both as to righteousness towards one another, and piety towards God, and so to come to baptism." For, said he, thus would baptism be acceptable to Him, if they would practice it not merely for putting away single sins but for the *sanctification* of the body after the soul had before been thoroughly purified by righteousness.

This baptism is evidently not to be identified with the daily bath of the Essenes, though the three principles taught by John are specified also by the Essenes, according to Philo.[2] Instead, it must have had for its purpose, as Hausrath[3] says, the entrance into a new special relation to God, the baptism being performed but once in life. Uppermost in the Baptist's mind obviously was the idea that only through repentance, a renewal of life, will the people attain the longed-for redemption, the change of heart being symbolized by the bath which makes man "born anew." So already Isaiah[4] admonished the people, saying: "Wash you, make you clean, put away the evil of your doings from before Mine eyes; cease to do evil, learn to do well." Likewise did Ezekiel,[5] when asking the people for "a new heart and a new spirit," hold forth the promise that God would "sprinkle pure water upon the people to cleanse them from their sins and impurities."[6] Zechariah[7] says in the same spirit: "In that day there shall be a fountain opened to the house of David and to the inhabitants of Jerusalem for purification."

The baptism, then, which John introduced was meant to be a spiritual regeneration of the people to prepare them for the Kingdom of God. Appearing in his rugged demeanor, his raiment of camel's hair, with a leathern girdle around his loins, and having wild honey for his food,[8] he impressed the people as being another Elijah, and he spoke with all the vehemence of the ancient prophets while announcing the day of wrath, of the divine judgment to come heralding the Messianic era. Far from displaying the tender qualities of Jesus, the Messiah he announces is a relentless judge who—figuratively speaking—"casts those trees that fail to bring forth good fruit into the fire," or "who cometh with the winnow in his hand and burns the chaff with unquenchable fire."[9] This is certainly a view widely divergent from that of Jesus. Hence it follows that the alleged relation of the Baptist

to Jesus as if he had actually been his forerunner, based
on Isaiah [10] and Malachi,[11] is only an artificial construction of the Synoptic Gospels. The actual fact is that
Jesus was baptized by him and afterwards, at the
imprisonment of the Baptist, or his death—here the
sources differ—took his place as preacher of repentance
in Galilee.

But Luke, to whose compilation we owe more details
about the Baptist, partly historical and partly legendary,
seems to have had before him a special treatise which
probably also contained the above-quoted description in
Matthew.[12] It apparently opened with the miraculous
story of his birth,[13] the prayer being falsely ascribed to
Mary, the mother of Jesus, the whole having all the
characteristics of an original Jewish legend. According
to this story, Zacharias, his father, was priest of the section of Abiah, and his mother, Elisabeth, was also of
priestly descent, both of an age when they could no longer
expect a child. But when Zacharias stood at the altar
offering incense the angel Gabriel appeared to him
announcing the birth of a son who should be named John,
who would be a Nazarite for life, filled with the holy
spirit and endowed with the spirit and power of Elijah to
turn the heart of the children to the fathers and the dis-
obedient to the wisdom of the righteous, thus to prepare
the people for the Lord.[14] As Zacharias would not
believe the message, he was struck dumb and told that
his mouth would be opened again after the birth of the
child. Elizabeth, when delivered of the child, offered
thanks to God for having been freed from her barren-
ness, the reproach of men, and Zacharias, filled with the
holy spirit, prophesied saying: "Blessed be the God of
Israel who has redeemed His people and raised a horn
of salvation for us through the house of His servant

David, salvation from our enemies and from the hand of all that hate us, remembering His oath he swore to Abraham."

This is evidently a Jewish concept and incompatible with the Christian concept of Jesus. Consequently, the relation of Elizabeth to Mary which follows here is a late Christian addition.

The Baptist, then, was the first to preach to the people, saying: "Repent ye, for the Kingdom of God is at hand." And as the crowds came to him to be baptized, he said: "O generation of vipers, who has suggested to you to flee from the wrath to come? Bring befitting repentance, and do not say we have Abraham for our father [that is, do not rely on the merits of the patriarchs] for I say unto you that God is able to raise up children (*Banim*) unto Abraham from these stones (*Abanim*)." [15] And when the crowds asked, What shall we do? he answered and said: "He that hath two coats, let him give one to share it with him that hath none," and he that hath food do likewise—an Essene principle. And when the tax collectors in the service of Rome came, he said to them: "Exact no more than is ordered to you"; and to the soldiers, likewise, he said: "Do violence to no man, neither accuse one falsely, and be content with your pay." What follows there, his reference to Jesus' baptism, is, of course, a Christian addition. [16]

Jesus of Nazareth was one of the many who came to John to be baptized, and his great career gave later on a new complexion to the history of the Baptist. According to Josephus, however, Herod feared the influence John exerted on the people and therefore he first imprisoned and then slew him. Strange is the story [17] that, when Jesus appeared as a preacher of repentance like John, Herod took him to be John risen from the grave.

But the Baptist remained a power even after his death and many followed his example in baptizing the people, as did Apollos.[18]   His work was apparently continued especially along the Jordan by a certain class named *Sabeans*, which meant the same as Baptists.[19]

CHAPTER III

The Jesus of the Gospels and the Historical Jesus

The history of Jesus is so wrapped up in myths, and his life as told in the Gospels is so replete with contradictions, that it is difficult for the unbiased reader to arrive at the true historical facts. But as the clouds in the sky hiding the orb of day rising in the east reveal its brilliant magnificence rather than obscure it, so do the legends clustering around a popular hero disclose rather than obscure the presence of a great personality impressing the people with power and charm. So do the beautiful tales about Jesus of Nazareth show that there was a spiritual daybreak in that dark corner of Judea of which official Judaism had failed to take sufficient cognizance. The stone that the builders rejected has become the cornerstone of a new world. In this light must we view the life of that personality whose very name was destined to divide human history into two.

The chief difficulty in ascertaining the real character of Jesus is that neither he nor any of his disciples wrote a word of the contents of the New Testament. Peter and John, the chief apostles, are characterized in Acts [1] as "unlettered and ignorant men," and Paul, whose Epistles represented Jesus as a supernatural being, while relating what he learned about him, did not even know him in person.

In fact, Jesus spoke only in Aramaic, which was the

vernacular, and we have only three or four sayings of his
preserved in this language: *Talitha Kumi*—"Little maid,
arise!" [2] *Ephphatha*—"Open thy mouth"; [3] and the well-
known words: *Eli, Eli, Lama Sabachtani*—"My God,
my God, why hast Thou forsaken me?" [4] the Aramaic
translation of Ps. 22:2—which is a cry of despair in the
agony of death on the cross, changed by Luke [5] into the
submissive words of Ps. 31:6: "Father, into Thy hands
I commit my spirit." All the apostles spoke in Aramaic,
and hence the collection of Jesus' sayings and the story
of his life first appeared in Aramaic. It took about two
generations to have them translated into Greek; and
many words or sentences were probably misread or misunderstood by the translator. Take for instance the
well-known sentence: [6] "Leave the dead bury their dead!"
which is both cruel and senseless. It probably read:
"Leave it to the men of the town (מְתֵי הָעִיר) [that is,
the burial society] to bury the dead, and follow me."

We must bear in mind also that the Gospels were not
intended to be biographies of Jesus, but were written
for the sole purpose of proving that Jesus was *the*
Messiah, in accordance with the expectation of the
Pharisean schools. Accordingly his genealogy had to
be traced back to David of Bethlehem. This was done
by Matthew who followed some tradition showing thrice
fourteen generations leading up to *Abraham,* with especial reference to Tamar, Rahab, Ruth, and Bathsheba, [7]
and also by Luke who gives the genealogy in reverse
order leading up to Adam through a different line of
David's royal house. Both, however, know only Joseph
to have been the real father of Jesus. Another condition
of the true Messiah was that, like David, he must have
been born at Bethlehem, according to Micah 5:1; so some
accident had to be invented causing the family of Jesus

to move temporarily from Nazareth, where they lived, to Bethlehem, which was done differently by Matthew and Luke. Likewise are the Bethlehem legends different in both, and we know not which is more beautiful, the one telling in oriental style of the three Magi who follow the star of Bethlehem until they find the babe Jesus and worship him, or that of the shepherds in the field who hear the song of the angels over the city of David: "Glory to God in the Highest, peace and good will among the men on earth." Two other childhood stories are told in Luke. According to the one, Jesus the babe is brought by Mary into the Temple where two (Essene) saints, Simeon and Anna, who had been waiting for "the consolation of Israel" or "the redemption of Jerusalem," were privileged to see and hail the new-born Messiah at the Temple. According to the other, the twelve-year-old Jesus amazed the teachers at the Temple by his wise answers, and when missed by his parents told them: "Wist ye not that I must be in my Father's house?" [8]

None of these childhood stories is given in Mark, who begins the history of Jesus, "the son of God," with his baptism by John the Baptist, as does also the fourth gospel. This story, however, is told differently by the four gospels, but, as far as we can see, it appeared in its more original form in the Gospel for the Hebrews, which was written in Aramaic and used by the Church fathers Origen and Jerome. According to it, Jesus was induced by his mother and brothers to go to John the Baptist to be baptized like the rest and obtain forgiveness, and so forth. But this is scarcely compatible with Luke, who tells us that Jesus was about thirty years old when he was baptized; besides, the four gospels state that he went of his own accord.

According to Matthew, John hesitated to baptize him,

he being his superior, while the other gospels recognized him at the baptism as the Son of God by the miracle of the descent of the holy ghost upon him. The three synoptic gospels, however, tell how Jesus, as he rose from the water, looked, and behold, the heavens opened and the holy spirit descended upon him amidst a great light in the shape of a dove, while a heavenly voice was heard, saying: Thou art My beloved son, on this day I have begotten thee.° So Luke and the Gospel of the Hebrews. The latter part of the verse was apparently changed when the belief arose that Jesus was born as the son of God by his very birth through the holy ghost. Of course, the unchanged Psalm verse was addressed to Jesus and emphasized that only then he became the Son of God, while the other would or should be heard by those standing by as well. At any rate the underlying idea of the original story is that through the holy spirit, which in the Aramaic language is feminine, *Ruha Kadisha,* Jesus became the Son of God. Thus Jesus actually speaks in the Gospel of the Hebrews of the holy ghost as his *mother.* But when the story was translated into Greek, in which holy spirit is of the neuter gender instead of feminine, it could no longer be taken in the former sense, and so the more sensual pagan concept of the deity offered itself. Mary then took the place of the holy ghost, while the holy ghost took the place of God, and Jesus became the Son of God not through baptism but by his very birth.

Now, the baptism story is followed by that of the temptation, which relates how the holy spirit (in the Gospel of the Hebrews, called his mother by Jesus) carries him into the wilderness up to a high mountain (Tabor) to enter into a combat with Satan, the ruler of this world, in order to prove that he is really the Son of God by the rejection of all terrestrial greatness and power. Instead of this scriptural combat, described by Matthew and Luke, Mark relates that he was carried up to the upper sphere of the world where he was with the Hayyot, that is, the holy beasts that carry God's throne-chariot—the translator erroneously took the word to mean wild beasts—and where the angels ministered to him. Of course, this proved him to be the Son of God.

Coming now to the basic facts of the history of Jesus, we must first take notice of what the historian Josephus wrote about him about sixty years after the crucifixion.[10] We shall put the words which only a Christian, and not the Jew Josephus could have written, in parenthesis:

There was about this time Jesus a wise man (if it be lawful to call him a man, for he was) a performer of miracles, a teacher of such men (as receive the truth with pleasure) as love to follow new—that is, revolutionary—things. He drew over to him many of the Jews and many of the Gentiles. He was proclaimed the Christ, and when Pilate at the denunciation of the principal men among them had condemned him to be crucified, those that were at first captivated by him did not cease to adhere to him (for he appeared to them alive again on the third day, as the divine prophets had told about this and many other wonderful things about him), and so the tribe of the Christians named after him is not extinct to this day.

That the historian mentioned Jesus as "the so-called Christ" in connection with the death of James, the brother of Jesus, at the hand of the Sadducean Sanhedrin, is the best proof that he had written about him before. Of

course, Josephus could as little imagine that the Galilean
wonder-worker, or prophet, as they at first called him,
would become one of humanity's greatest personalities,
filling the world with his fame, as could his contemporaries among the Rabbis, even if they heard of his
appearance and achievements in the little corner of the
Lake Genezareth where the fishermen and the shepherds
began to worship him. He at first appeared as the successor of John the Baptist, preaching like him: "Repent,
for the Kingdom of God is at hand," but then his chief
practice was that of a healer in Galilee and its Syrian
border. Like the Essenes, he went about casting out
demons of the various diseases, such as epilepsy, par-
alysis, and lunacy, also blindness, which were believed to
take possession of men. He cured them by some magic
formula he whispered, at times by the touch of the hand,
or putting spittle upon the affected organ, parallels of
which cures we find in the Talmud.[11] In numbering such
cures, Mark is more moderate than Matthew, who likes
to exaggerate. As a rule people gathered at the close
of the Sabbath at the Synagogue, waiting to be cured by
him.[12] He did not mind curing the diseased on a Sabbath,
thereby provoking the Pharisees, and argued against
them that the Sabbath was given to man (*Bar Neshu,*
"the son of man") and not the man to the Sabbath, a
maxim expressed also by Simon ben Menasia.[13] The
legend about the Gadarene swine,[14] into which he caused
to enter a legion of demons he had cast out of a madman
and which were driven by him into the lake and drowned,
reflects his fame as an exorcist, whatever the real facts
may have been. As to the various miracles ascribed to
Jesus in the Gospels, Klausner, in his *Jesus of Nazareth,*[15]
properly distinguishes *five* classes: (1) Miracles due to
a wish to fulfil some statement in the Old Testament or

to imitate some prophets, that is, like Elijah and Elisha, who are represented as having raised children from death, or to have satisfied five hundred men with bread to spare; or miracles which are expected to occur in the Messianic time;[16] (2) Miracles which grew out of poetical description; (3) Illusions or apparitions, such as Jesus walking on the sea, or his rebuking the wind and waves; (4) Acts only apparently miraculous; (5) The curing of seemingly sick ("nerve-cases"), that is, psychological acts. On the whole, we may say: Miracles happen wherever the belief in miracles prevails.

So we rather omit the entire miraculous part of the life of Jesus and instead dwell on the wondrous power he exerted upon the people by his great sympathy with the afflicted and the downtrodden, and the gentleness and grace with which he appealed to the souls of all, electrifying and fascinating them by his fine observation of nature's beauty and the manifold richness of the simple human life around him. Indeed we do him little justice when, in comparing him with Hillel, the great and meek teacher, we fail to give him credit for the simplicity and incomparable humanity in which the man of the people eclipsed the Pharisean schoolmen. After all, the formalism and sternness of the Law, the Halakic rules, constituted the main object of the Pharisean schoolmen, even of Hillel, the great master whose maxims, principles, and ideals have for all times shed the brightest light on the doctrine of Judaism. While ignoring and censuring this very part of Pharisaism, despite all the limitations of his social circle, he became the boldest and most unique ethical teacher. He was an idealist of the highest type and cared not for the requirements of civilization, such as industry, science, and art. Waiting only for the approaching new world, the Kingdom of God that was at hand, he was satisfied to have his disciples consider the birds of heaven which sow not nor reap, nor gather into barns, but are content to be fed by God, the heavenly Father. So should they not be anxious for their life, for what they eat or drink. "Are ye not of much more value than they?" [17] "And why are you anxious for your raiment?" "Consider the lilies of the field, how they grow; they toil not, neither do they spin, yet Solomon in all his glory was not arrayed like one of these." "But if God doth so clothe the grass of the field which is today and tomorrow is cast into the oven, shall He not much more clothe you, O ye of little faith?" [18] "Your heavenly Father knows that you have need of all these things. But seek ye first the Kingdom and His righteousness, and all these things shall be added to you." Of course, only one "whose Kingdom is not of this world" could speak thus.

That Jesus was a perfect Jew he shows by his declaration of the *Shema:* "Hear O Israel, the Lord our God, the Lord is One," as the first and highest commandment before he quotes the following verse: "And thou shalt love the Lord thy God with all thy heart," and so forth, from Deut. 6:5, and the second half-verse from Lev. 19:18: "Thou shalt love thy neighbor as thyself." [19] It is significant, however, that the other gospels omit the Creed, the Shema. In like manner, Jesus' declaration of loyalty to the Law has found its place only in the Sermon on the Mount in its most pronounced form,[20] though it is least in accordance with the tenor of the Sermon: "Think not that I come to destroy the Law or the Prophets. I come not to destroy but to fulfil. For verily I say unto you, Till heaven and earth pass away, one iota or tittle shall in no wise pass till all things are accomplished. Who, therefore, shall break the least of these commandments shall be called least in the Kingdom of heaven, but whosoever shall do and teach them shall be called great in the Kingdom of heaven."

On the other hand, it is not in Matthew's Sermon on the Mount, but in Luke's Sermon in the Field [21] that we find the genuine teachings of Jesus. These are addressed directly to the poor, the hungry, to them that weep and suffer, and so on; whereas Matthew's sermon speaks in a general way: Blessed are the poor, adding the words in spirit, and instead of the hungry, those that hunger and thirst after righteousness, and so forth. It is plain that Luke's Beatitudes and Woes are more simple and original and had in view the older Judeo-Christian community, which was known as the *Ebionim;* [22] whereas Matthew's Beatitudes, as well as his Woes, were aimed at the Christians of the whole Church. Evidently at first a large part of the audience was formed by the poor and the downtrodden, who above all needed consolation and encouragement. Besides, the Essene rule of voluntary poverty was in vogue among them. Accordingly, when a rich ruler came to Jesus, stating that he had observed the Commandments from his youth and asked what more he had to do to inherit eternal life, he was told to sell all he had and give it to the poor in order to obtain the treasures of heaven instead. But when he failed to heed this admonition, Jesus said to his disciples: "How hard it is for those who possess riches to enter the Kingdom of God. It is easier for a camel to go through a needle's eye than for the rich man to enter the Kingdom of God." So when Peter said to him: "Lo, we have left house or wife, or brethren or parents or children and have followed thee," Jesus answered: "There is no man that hath left house, or wife, or brethren, or parents, or children for my sake (Luke, better, for the sake of the

Kingdom of God) who shall not receive a hundred-fold in this time or in the world to come." [23] In the same spirit he takes as his text for the first sermon at Nazareth [24] good tidings to the poor, as the Septuagint read in Isaiah 61:1 *Aniyim* instead of *Anavim*. Luke alone contains the story of Lazarus, the poor, who, in contrast to the rich man, finds a place in Abraham's bosom, which means admission into Paradise. [25]

Another feature peculiar to Luke's collection of the sayings of Jesus is his love for the repentant sinner. This is voiced in the striking parable of the lost sheep, for the finding of whom the shepherd leaves the other ninety and nine, or of the lost piece of money for the seeking of which the woman leaves the rest at her home; and above all the touching story of the prodigal son whose return the father celebrates by a festive meal. [26] The idea, similarly expressed also in the Talmud, is that there is more rejoicing over the sinner that has repented than over all those who need no repentance, having been righteous always.

And here we touch upon a principle which became the very *leitmotif* of Jesus' activities, raising him above both Pharisean and Essene teachers. The latter blamed him for associating with sinners, publicans, non-observants of the Law, the untaught and unchaste women, all of whom they avoided in order not to be contaminated by their contact. He, on the contrary, made it his maxim that they that are well are in no need of the physician, but they that are sick; and "I am not come to call the righteous but the sinners to repentance." [27] Because he was frequently found sitting and eating with men and women of unsavory reputation, the Pharisees declared him to be in league with Beelzebub or Satan, the spirit of uncleanliness, by whose power he effected his exorcistic cures,[28] whereas his followers regarded him with all the more admiration.

To come back to the comparison of Matthew's and Luke's Gospels, we must not fail to notice the pronounced anti-Mosaic spirit of the former, which not only ignores the broadly human exposition of the Decalogue and the other Mosaic laws, but goes so far as to make the Mosaic law teach: Thou shalt love thy neighbor and hate thine enemies, for which there is nowhere in the entire Hebrew Scripture, nor in Rabbinical teachings, the slightest support. On the contrary, these contain in essence the ethical teachings of the Sermon on the Mount. The fact is that exactly as the Hasidim taught that one should not be satisfied with the mere observance of the letter of the Law but should "go beyond the line of the statute"— *Lifnim Mishurat Ha-Din*—so Jesus tells his disciples to "exceed in righteousness the Scribes and the Pharisees." [29] Accordingly, he expands,[30] exactly as do the Rabbis in the Talmud and Midrash, the Commandment "Thou shalt not kill," so as to make it include even anger which may lead to murder; or the prohibition of adultery to include even lustful glances at one's neighbor's wife; or that of false swearing to include all kinds of swearing, to have your speech Yea, Yea, Nay, Nay—as is expressly taught in the Talmud and likewise by the Essenes. The law, demanding "an eye for an eye and a tooth for a tooth," was altered in practice long before Jesus' time. "Love thy neighbor," too, is extended to enemies, exactly as was taught by the Essenes, according to the version of Hippolytus, as we saw above. That the giving of alms should be done in secret was taught and practiced both by the Essenes and the Rabbis. Also, what is said in regard to prayer and fasting has its parallels in the Rabbinic sources. And what is said about the treasures to be laid up in heaven, where neither moth and rust can consume them nor thieves steal them, has its origin in the Talmudic story of the King of Adiabene who was converted to Judaism.[31] As to "the narrow gate" through which the few righteous enter the realm of bliss, while the majority of souls enter the wide gate which leads to perdition,[32] the Testament of Abraham, a Jewish Apocryphal work, offers the explanation, and it certainly is not original with Jesus. Even the plea, so antagonistic to all civilization, not to be anxious concerning tomorrow's food and raiment, but to consider the birds of heaven which neither sow nor reap while our heavenly Father feedeth them, and the lilies of the field which neither toil nor spin, yet Solomon in all his glory was not arrayed like one of these, is a picture probably suggested by the purple lily of Palestine called the "royal lily," *Shoshanat Ha-Melek,* and not to be "of little faith" has its parallel in the sayings of Eliezer of Modin and Simon ben Johai.[33]

Again, when Jesus for the sake of relieving the sick performed his cures on the Sabbath,[34] he followed the maxim expressed by the Rabbis in almost the same terms that he used: "The Sabbath is handed over to you, not you to the Sabbath."[35] The phrase: "The Son of man is the Lord of the Sabbath," refers not to Jesus but to man in general. Like this another passage has been misunderstood by the Evangelist, to wit, the one about the disciples plucking grain,[36] which refers to the new corn which should not be eaten before some has been offered on the altar.[37] This alone accounts for the fact that Jesus referred to David who ate the holy bread when hungry.[38] It simply shows that Jesus did not heed slight transgressions against the Halakists.[39] So he could not consider the eating with unwashed hands, which was a Pharisean custom based by some on Lev. 15:11; Ber. 8, 2,

as a sin. The beautiful words he spoke against the Pharisees who blamed him for it, about what really defiles,[40]
must not be stressed as if he permitted the transgression
of the dietary laws, as Peter also observed them until he
had his vision.[41] Bold sayings, such as "The eye that lusts
and the hand that causes sin must be cut off," we find used
by R. Tarfon,[42] as well as by Jesus.[43] How far, in fact,
Jesus was himself indebted for the Logia—Sayings—
credited to him, to the ethical teachings of his predecessors, such as are found in the Didache [44] or in ancient
Rabbinical sayings, needs further investigation.

The assumption that he was a *universalist,* preaching
to the Gentiles as well as to the Jews, is contradicted by
his own words: "I was not sent but unto the lost sheep of
the house of Israel";[45] and to his apostles: "Go not into
the way of the Gentiles . . . but go rather to the lost sheep
of the house of Israel." [46] Still stronger are his words:
"Give not that which is holy unto the dogs, neither cast
ye your pearls before the swine." [47]

In choosing twelve apostles from his disciples,[48] he
apparently had the twelve tribes of Israel in view, as he
promised them [49] that they would, at the time of regeneration when the Son of Man sits upon his glorious
throne, likewise sit upon twelve thrones and judge the
twelve tribes of Israel. Luke,[50] obviously with a view to
the seventy nations, has seventy apostles in addition.

The central thought and hope of Jesus, as of all his
Essene and Pharisean brethren, was the *Kingdom of God,*
the Hebrew *Malkut Shamayim,* which Matthew trans-
lates literally the "Kingdom of Heaven." This meant
originally, as in Daniel and all the Apocalyptic writings,
the end of the four world-kingdoms and the reign of
Israel's only God. For its expected advent John the
Baptist, in common with all Essenes, prepared himself

by repentance and the leading of a holier life. As the
Synagogal liturgy had it probably long before him, Jesus,
in the so-called *Lord's Prayer*, prayed for the speedy
advent of the Kingdom of God, which is sufficient proof
that he did not claim to be its mediator himself. He
expected it to come, however, in the immediate future
and possibly in the lifetime of his hearers.[51] All the
passages speaking of the Son of Man were taken over
from the Apocalyptic writings and were only later applied
to Jesus, as is especially shown in Matthew;[52] so is the
belief in the sudden coming of the Messiah older than
the New Testament. Consequently, none of those passages, such as [53] "The Kingdom of God cometh not by
calculation" (false observation);[54] and "the Kingdom of
God is *amongst* (not within) you"; or it "comes like a
thief in the night";[55] likewise, all the admonitions to
"watch, for ye know not when the Lord of the house
cometh," [56] are genuinely original sayings of Jesus. Even
the parables of the faithful and the unfaithful servants
and the watchful and the unwatchful virgins [57] have their
parallels in ancient sayings of the Talmud.[58] Also, "The
Messiah comes when least expected" is Rabbinical.[59]

That the Kingdom of God at first was conceived by
Jesus as having a worldly character may be learned from
his own statement to John, according to Papias,[60] that it
will offer plenty of fruits of marvelous size for the benefit
of the righteous.[61] Sayings, such as "I have not come to
bring peace but the sword," [62] and "I have come to cast
fire upon the earth," announcing discord among the
people of the same household, which are hard to reconcile
with Jesus' attitude elsewhere, are probably placed in his
mouth in view of later events in the Church. When he
spoke of "the mysteries of the Kingdom of God" [63] and
"Things hidden from the foundation of the world," [64] he

apparently referred to the End of the Kingdom of Satan, which was Rome.[65] In general, however, these parables speak of the slow working of the Kingdom; and not all of those given in Matthew appear to be genuine, nor their interpretation to the disciples.

When the Pharisees and Herodians tried to ensnare him by the question whether or not it was lawful for the Jewish people to pay tribute unto Caesar—that is, to Rome, the oppressor, he evaded the test by answering: "Render unto Caesar the things that are Caesar's, and to God the things that are God's." [66] In like manner, the Sadducees, who denied the Resurrection and the advent of the Messianic Kingdom, asked Jesus in connection with the Mosaic law of the Levirate the question in regard to the woman who had successively been married to seven brothers, whose wife shall she be in the Resurrection? Whereupon he replied: "In the resurrection they neither marry nor are given in marriage, but are as the angels in heaven," and then he argued from Scripture which says: "I am the God of Abraham, the God of Isaac and the God of Jacob," [67] that "God is the God of the living, not of the dead"; to which some of the Pharisean scribes gave their approval.[68] When afterwards he arraigned the house of the high priest Hanan for their greed, he voiced the same condemnation as did some of the Essenes;[69] but he went so far as to call the Temple "a den of thieves" and to seize the tables of the money-changers and drive off the owners thereof, which finally led to the great catastrophe caused by the priesthood who accused him before Pilate.

Also, in castigating many of the Pharisees for their hypocrisy, he did not stand alone, as an oft-repeated statement in the Talmud charges five classes out of seven of the Pharisees with being hypocrites.[70] The Gospel

records, however, especially Matthew, soon identified the
very name Pharisees with hypocrites, and whereas the
authentic older records relate that Jesus was seized by
the high priests and the (Sadducean) Sanhedrin and
delivered over as a revolutionary [71] to the Roman
authorities for execution [72]—John [73] tells of the high
priests' fear of the Roman prefect—the Pharisees were
later added to the list of his assailants. [74]

The very acme of these accusations of the Jewish
people in general—not to mention the late fourth gospel,
which calls them Christ-killers—is reached in Matthew, [75]
where the Jewish masses are represented as shouting
forth that Jesus, and not the rebellious Barabbas, must
be crucified; and when Pilate washes his hands before the
multitude saying, "I am innocent of this blood," the whole
people cries forth: "His blood come upon us and our
children"—a malicious slander, which can only be read
with a shudder, as it created all the Jew-hatred and the
slaying of the millions of Jews throughout the centuries.
Elsewhere we read that the people clung to Jesus [76] and
lamented over his death. [77]

The facts, however, speak for themselves. The Roman
soldiers nailed him to the cross, hailing him mockingly
as King of the Jews, after Pilate had himself scourged
him. [78]   The crucifixion was the Roman method of punishment for the rebel, and in three languages, Hebrew,
Latin, and Greek, were inscribed on the cross the words:
"Jesus of Nazareth, the King of the Jews." [79]   The fact
that Jesus was left in haste by his own disciples [80] in order
not to be caught with him, and that Peter denied him
three times, shows that they feared to meet the same
punishment as their master.   But the statements that the
high priests found him guilty of blasphemy for having
claimed to be the Son of God, or that the Pharisees

accused him of the violation of the Sabbath or of having
spoken against the Temple, must be dismissed as spurious.
Likewise, the statement that the high priests and the
Sanhedrin held a trial on Passover morning, or on Passover eve, must be dismissed as unhistorical, as the Jewish
law made that impossible.

There is only one thing that stands out as historically
well established, and that is that Jesus was crucified on
the fourteenth of Nisan, which was also Sabbath eve.[81]
But as on this very day the Passover lamb was slaughtered and eaten, Jesus was spoken of, as we learn from
Paul's saying,[82] as the Christian Passover lamb. Not
satisfied with the symbolic figure, the Christian tradition
went further and rather inconsequently placed the Last
Supper, which Jesus took with his disciples, on Passover
eve when the Passover lamb was slaughtered and eaten;
so that Jesus was represented as having actually celebrated the Passover eve feast the very same night that
he was seized by the Romans to be crucified.[83] Moreover, the Gospels represent him as having then told his
disciples to eat of the lamb as symbolic of his own body,
and drink of the wine as symbolic of the blood of the
new covenant which was to be shed for the forgiveness
of sins,[84] and this has found a place also in I Cor. 11:24f.,
where it is emphatically presented as if Paul had received
it as a special instruction from Jesus—whom he did not
even know! It is easy to understand that the Last Supper,
which the Apostles had in common with their master,
in view of the tragic events which followed, made a
mighty and permanent impression upon them, so as to
become elaborated into the solemn conclusion of a new
covenant by him; while, in fact, it was originally only one
of the love feasts [85] which the Essenes had introduced.

Of the historical connection between Jesus and the

Essenes we have a direct proof in the fact that Joseph of Arimathea—or *Ramathaim*—called the eminent counselor of "the city of the Jews," [86] a name which apparently read originally the city of the Hasidim or a colony of Hasidim or Essenes,[87] "who was waiting for the kingdom," was anxious to provide a singularly honorable burial for Jesus.[88]

It is unnecessary to dwell at length on the various legends concerning his resurrection, which Jesus himself was believed to have foretold.[89] Interesting it is to note that the women of his acquaintance, particularly Mary Magdalene, are said to have gone to his tomb to give him the last ointment, only to find it empty, and then to be told by an angel of his resurrection. Paul [90] has no reference to these women, but affirms that Jesus revealed himself first to Peter, then to the other apostles, and finally to five hundred of the brethren, before he appeared to him. More important still is his declaration [91] that if Jesus has not risen from the dead, then his own preaching and the whole Christian faith were without truth. Henceforth the belief in Jesus' resurrection became fundamental for the Church.

But it was Peter who, according to Matthew,[92] was declared by Jesus to be the *rock* (Petra) upon which he would build his *Church,* and who was given the keys of the Kingdom of heaven after he had acknowledged him to be "the Messiah, the son of the living God." Compare this with the Midrash Yalkut to Isaiah,[93] where Abraham is declared to have been the rock upon which God built His Kingdom.

In summing up the history of Jesus, it must first be stated that he was not the founder of Christianity, as he still is regarded by many. As a disciple of John the Baptist, called "a prophet of God," he followed his calling to prepare the people for the advent of the Kingdom through repentance of their sins, and, as he felt himself imbued with the holy spirit, he achieved greater success than John did as a preacher among his Galilean countrymen, he being the eminent healer of the diseased, which John was not. He traveled from place to place throughout Galilee and the neighboring towns, attracting the masses and winning his faithful apostles for his task as healer and preacher. He shared the belief of his co-religionists in God as Father of the people of Israel in particular, as they are the true sons of the Kingdom from which non-Jews were excluded,⁹⁴ and he cherished especially the Apocalyptic dreams and visions of the coming Day of Judgment, with its visitations for the sinners and rewards for the righteous in the hereafter. Love of God and of man constituted for him the substance of the Law,⁹⁵ as taught previously in the Testaments of the Twelve Patriarchs and by Hillel and his disciples; but he insisted above all on the inwardness of religion. While looking for the advent of the Kingdom of God during his own generation,⁹⁶ in his parables he spoke of its going through the process of slow ripening,⁹⁷ owing to the gradual conquest of the Satanic powers of evil. In overcoming Satan he apparently claimed supernatural powers, but he never claimed sinlessness. On the contrary, he declined to be called the good one, God alone being really good. At the same time he told his disciples to be guileless like little children; and his words: "Be perfect as your Father in heaven is perfect!" are only a paraphrase of the Mosaic command: "Be holy, for holy am I, the Lord your God."

Jesus was by no means a social reformer. He despised the owners of wealth and extolled the poor; and though he was the son of a carpenter, he never encouraged, in fact rather discouraged, industry, which forms the main factor of civilization. Nor did he ever dwell upon the blessings of home; quite the contrary, he favored the ascetic abstinence from marriage, chiefly in view of his expectation of the speedy advent of the new state of life in the Kingdom of God. In claiming to be in a unique sense the Son of God, he went so far as to make himself the mediator between God his Father and the rest of mankind.[98] Still, he was far from ascribing to himself a divine character, as is done in the fourth Gospel and by Paul. The title Son of God is given in the Scripture to kings, to Israel, and, in Ps. 2, to the Messiah; but nowhere does it denote more than a distinction from others, an aloofness above the rest of men. Just what meaning Jesus applied to this title assumed by himself, it is difficult to say. He appears, however, to have regarded it as inseparable from the Messiahship, yet only in a spiritual sense. Only his disciples ascribed to him a divine personality, and his descent from David was never urged by him, though he may have allowed himself to be called by the term which the people of his time applied to the Messiah, "the Son of David." In fact, he disclaimed the descent [99] which the Gospel legends later on asserted in artificial genealogies.

Those that would rank Jesus among the Prophets of Israel overlook the important fact that the ancient prophets spoke simply as the mouthpiece of God, never obtruding their own selves in their prophecies; their "I" was God who spoke through them. Quite different was the attitude of Jesus. His "I" was in the foreground. In his "I say unto you" in the Sermon on the Mount, if genuine, he puts himself in contrast to the past Revelation, and his claim that the way of reaching God his

Father was through him, His son, which runs through all the Gospels, led the way to his eclipsing God in the Christian system.

As was stated at the beginning of this chapter, he could never have spoken the words: "My God, my God, why hast Thou forsaken me!" if he had had a foreknowledge of his tragic end foreordained by God and had been ready resignedly to submit to it. On the other hand, it was just this cry of despair, taken from the twenty-second Psalm, which gave rise to the description of his maltreatment by the Roman soldiers at the crucifixion, in fulfilment of the prophecies contained in the Psalms, as claimed by the Gospel writers. In fact, all the Biblical passages quoted or used for the delineation of the history of Jesus as the Messiah, and the Messianic application of those passages by the Rabbis, still deserve close study, such as was undertaken by Wünsche and others.

Taken all in all, and leaving aside the popular legends and the assumed Messianic characteristics taken from the Scriptures, in fact all the supernatural elements of his history, we cannot fail to admit that Jesus' great sympathy with the outcast and despised, which was his outstanding characteristic, made him a redeemer of men and an uplifter of womanhood without parallel in history. All the more pity it is that he was so little known outside of his Galilean circle, and that the tragic fate he met in Jerusalem as the Galilean Messiah rather obscured his real greatness as the friend of humanity. Providence, however, assigned to him a place in history which no one, either before or after him, has occupied. That it took nineteen hundred years to bring his true value to light is the shame of the Church that deified the man instead of following his example.

CHAPTER IV

The Beginning of the Church

It was by no means either the life of Jesus or his teachings, however unique in grandeur of soul the one or in loftiness of spirit the other, that created the Christian Church, but rather his followers' visions of his *resurrection,* which gave unity and stability to their belief in him. It was a new Messiah, one totally different from the one expected by the members of the Synagogue, that kept the small band of believers together, a Messiah who had died and risen from among the dead to start the new world for them. That they saw him was sufficient for them to keep them waiting for his return in glory to bring about the Kingdom of God for which they were all looking and praying. In the light of this resurrection the whole past, the life of their master and the old prophecies, had to be reconstructed.

The resurrection, which, from a mere Pharisean hope, had for them become in Jesus an actual fact, changed the whole aspect of life for these believers. Nor could it be otherwise. Nothing better characterizes the terrible situation of the disciples when their master had been taken from them to suffer the tragic fate of crucifixion by the Romans than does the quotation from Zech. 13:7: "Smite the shepherd, and the sheep shall be scattered." In their despair and bewilderment they had fled in haste from Jerusalem, and they rallied again in Galilee in momentary security from the Roman powers, buoyed up

by the common conviction that their Messiah had risen to
a new life. The story that in that fatal night previous
to his crucifixion Jesus had told his disciples, in view of
the coming event, that he would go ahead of them to
Galilee and appear to them there,[1] whatever its legendary
part, at least confirms the fact that the fugitive disciples
rallied in Galilee and had there the vision of Jesus appearing to them. But there is one story which appears to rest
upon a certain fact. It is the one which relates that Peter
was at first the only one who "acknowledged Jesus to
have been the Messiah, the son of the living God," and
this happened to have taken place in Cesarea Philippi in
Galilee.[2] Now it is out of the question that this had happened in the lifetime of Jesus, as the whole attitude of
Peter afterwards contradicts such an assumption. It is
different when we place the story after the death of
Jesus, as we have the testimony of Paul[3] that Peter was
the first to whom the resurrected Jesus appeared. This
would throw a special light on the words of Jesus declaring Peter to be the rock (*petra*) upon which his Church
would rest. At any rate, we have here the remarkable
statement that in Galilee, under Peter's leadership, the
Church was founded.

In striking contrast to these Gospel records, the Acts[4]
relate that Jesus after his resurrection stayed with his disciples for forty days, discoursing of the affairs of the
Kingdom of heaven that had come, and that he expressly
warned them not to leave Jerusalem, but to wait for the
fulfilment of the promise of God his Father that they
would in Jerusalem be endowed with the power of the
holy spirit and become witnesses to his resurrection on
the *third day*—after Hosea 6:2. So also Luke 24:48-49.
Evidently the Church at Jerusalem purposely ignored the
claim of the Galileans to have been the starting point of

the Church by the rally of the fugitive disciples of Jesus and claimed it for itself in order to make the holy city the only center of the new dispensation. But the claim of being the first·true Church was based by it on the great miraculous event which, according to the Acts,[5] created the Christian Pentecost to be a substitute for the Jewish Pentecost, just as the Last Supper previous to the crucifixion was rendered the substitute for the Jewish Passover eve. Of course, as the latter was merely a late construction of the actual event, so was the Pentecost event fashioned after the Jewish Pentecost, which was taken by the Rabbis to have been the day of the divine revelation on Sinai at which the Ten Commandments were given forth in seventy tongues of fire to reach the seventy nations of the earth. The inarticulate voices stammered forth by the large ecstatic assembly under the influence of the holy ghost, and called "speaking in tongues," of which Paul also speaks at length,[6] are taken to have been the languages of the various nations corresponding to the Sinai miracle. At the same time, we are told, that Peter stood up among the apostles and, referring to the words of Joel:[7] "It shall come to pass afterward, [says the Lord], that I will pour forth My spirit upon all flesh, and your sons and daughters shall prophesy," said that this prediction had now actually been fulfilled; whereupon all were baptized by the holy spirit. The numbers, 120 and 3,000, given of the assembly by the writer are, no doubt, exaggerated, and it is much more likely, as Hausrath suggests, that Paul's statement[8] that, after Peter and the other apostles, Jesus had appeared to five hundred at one and the same time, refers to the Pentecost event.

These ecstatic outbursts under the influence of the holy spirit manifested in the "speaking with tongues" and prophesying apparently became a standing feature of the early Church, as is seen also in Acts [9] as well as in Paul.[10] The claim of having been "baptized by the holy spirit" seems to have given them the name of "saints," [11] as Paul calls them.[12] Especially were the "saints of Jerusalem" spoken of as a privileged class. Possibly "the holy Congregation of Jerusalem," frequently mentioned in the Talmud in the second century, was an Essene organization existing before the rise of Christianity. At any rate, these early Christians constituted themselves no longer as a *Synagogue*, a name henceforth retained exclusively by the Jewish Congregations, but as a Church—Ecclesia—namely, "the Church of God," corresponding to the Biblical *Kehal Yahweh*, "Assembly of the Lord," being more expressive of the totality of the people of God, and corresponding more to the name *Keneset Yisrael*, "the Congregation of Israel." In this sense the name Ecclesia is used in Ben Sira, the Book of Maccabees, and other Apocryphal books; and in James, an original Jewish work, as was shown by Spitta and myself,[13] and particularly in *Hermas*, where Ecclesia is the Personification of Israel, as shown by Spitta. Owing chiefly to Paul's Epistles, Ecclesia— Church—became the exclusive name for the Christian Church, whereas the Judeo-Christians adhered as a rule to the Jewish name Synagogue.

Not to dwell on the miraculous cures performed by exorcism in the name of Jesus the *re-risen* by the apostles, especially by Peter on whom the Acts [14] lay so much stress as having made many converts, we are told that the early Christians were kept together by three features which were obviously taken over from the past: their *common* possessions, their *common* meals, and their *common* prayers. The communistic principle which induced them

to sell their property and lay the money at the feet of
the apostles for an equal share to be handed over to all [15]
is already expressed in a number of sayings attributed to
Jesus, which implied renunciation of private possession
and private enterprise. But the conditions of the Galilean
community in Jerusalem, which offered to the newcomers
little chance for either agricultural or industrial occupations, themselves favored the communistic life. Especially were "the saints of Jerusalem in need of provisions
in their great poverty." [16] As we know very little concerning those early communities, we cannot tell when
arose the name *Ebyonim*, "the Poor," with reference to
Deut. 15:7—by which the Judeo-Christians were afterwards called; nor do we know whether there was voluntary poverty or not. As to the common meals, it is significant that no reference is made to the Last Supper,
nor are they in any way declared to be memorials of
Jesus. Hence, we are forced to regard them simply as
typical love feasts (Agapae). And as in those meals
in which Jesus, the living or the re-risen, participated,
"the breaking of the bread" was the outstanding feature, that is, that the one presiding at the table while
breaking the bread would offer the thanksgiving—called
later "the Eucharist," so here also.

The Eucharist formula in the Teaching of the Twelve
Apostles [17] is, of course, of later origin. The Agapae
themselves, even in the second century, retained their
simple character of communal meals, and the widows and
the orphans became the chief beneficiaries. For their
common prayer, they assembled in the so-called Porch of
Solomon in the Temple. [18] There is but one time of the
day mentioned for their common service, the ninth hour
or afternoon service, [19] but in all likelihood they held
service three times a day, as did the rest of the Jews.

When we are asked, however, who formulated the prayers for the newly formed Church, we are at a loss to answer. Neither Peter nor John can well be supposed to have done so, as they are characterized as ignorant men.[20] We are thus led to assume that a new element joined the new Church which was ready to acknowledge the crucified Jesus as the expected Messiah and helped in its formation. Such was to a large extent the Essene order, to the consideration of which we shall devote the next chapter.

CHAPTER V

THE ESSENES AND THE EARLY CHURCH

The question occasionally has been asked but in no way satisfactorily answered: How did it come about that the Essenes, to whom both Philo and Josephus give so prominent a place in the history of those times, are nowhere mentioned in the New Testament? It is true that Jesus and his disciples living in Galilee scarcely came in contact with the Essene order, though they may have indirectly been influenced by its teaching and habits. But there were the writers of the Gospels and the Church of Jerusalem who must have come across the Essenes in some way or other. The answer is given by the fact that some of them actually are referred to under the name of such as were looking "for the consolation of Israel" or "for the redemption of Jerusalem," or "for the Kingdom of God," [1] and they are represented as believers in Jesus as the Messiah. Not as a class, then, but individually many Essenes may have joined the Church, seeing their great hope fulfilled in Jesus, while accepting the belief in his resurrection.

But there are other indications which are of even greater weight. There are in the Gospels a number of important Apocalyptic passages which cannot have been developed on Galilean soil or produced by Jesus and his disciples. They form parts of the Apocalyptic literature which are the products of the Essenes, and though ascribed to Jesus they prove, on closer scrutiny, to have been taken from other sources and to belong to other periods. For instance, the larger part of Matthew ch. 24, to which Mark ch. 13 corresponds, and Matthew 25:31-46, in which the Messiah is described as "the son of man coming on the clouds of heaven with great power and glory," and in which the son of man is pictured as "sitting on the throne of his glory, judging all nations gathered before him, and separating the sheep on his right from the goats on his left, declaring the former to inherit the Kingdom prepared for them since the foundation of the world, and condemning the latter to the everlasting fire prepared for the devil and his hosts," are Jewish Apocalypses written shortly before the capture of Jerusalem, neither the name of Jesus nor any other feature indicating a Christian character. Moreover, none of the passages in which Jesus speaks of himself as the Son of Man in the eschatological sense is genuine. Only the Essene Apocalyptists could have put them into his mouth as predictions of his own tragic end.[2] As a matter of fact, the entire Apocalyptic literature, from the Books of Enoch on, which was rejected by the Synagogue as being in conflict with the view that after the last three canonical prophets no prophet was to be recognized, could only have come into the possession of the Church through the Essenes who joined it. No one can read the instruction given by Jesus to the apostles regarding their travels[3] but find its striking similarity to the Essene restrictions;[4] yet we can scarcely believe that those restrictions emanated from Jesus. Likewise, the monition to go through the narrow gate[5] points directly to the Testament of Abraham or some similar work, without which it is scarcely understood. Many a passage in the Gospels bears the earmark of the Essene and Apocalyptic literature with which Jesus himself could not have been

familiar.[6] Nor are we going too far when we assert
that the Didascalia, known as the Apostolic Constitutions, reflect the influence of, if they did not actually
emanate from, the Essenes.[7] That the Seventh book of
the Apostolic Constitutions contains prayers composed by
the Essenes before the Christian Era, I have shown elsewhere.[8]

CHAPTER VI

THE EARLY CHURCH AND THE SADDUCEAN AUTHORITIES

It is amazing to find even New Testament critics accepting as authentic (despite the contrary tenor of the older records, including the predictions ascribed to Jesus concerning his end) the story of the late Romanizing Gospel writers that the Jewish people had a hand in delivering Jesus over to Pilate for his crucifixion as a rebel; yea, that they urged him at the last moment to have him slain, while they assert that after his death a reaction took place among the Christians themselves in favor of the Jews, which led to the election of James, the elder brother of Jesus, as recorded in the Acts. But there was no reason for the Pharisees to deal so harshly with Jesus as claimant to the Messiahship, though they would not acknowledge his claim; nor were any of the charges, even if made against him, a mortal sin according to the Law. Only the Sadducean council and the priests were fierce opponents of the Messianic movement, and when the death of Jesus, far from putting an end to it, gave it a new impetus, owing to the belief of his followers in his resurrection and the miracles wrought by his apostles in the name of the re-risen Christ, the Sadducean authorities tried their utmost to suppress it, imprisoning Peter as the chief leader and forbidding expressly the invocation of the name of Jesus. All the more numerous and strong grew the young Church, no matter whether the bold aggressive speeches against the Sadducean priests given by the writer of the Acts are genuine or not. At any rate they let the matter rest for a while.

The crisis came, however, when the Hellenists who had joined the Church took a more prominent position in regard to the administration of the charity, after having expressed their dissatisfaction at seeing the widows neglected; and accordingly *seven* men were selected out of their own midst to take charge of it. But then one of these, Stephen, gave vent to views which could only exasperate those adhering to the old doctrines and practices. Addressing the assembled people, he said that Jesus on his return from heaven would destroy the Temple and abolish the Law. This so provoked the multitude that they drove him out of the city and stoned him to death, and the rest fled. And there it happened that Paul, called by his Hebrew name Saul, who still shared in the fanaticism of the assailants of Stephen and his associates, took part in their persecution, going as far as Damascus at the order of the high priest to spread terror among the fugitives in the Synagogue there. But then the strange thing happened that he was seized with awe and regret at his own doings and he heard a heavenly voice saying to him—so we are told in Acts [1]—"Saul, Saul, why persecutest thou me?" and after this strange vision, while for days in an epileptic state, he became the most zealous adherent of Jesus. Thus Stephen's martyrdom led to Paul's creation of the Church for the Gentiles.

All the more strenuously did those of the Jerusalem Church for a long time adhere to their Jewish views and customs under the guidance of the apostles, opposing with all their might the attempts at breaking with the Law. The difficulty is that the whole history of Judeo-Christianity is but little known, and it is chiefly through Paul's

Epistles, particularly the Galatians, that we obtain glimpses of it, while the writer of the Acts tries to reconcile the views of Peter and of Paul by all sorts of compromises. So we are left in the dark as to what induced King Herod to slay the apostle James, the son of Zebedaeus;[2] possibly his boldness, which gave him the name of Boanerges, the "Son of Thunder,"[3] had provoked his anger. On the whole, however, years of peace followed,[4] during which many Pharisees joined the Church. The increased zeal for the Law was especially manifested by the rise to power and authority of James the Elder, the brother of Jesus, surnamed the Righteous, who believed in the Messiahship of Jesus, the re-risen, probably since the Pentecost vision of the five hundred. According to the description of Hegesippus, a Judeo-Christian of the second century,[5] he led the life of an Essene saint, being a Nazarite for life,[6] avoiding wine and intoxicating drink and animal food, using neither a razor for his hair nor a warm bath for his body, and wearing no wool but only linen garments. He used to pray in the Temple for forgiveness on behalf of the people, lying on his knees which became hard like those of a camel, and he was called by the significant name *Kebal Am,* which meant the protection or bulwark of the people. Josephus [7] also tells us that he stood in high esteem among the people, and when with his companions he was charged by the high priest with violation of the Law and finally executed, by being cast down from some elevated spot and then stoned, the foremost citizens were greatly provoked by this arbitrary act of the Sadducean council.

Hegesippus [8] presents the legendary story that the Scribes and Pharisees first entreated James to persuade those that had come for the Passover season to celebrate the feast in the Christian manner—that is, regarding

Jesus as the Passover lamb—not to do so and, instead, to address the people from the high pinnacle of the Temple in this spirit, telling them of "the gate of the Lord into which the righteous enter." [9] (Jesus is certainly an error of the writer.) But when he spoke of Jesus as sitting at the right hand of God who would speedily come back on the clouds of heaven, the Scribes and the Pharisees—obviously a misstatement for the Sadducees—cast him down, and, while the *Rechabites* pleaded for his life, saying the righteous one prayeth for you, a fuller in the crowd struck him on the head and killed him. He was then buried in a spot near the Temple, and in punishment for the crime the Emperor Vespasian came and began the war which put an end to the Jewish State.— The fact is James the Elder was killed five years before the destruction of the Temple.

It was chiefly due to his paramount influence that Paul and Barnabas were called to task for their arbitrariness in admitting a heathen without circumcision and without obligation to observe the Law; but, owing to their great success, a compromise was reached at the apostolic convention, where it was decided that the heathen proselytes should be bound to observe the so-called Noahidic laws of which the abstaining from idolatry, from fornication (incest), and from eating strangled animals and blood are singled out.[10] How far and how long this agreement was adhered to by the Paulinian Church, we cannot tell, as freedom, or emancipation, from the Law was made its leading principle by Paul. After all, these proselytes who observed only the Noahidic laws were to be only semi-proselytes, according to the Rabbinical system, by virtue of which there existed two classes of converts, the proselytes who by the rite of circumcision adopted the whole Mosaic Law and became full members of the Jewish community, and the others who became only half-Jews. In contrast to this division, Paul created his system of belief in Jesus as the atoning Christ, which rendered all alike, those born as Jews and circumcised on the eighth day after their birth and the converted heathen. Outside of Palestine, where instead of the Rabbinical terminology the Hellenistic propaganda laid all the stress on the worship of the only One God and the observance of ethical laws in general, this division between full Jews and half-Jews was not brought out so strongly, and so the way was paved for the Paulinian Church which did away with the whole idea of the Law.

On the other hand, the Judeo-Christians remained loyal to the Temple as long as it existed, offering their prayers there, and some leading the life of Nazarites. They observed the Mosaic Law, keeping the dietary laws; they even wanted Paul to manifest his adherence to the Temple by asking him to become a Nazarite. But their relations became ever more strained, as may be learned from Paul's Epistles, though at first the latter sought to maintain a certain friendly relation by collecting money everywhere for the support of the poor of Jerusalem. As he became an outspoken opponent of the Law, he was nicknamed Balaam.[11] When the Roman conquerors no longer permitted the Jews to stay at Jerusalem, the Judeo-Christians fled beyond the Jordan and there started various communities; but lacking a firm organization they divided into different sects, under such names as Nazarenes and Ebionites. There is, however, nothing definite known about them. Apparently they preferred the name Synagogue to that of Church (Ecclesia) and at no time did they apply the name Christian to themselves, as, in fact, only the heathen of Antioch gave that name to the Paulinian Christians,[12] believing that Christus or Chrestus was the proper name of Jesus their master whom they worshiped; and only gradually was the name adopted by the latter. This much is certain, that Judeo-Christianity in upholding the Jewish ideal of Law against the Paulinian antinomism worked as a wholesome positive force against the negative attitude of the latter. Only the fact that the Apocalypse of John, popularly known as the Revelation, found a place in the New Testament, shows that for some time Judeo-Christianity had to be reckoned with. How much of the Judeo-Christian element has been embodied in the Synoptic Gospels is a matter of dispute.

CHAPTER VII

THE SO-CALLED APOSTOLIC LITERATURE, COMPRISING THE TEACHING AND THE LITURGY OF THE EARLY CHURCH

Before we turn to the system of Paul, the real founder of the Christian Church, which by its spreading over the various lands became the Catholic Church, we must get a deeper insight into the teaching and the liturgy of the early Church ascribed to the Apostles. It has escaped most of the modern Church historians that the Apostles themselves could not quote from the New Testament or the Gospels, which did not exist in a fixed written form in their time, and that only the Old Testament, including Sirah, could be quoted by them as "Scripture." In this light, then, we have to examine, on the one hand, the Didache, presented as the Teaching of the Twelve Apostles, and the Didascalia, presented as the Apostolic Constitutions, though composed much later, as they claim at the outset to be "the Catholic teaching."

I

THE DIDACHE

It has been recognized by such leading critics as Rendel Harris,[1] Charles Taylor,[2] and Adolph Harnack[3] that the Didache is based upon a Jewish Manual for Proselytes, which bore the title, "The Two Ways," after its beginning: "There are two ways, one of life and one of death." Possibly the title "Teaching of the Lord to the Gentiles" was originally Jewish, before the words "Through the Twelve Apostles" were inserted by the Christian writer. At any rate, the first paragraph has preserved the Jewish original. The idea of the two ways opposing each other is derived from Deut. 30:15-19 and Jer. 21:8, and it occurs in Ber. 28b [4] and in the Testaments of the Twelve Patriarchs, Asher I, where the two commandments: Love of God and love for one's neighbor, are found combined for the first time. The negative form of the latter given in the J. Targum to Lev. 19:18; Tobit 4:15; Philo [5] and by Hillel [6] is the best evidence of its Jewish origin, the Gospels [7] having it in the positive form.

On the whole, it seems that the Christian composer of the Didache, while including citations from the Sermon on the Mount in Chapter I, omitted purposely such parts of the Jewish original as pertain to the duty toward God as implied in the first part of the Decalogue, and at once took up those dealing with man contained in the second part of the Decalogue, as does Jesus in Matt. 19:18-20, and we may compare the story of Hillel converting the heathen. [8] But these duties are enlarged in accordance with the Jewish principle often quoted in the Talmudic sources: "Flee from evil and from whatsoever is like it," with which Chapter III opens, corresponding to the ancient Rabbinical maxim: "Make a fence around the Law." Thus, it warns against anger as it may lead to murder, against lust and lasciviousness leading to adultery, against lying as leading to theft, against irreverence to God as leading to idolatry. Chapter IV refers chiefly to what is implied in the duty toward God, such as reverence for His word and its teachings, for parents, respect for every man born in the image of God, and avoiding hypocrisy. Genuinely

Jewish is the monition to keep the commandments of the Lord, none to be added and none to be taken away,[9] which could scarcely have emanated from a Christian writer.

Chapter V presents the prohibitory laws under the heading of the "Way of Death." As in the former chapters, the enumeration shows lack of order. But all the mandatory and prohibitory precepts have their parallels and origin in the Jewish sources. Finally, in warning against erroneous teaching, Chapter VI, speaking in the Jewish spirit of the Yoke of the Law, characteristically distinguishes the two classes of proselytes, those that accept all the laws including circumcision, the Sabbath and the dietary laws and the semi-proselytes who are to observe only the Noahite laws, though of the latter it specifies only the meat sacrificed to idols.

The second part of the Didache is exclusively Christian in character, treating as it does of Baptism, the Eucharist, the Lord's Prayer, the Christian ministry, the Anti-Christ, and the Reappearance of Christ. At the same time there are indications that here also the Jewish original formed some kind of a basis. First of all, there were the two Jewish fastdays of the week, Monday and Thursday, probably a survival of the former Maamadot, which are here transferred to the fourth and sixth days of the week;[10] and so are the three prayers each day taken over from the Synagogue. Likewise, the baptism of proselytes in living water[11] is of Jewish origin. Equally, the change of the Jewish Sabbath as the day of the Lord to Sunday as "The Lord's day of the Lord"[12] points decidedly to the Jewish original, all the more so as the ancient Jewish observance laid stress on rendering the Sabbath a day of peace when all kinds of strife were to be avoided.[13] Less clear is the depend-ence of the thanksgiving formula for the wine and bread upon the Jewish custom. Whether the Psalmist's name for the son of David, "the vine," [14] suggested to older Hasidean circles the connection of the benediction over the "fruit of the vine" with the Messiah, we do not know; it is not likely that the words of Jesus in Luke 10:34, had no precedent for this combination in Jewish circles. As to the formula for the broken bread, we may well assume that a Hasidean benediction over the bread, lost to us, contained a reference to Israel being scattered all over the earth and to be gathered again for the Kingdom of God, and was utilized by the Christian composer.[15]

Altogether the Didache, as we have it, is a work of the beginning of the second century, and a compilation rather than a unit. The reference to "the saints" who should be preferred for support [16] shows the *Hasidean* character of the work,[17] as the word cannot be applied to the Christian members of the Church.

Especial attention must also be called to the significant fact that the Old Testament quotations are introduced by the words "Says He," thus referring to God, whereas the New Testament quotations are introduced by the words "Our," or "The," "Lord Jesus says."

II

THE APOSTOLIC CONSTITUTIONS

As for the Apostolic Constitutions they contain the regulations of Church life of the early period, and originally bore the title of *Didascalia,* "The Instruction," comprising at the outset only the first six books, the latter two, though partly older, having been attached much later. We are at a loss to understand how Lagarde [1] and most modern scholars could arrive at the conclusion that the much shorter version, consisting of the Didascalia preserved only in the Syriac and other translations, is the original work, of which the Apostolic Constitutions is an amplification.   As has been shown by Bickell,[2] the former is a mere condensation of the latter, accentuating its strict Catholic character with the omission of every Jewish feature; and while referring to the Didache,[3] it claims to offer the direct outcome of the discussion of the twelve apostles, adding to it words of the Apostle Paul, of the much later Syrian Apostle Addai, and of the very late Canons of the Church.   As a matter of fact, the Apostolic Constitutions prove on closer examination to be based, as is the Didache, upon an original Jewish work, transformed, by extensive interpolations of very late periods and by many alterations, into a Christian document of great authority.   The original writer quotes the Scripture after the Septuagint version, and he must have been in possession of Apocryphal works containing Haggadic and Halakic material not found in other sources; while the Christian interpolator is easily recognized by interruptions and ill-fitting references to the New Testament, and by occasional outbursts of Jew-hatred.   For instance, as the prophet Isaiah calls the house of Israel the vineyard of the Lord of hosts, and the men of Judah the plantation of His delight,[4] so in the introductory sentence of the Didascalia the Catholic Church rather oddly is called "the plantation of God and His beloved vineyard," no doubt after the example of the Jewish original, which contained many of the following sentences speaking of those who believe in "God's unerring religion who will partake by their faith in His everlasting Kingdom" who are here told to "hearken to His holy Instruction" (Didascalia).   All the references to Christ instead of "the Lord our God" are Christian insertions, as is shown by the context.

The first book, after a general introduction which is now Christianized by a number of interpolations, deals with the conduct of the individual and, beginning with the last of the Ten Commandments, dwells on covetousness while referring to the Golden Rule [5] in its negative form,[6] as the J. Targum (ib.), Tobit 4, 15 and Philo have it, and not in the positive form of Matthew, it warns against lasciviousness on the part of men and women, thus presenting the Rules of Modesty, *Hilkot Zeniut,* which have many parallels in the Rabbinical treatises on the subject.[7] In the second paragraph, likewise, the Old Testament quotations are genuine, not those from the Gospel. Most significant is the reference to the various Mosaic laws, such as Lev. 19:27 and Deut. 22:5.[8]

The warning against the alluring immodesty in dress by the men, which may cause "the stumbling" of women,[9] with special reference to Deut. 22:5 and Lev. 19:27, taken to be prohibitions of certain forms of dressing the hair and the beard, and likewise the warning against all kinds of frivolous attire and unseemly conduct of women by which men might be seduced to sin, including also the unveiled hair, is characteristically Jewish, and was copied by Paul,[10] *not* the reverse. The original sentence: "Let the wife subordinate herself to her husband, for the head of the woman is man, and of the man who walks in the way of righteousness, God, his Father, who is over all," [11] following Paul,[12] has an additional reference to Christ as the head, which is altogether out of place here, as also in the next sentence. Two chapters on woman are quoted from Proverbs, but there is no reference to any New Testament woman.

Book II deals elaborately with the functions, the powers, and the qualifications of the Bishop, *Episcopus* or Overseer, the Rabbinical Parnas, *Pronoos,*[13] and the

whole system appears to have been worked out by the
Judeo-Christian Church, whose main attention was
directed to the work of charity, the chief beneficiaries
of which were the widows. The necessary qualifications
of the Bishop are derived from the Law. He is held
responsible as the shepherd for his flock.[14] Great stress
is laid upon his possessing tender-heartedness and compassion. He is charged, above all, with providing for the
poor, especially the widow. Mention is made in Book II,
25 of the tithes and first fruits, which according to the
Mosaic Law are given to the Levites and the priests, and
likewise of the free-will offerings that should be given
to the Overseers for the poor, the orphan, the widow, the
afflicted and the strangers in distress. And as the Tabernacle of the Testimony, being a type of the Congregation,
so should the laborers, like the Levites of yore, obtain
their share for themselves and their families. In this
connection reference is made to the threshing ox which
should be allowed to eat, according to Deut. 25:4, and
this is apparently Paul's source.[15] Moreover, the
Bishop must not be a proselyte and, like the priest, he
must be free from blemish. In order to be able to instruct
the people in the Law,[16] he must be sober-minded, and
not greedy, suffer rather than inflict injury upon any one,[17]
as a good shepherd expel bad sheep from the flock,[18] such
as Achan and Gehazi—not mentioning New Testament
persons. Sinners should be separated, like Miriam, from
the Synagogue for longer or shorter periods (*Apo syna-
gogos*). The entire disciplinary system of excommuni-
cation is Essene.[19]

Compassion with the penitent sinner is especially
demanded and the example of Manasseh given at great
length from an Apocalyptic writing; whereas the futility
of hypocritical penitence is illustrated,[20] as in King Amon.

Without any reference to Jesus, only Noah, Lot, and Rahab are singled out as objects of divine pity,[21] and Ezekiel [22] offers the type of the good shepherd. Very skilful in the following chapter is the transmutation of the original "Congregation of Israel" which escaped the ten plagues and received the Ten Commandments, having Yod as its first letter and named after God whose first letter also is Yod (Yahweh), into the Christian Church named after Jesus; betraying at the same time the Jewish original. Significant and at the same time offering the proof of its Jewish provenience, is what is said in Ch. XLVII, that inasmuch as the Lord's Day, the Sabbath, should be a day of peace and not of contention, the judicial court should have its session on the *second* day of the week—the *fifth* being omitted—so that in the interval the controversies might be readjusted.

The repeated statement that the widows and orphans are types of the altar of burnt-offering and the virgin-widows of the altar of incense,[23] seems to reflect a favorite idea of the early Judeo-Christian Church, and there arose most likely also the peculiar institution of the order of pious widows spending their lives in prayer, like Judith, and in charity work, they being as a rule too old to remarry. At least, we find no parallel of that institution in the Synagogue, though possibly Anna, the Essene saint,[24] was a pattern of it.

This is not the place to dwell on the entire system of Jewish charity and its influence upon, if not its full adoption by, the Church.[25] The Apostolic Constitutions offer in Books II to V sufficient evidence of the Jewish origin of the principal Church work in the field of charity, as has already been stated. But it is also characteristic of the Jewish spirit to find in Book IV a distinct place assigned to the treatment of the orphan, and the two opening paragraphs deserve to be quoted in full: "When any [Jewish child]—the text has it 'Christian'—becomes an orphan, whether it be a young man or a maid, it is proper that one of the brethren who is without child should take the young man (or maid?) and adopt him (or her?) in the place of a son (or daughter?), and that he that hath a son of that age who is marriageable should marry that maid to him, for they that do so perform a great meritorious work (*Mizwah*) in becoming fathers to the orphan and shall receive the reward of this benevolence from the Lord God.   But if anyone that walks in the way of man-pleasing is rich and is ashamed of adopting an orphan, the Father of the fatherless and the Judge of widows will make provision for the orphan, but he himself shall have an heir who will spend what he has spared, and it shall happen to him according to what is said: [26] 'What things the holy people have not eaten the Assyrians will eat,' as also Isa. 1:7, which says: 'Your land strangers devour it in your presence.' "   "Be therefore solicitous, ye Overseers, about their sustenance that they be not in want of anything; exhibiting to the orphans the care of parents, to the widows the care of husbands; to those of suitable age the state of marriage; to the mechanics work; to the unable sympathy; to the strangers a home; to the hungry food;. to the thirsty drink; to the naked clothing; to the sick visitation; to the imprisoned rescue."

It must be noticed that in the enumeration of these different modes of charity, which of course have their analogies in the Rabbinical writings, no reference is made to those spoken of in the twenty-fifth chapter of Matthew by the Son of Man as Judge of the nations.

Above all, there is shown great solicitude for those who are orphans: "As to the maiden till she arrives at the age of marriage, when you will give her in marriage to a brother; and assist the young man that he may learn a trade to maintain himself by its practice . . . and not need to take the place of the orphan, the stranger, and the widow." Here may be mentioned the exquisite passage in the Midrash [27] to Exodus 33:22, which tells that when God revealed His glory to Moses, He showed him the treasures preserved for the benefactors among men and particularly those to be bestowed upon those who raise the orphan. Strictly Jewish is also the warning [28] not to receive charitable gifts from the various classes of sinners, as being like bringing abominable things to the altar of God. [29]

The frequent admonition to observe the laws of God and to esteem them more honorable than the necessities of life, [30] together with the warning against visiting the theaters, the sports and the assemblies of the heathen (Hellenes), points to a Jewish origin; and no less so the special statement that for the sake of redeeming a captive and saving life such visitation is permitted. Unsavory remarks concerning the Jews interspersed here betray the late Christian interpolator.—Among the many sentences that have found a place in Paul's Epistles, while taken from the Jewish Didascalia, must be mentioned Ephes. 4:26: "Be ye angry and sin not; let not the sun go down upon your wrath." [31]

Concerning the essential features of the Church as a house of prayer and instruction, it is important to know that it was shaped by the early Christians after the pattern of the Synagogue, while the Christian elements were gradually added to it. Accordingly, "the Reading from the Law" and "the Instruction out of the Scriptures" followed by Psalm-singing, [32] or as the more explicit description of the divine service at the Church has it, [33]

the Reader standing in the center (on the *Bema*) reads
two lessons, one from the Book of Moses, the other from
the Prophets, and is followed by the singing of Psalms,
after which come two corresponding readings from the
New Testament, the Epistles and the Gospels,—all this
became the regular order of the Church service.   But long
ago attention was called by Franz Mone,[34] to the occurrence of prayer formulas addressing God as "the God
of our fathers Abraham, Isaac, and Jacob," [35] showing the
Judeo-Christian origin of these prayers.   Close analysis,
however, of Books VII and VIII, which, while added
later to the Didascalia, are compilations of much more
ancient material, shows how out of the original Jewish
prayers the Church liturgy gradually emanated.   As
shown in the art. "Didascalia" in *J. E.*, and more exten-
sively in "The Origin and Compilation of the Eighteen
Benedictions, etc.,[36] chs. 33-37, contain the Seven Benedictions of the ancient Jewish Ritual turned into a new
shape by Greek-speaking, probably Essene, Jews, but
Christianized by a few verbal changes or additions. And
there are other prayers in Book VII that have undergone
the same transformation, as is shown in Ch. XXVI, for
instance, where God is addressed as "the God of our
holy and blameless fathers, Abraham, Isaac, and Jacob,"
and given thanks for "having planted the—a—Law in
our souls."   But when we come to Book VIII, which
contains the so-called Clementine Liturgy, we can easily
discern its adaptation of large portions of those Christianized Jewish prayers in Book VII, with elimination of
their Jewish character, excepting perhaps such passages
as "the God of Abraham, Isaac, and Jacob" in Ch. XL
and "the pious that are sent into the bosom of Abraham,
Isaac, and Jacob" in Ch. XLI.   Likewise, many formulas
and phrases in the various Church liturgies, which have

one common origin, dating back to the beginning of the second century, can be traced back to Jewish sources. Moreover, as the Didache, called the Teachings of the Twelve Apostles, has been recognized as the Christianized Jewish Manual of Proselytes, so may some prayers in the Church Liturgy have been derived from the Jewish liturgy, though no longer known to have been Jewish; thus, for instance, prayers renouncing paganism as Satanic and leaning to monotheism, or the prayers for the Jewish proselytes after their baptism (Proselytes' Bath).[37]

At a later stage when Christianity claimed to represent true Israel, the Temple with its sacrifices and priesthood became the type of the Church, not the Synagogue which had neither the sacrificial cult nor the priesthood. The idea that in Christ the Law found its fulfilment in a higher sense at once made the Communion service, called *Amphora*, "sacrificial offering," the higher substitute of the Temple sacrifices, inasmuch as the symbolic offering of the blood of Christ had been declared by him at the Last Supper to be the sacrificial cult of the New Covenant. Even the Veil of the Temple was given a place in the Church service.

At the same time the Apostolic or Judeo-Christian Church sometime observed the Jewish Sabbath alongside of the Sunday, the day of the Resurrection, which the Ebionites called the Lord's Day, or the Day of the Lord, in distinction to the other,[38] while we learn from Jacob of Edessa that the Armenians, having at first been Judeo-Christians, observed, besides the Biblical law regarding the *unleavened* bread for the Passover, the laws of Clean and Unclean with regard to their Church, and likewise the Dietary Laws and Circumcision.[39]

As extensive Christian passages of various periods with

an occasional expression of Jew-hatred predominate in parts of the whole work, it was quite easy at a superficial glance to regard the Apostolic Constitution as an altogether Christian product of the third century, as is done by most modern writers. Quite different, however, is the impression that Books VII and VIII make on the reader. Aside from the Didache, which has more Jewish elements than the other version, as stated above, the prayers contained in these books for the most part have a distinct Jewish character and thus evidence their Jewish origin, as is especially shown by such words as "the God of our fathers, Abraham, Isaac, and Jacob." Here we cannot escape the conclusion, which is confirmed by a study of the entire ancient Church liturgy, that the early Church took over the Jewish liturgy as far as it was accessible in its Greek—if not also in the Syrian—form and adapted it to its needs by introducing Christ for the Logos—or Memra—as mediator between God and the world, and similar changes.⁴⁰ This could only have been the work of Judeo-Christians in the second century, when Paulinian Christianity had no share as yet in framing the constitution of the Church. It is not too much to say, therefore, that the transition from the Synagogue to the Church was affected by the Judeo-Christians, many of whom were probably Essenes.

CHAPTER VIII

Paul, the Apostle to the Heathen, and the Christian Church

While Judeo-Christianity, centered in the Church of Jerusalem under the direction of the Apostles and of James, the brother of Jesus, adhered in principle to the Mosaic Law, making concessions to the heathen world by admitting such proselytes as would observe the Noahidic laws and above all become worshipers of the One God, there arose Hellenists who, dissatisfied with the distinction between semi-proselytes and full Jews, made the belief in Jesus the watchword for the formation of a universal Church. It was Stephen, primarily, who came forth with the declaration that the return of the risen Jesus from heaven would mean the abolition of the Temple with its sacrifices and of the entire Mosaic Law; and Stephen's martyrdom and the persecution of his followers gave rise to the new movement in Antioch whither the latter had fled, starting the Church among the heathen there under the name of Christians—a name probably given them by such as took *Christus* (or Chrestos) to be a deity.[1] How far those Hellenists went in their effort to win Jews in other places or districts is not stated; in all likelihood they were unsuccessful. The movement required more powerful leaders, and they came in the persons of Barnabas and Paul, who joined those in Antioch. But the real founder of the Christian Church was Paul, who stepped forth with a system of his own.

The twelve Apostles, as the disciples of Jesus, retained

more or less the Jewish spirit of their master, as voiced in the Synoptic Gospels. Paul, however, first saw Jesus in a vision at Damascus after he himself had persecuted Jesus' followers, and in that vision Jesus appeared to him as a supernatural being, totally different from the human figure the Apostles had seen as having risen from the grave, and upon that peculiar experience he construed his system, apparently the result of many years' thinking.

Only those unfamiliar with Rabbinic theology— as are almost all Christian writers—can find traces of the Rabbinical schools in his writings. Least of all, had he really sat at the feet of Gamaliel, the mild Pharisean teacher, as the Acts of the Apostles state, could he have become the fierce fanatical assailant of the followers of Jesus. Here, as we are clearly told, he acted under the direction of the ·Sadducean authorities, and it is rather surprising that he alludes nowhere to the wide difference between the Pharisees and Sadducees, speaking always with the same disdain of the Jewish people in general. Nor must we stress his claim of being "a Hebrew of Hebrews" too much. Even his calling himself a member of the tribe of Benjamin appears to rest solely on his name Saul, as we find nowhere that genealogical lists were kept in those days. As a matter of fact, his antecedents, until he came to Jerusalem after the death of Jesus, were those of a citizen of Tarsus, a commercial city of Cilicia, brought up under Hellenic influences in a strictly Jewish household and imbued with Philonic and similar ideas. The Scripture he knew only from the Septuagint version, and to its interpretation he applied the allegoric method after Philo's example. He was moreover, probably more familiar with the Apocryphal Book of Wisdom and the Apocalyptic writings, such as the Books of Enoch, than with Greek literature in general.

What is generally looked upon as the miracle of his conversion can be accounted for only physiologically by the fact that with his feeble body he was subject to epileptic attacks, a neurotic disease which he calls "a thorn in his flesh" and which the Greeks called "the holy disease," as it frequently put men into a state of ecstasy, making them see visions and hear articulate or inarticulate sounds.[2] Thus, there may be a historical kernel to the story related three times in the Acts that he heard the words of 1 Sam. 24:15: "Saul, Saul, why persecutest thou me?" Psychologically there must have been in the background of his mind the Philonic figure of "the archetypal man," the *Adam Kadmon* of the Cabbala, the image of God, the first-created heavenly man who preceded the earthly man, whom he afterwards identified with Jesus, the son of God. Hence, his claim that he had a direct revelation of Jesus sending him forth as apostle to the heathen; and upon it he built his theology which proved so alien to the Jewish mind, as when he tells that God in His grace delivered His own son to be a ransom for sin-laden humanity, or that the heavenly Jesus humbled himself of his own accord to descend into the realm of flesh to redeem mankind from death caused by the first sin and lift it up to eternal life.

It is difficult to say how far he was influenced by pagan notions, such as found expression in the Hermes literature, as shown by Reizenstein in his *Poimandres*.[3] Certain it is that his Monotheism was not as sublime and absolute as that of the great prophets through whom God said: "I will not give My glory to any other being";[4] it was obscured and infringed upon by the exaltation of Jesus who, rather than God, was declared to be "the head above all"[5] and was called "The Lord." In Titus[6] he is even called "Our great God and Saviour, Jesus

Christ." Only from the Gnostic literature could he have derived the idea of the *pleroma,* the fulness of the God-head dwelling in Christ as the head of all principality and power.

But it is mainly Paul's attitude towards the Law that placed him in sharp contrast to Judaism. In a spirit of what can only be called sophistry, he argued that it is the very Law that begets sin by way of transgression. "I had not known lust, except the Law had said 'Thou shalt not covet,' " he says.[7] Nor has he any faith in the moral power of man, as he says: "I know that in me there is no good thing,"[8] for the flesh is beset by sin and altogether of the evil one, and it can only be overcome by the spirit of Christ, who is "the end of the Law" because he is the beginning of the resurrection.[9] And what is the *leitmotif* of all these sayings of his? That "hardness in part hath befallen Israel," he gives out as a mystery, "until the fulness of the Gentiles may come in."[10] In other words, he imputes his own partiality for the heathen world to God himself, and he quotes the Scriptures to prove that the Jews by their very Law had fallen from grace, whereas the heathen who have faith—not the simple childlike faith in God, but in Christ's atoning power—are saved from the coming wrath of God. It may be questioned whether Paul after his conversion had any sympathy with the Jewish people whose Law he declared to be a curse from which the crucified Christ —himself "a curse" (accursed of God, according to the Law)[11]—was to redeem the believer. We certainly need not be surprised to find him hated and frequently punished as transgressor by those whose holiest feelings he so rudely offended by his preaching and practicing. It is true that his primary motive was to tear down the partition wall between Jew and Gentile and do away with the distinction between proselytes and semi-proselytes and the genuine Jew. For this very reason he pointed to Abraham, whose faith is declared to be his saving power,[12] and who is called the "father of the Gentiles" and not merely of the nation of Israel,[13] rather than to the Law which came so much later.

We certainly cannot help admiring the wonderful mental and spiritual power of the man who had the courage to say that there should be "neither Greek nor Jew, circumcision nor uncircumcision, bondman nor free, but Christ in all," that "all should become a new creature"; the mighty genius who, welding together, consciously or unconsciously, the various elements of pagan and Jewish thought, made the building up of a universal religion his great aim, and in battling and suffering for his views of life, like one of the great prophets of Israel, exhibited a heroic spirit that places him among the greatest of men. Nor can we deny him the credit of having brought the teachings of the monotheistic truth and the ethics of Judaism, however mixed with pagan elements, to the heathen world in a form which appealed most forcibly to an age eager for a God in human shape and for some means of atonement in the midst of a general consciousness of sin and moral corruption. Different from Simon Magus, his contemporary, with whom he was at times identified by his opponents and in whose system sensuousness, profanity and vulgar witchcraft predominated, Paul with his austerity and asceticism made Jewish earnestness his aim, while seeking to establish the Kingdom of God to whom also his Christ subordinated himself, so that when his task of redemption was completed God might be all in all.[14] He was indeed an instrument in the hands of Divine Providence to win the heathen nations for Israel's God of righteousness. At the same time he acknowledged himself that his scheme of salvation was "a stumbling block to the Jews and folly to the Greeks." [15] What he calls the mystery of the Cross, is really a surrender of reason. It is not righteousness, nor personal merit and the greater effort to overcome sin, but some arbitrary act of divine grace which justifies man and secures his salvation. Men are no longer divided into Jews and Gentiles, but what is a great deal worse in its ultimate effect, into believers and unbelievers, that is, into such as accept the dogma of no salvation except by the belief in the atoning power of Christ's blood and such as would not accept it.

At all events, Paul by his bold adverse attitude toward the Law succeeded in attracting the heathen communities in Asia and Macedonia and Greece and turned them from idolaters into worshipers of God, implanting into their hearts a higher ethical conception of life, as indicated by the list of vices they would have to avoid and of the virtues to be pursued, which the manual for Jewish proselytes also contained.

As there is a great difference between the Epistles of Paul, most of which are now, contrary to the Dutch school of critics, accepted as genuine, and the Acts, written about a century later, as to the missionary work of Paul in the various lands and cities, it is difficult to say whether Paul at first carried out the plan agreed upon by him and the apostles at the covenant of Jerusalem, according to which as stated in the Acts [16] the heathen had to bind themselves to observe the Noahidic laws in order to be admitted as proselytes, or whether Paul ignored those conditions from the very start. The probability is that wherever there was a synagogue, where Jews and semi-proselytes, the so-called God-worshipers, met together, Paul found the soil prepared for his missionary work, winning an increasing number of heathen converts by his powerful preaching. After all, it was not a cultured class, but the lower element of the cities, the slaves and, principally, the women, that he won over to his views, and these were scarcely able to follow his theological arguments, based mainly on his construction of scriptural words. In fact, the Paulinian theology was soon given up by the Church, especially when the rejection of the whole principle of Law led to libertinism, so as to give rise to the so-called Nicolaitans, or disciples of Balaam; and in the reaction that followed, the Catholic Church reverted to the adoption of those laws which are presented as the Apostolic Constitutions.[17] On the other hand, the Acts contain a great deal of romance rather than historic facts in the career of Paul, and a sample of this is given in the fictitious story of Paul's address to the men of Athens on the Areopagus.[18] It was to the center of the heathen world, the Roman metropolis, that Paul's career gravitated, and he seems purposely to have avoided the great Alexandrian metropolis, the center of Hellenism. To the Christian community of Rome, which counted also a large number of Jews and Jewish proselytes, he sent toward the close of his career those Epistles which give the best insight into his mode of preaching and which more than any other reflect his hatred of Judaism and the Jew, probably the result of his long and bitter conflict with his former brethren. Then he died a martyr for his faith, the victim of the Roman persecution of Christianity.

It is quite natural that a great personality such as Paul should have found disciples who not only spoke and wrote in his spirit, but also imitated him in sending out Epistles in his name. We have, therefore, a number of Epistles which circulated under Paul's name, but emanated from their hands, also such as were interpolated by them; but the critics do not agree as to which are genuine and which not. So it is more than doubtful whether the statement of his having received from Jesus—which can only mean by some kind of revelation—the story of his having instituted in the night of his betrayal the Lord's Supper, with the declaration that the bread and the wine offered were to symbolize the New Covenant, as stated likewise with some variations in the Synoptic Gospels,[19] is genuine. Neither do the words "New" and "Old Testament" in 2 Cor. 3:6, 14, which rest upon Jer. 30:31,[20] make the impression of being genuine, though the application of the reading from the Law of Moses to Ex. 24:7-8, has a ring of genuineness.

But especially noticeable is the change of attitude toward the Law in some of the Epistles, the so-called pastoral Epistles, such as 1 and 2 Timothy and Titus, which are no longer as hostile to the Law as Paul and rather oppose his asceticism. And whereas Marcion and other followers of Paul in their antagonism to the Law went so far as systematically to condemn, defame and profane not only the Old Testament but also the God of Israel, identifying Him in their fanaticism with the very sower of Evil, the Church in her reaction, following the lead of some Judeo-Christian writers, made certain essential institutions of Moses, such as the feast of Tabernacles with its sacrificial and priestly ritual, types of true worship. The beginning of such typology in the New Testament was made by the author of the Epistle to the Hebrews, who set up Jesus as the world's High priest, "a priest forever after the manner of Melchizedek."[21] So in the course of time the Church virtually abandoned Paul's

Antinomianism, and only Protestantism, in stressing the *faith* in Christ as the essence of Christianity, went back to Paulinianism.[22]

The Gospel of John, which has nothing to do with John, the author of the seven letters to the seven Churches of Asia, nor with the following Apocalypse or Revelation also ascribed to John the divine of the isle of Patmos, is a product of the second century, emanating from the Hellenistic or Philonic school in which the idea of the Logos, the Creative Word of God, or Memra, played a prominent rôle. It is apparently based upon an older gospel essentially different from the Synoptic Gospels in the entire construction of the history of Jesus and showing greater familiarity with Jewish customs, Jewish personalities, and Palestinian geography. Moreover, the formula: "That the saying may be fulfilled," in the latter chapters, shows its close connection with the Gospel of Matthew. Possibly the original gospel bore the name of John the son of Zebedaeus the apostle, "the disciple whom Jesus loved" and "who was leaning on his bosom," and a late compiler elaborated it into its present form in which lengthy speeches, disputes and prayers are ascribed to Jesus, which bear the stamp of fiction and on closer scrutiny prove to be allegorical interpretations of words or expressions he had or may have used. The whole Gospel is rather an apothesis of Jesus, intended to lift him from the very beginning of life above all human kinship, not as Paul did who fashioned him after the vision he had of the re-risen Christ as the archetypal man of Philo, calling him the image of God, but assigning to him the highest possible place in the cosmic realm by declaring him to be the incarnation of the creative word of God, the Logos or Memra, and thus identifying him with God Himself as the Light and the Life of the

World, from whom everything that exists emanated.
Accordingly, Jesus no longer speaks as a man to man,
but as the son of God in whom the Father lives and
through whom He speaks. As a matter of course, there
is no longer any place for the virginal birth of Jesus,
nor for words of despair and resignation at his crucifixion. He is only anxious to be "glorified" by being
"lifted up" [23] and thereby "glorifying his Father." John
hails him as "the lamb of God, which taketh away the sin
of the world," [24] a view which differs essentially from the
paschal lamb of the other gospels. And while he frequently speaks of himself as the Son of Man in the
Apocalyptic spirit, he declares himself to be "the living
Water" and "the living Food," with allusion to his flesh
or body and his blood taken at the Last Supper; or the
Bread of Life that came from heaven, the Manna; the
heavenly "Vine," his believers being the branches; "the
Good Shepherd," and the Door leading to the Sheep.
Furthermore, he says: "I am the Resurrection and the
Life," or "the Way and the Truth"—names that never
occur elsewhere in the Gospels.

While altogether ignoring the Mosaic Law, he
declares: "A new Commandment I give to you, that ye
love one another," [25] a declaration which is constantly
repeated by Christian believers to this very day, as if the
Golden Rule emphasized by Jesus himself had not first
been given in the Mosaic Law. [26] But the most prominent
feature of this Gospel of John is the intense hatred of
the kinsmen of Jesus, as if from the very outset they
had been his implacable enemies always plotting against
his life. [27] Yea more, the Jews are the sons, not of
Abraham, but of the Devil, the murderer from the beginning. [28] Thus, the writer discountenances the fact that
the twelve Apostles as well as Jesus were Jews, not to

mention James the Elder, the brother of Jesus, who was the saintly leader of the Judeo-Christian Church in Jerusalem. This Gospel is indeed a psychological problem, and most amazing is the fact that leading Christian theologians to this very day cherish it. We can only account for this writer's extreme hatred of the Jewish people by assuming that it was dictated by his animosity against the Judeo-Christian Church, which was still strong enough to oppose Paulinianism, while firmly adhering to pure Jewish monotheism and the Mosaic Law. In fact, many of the arguments put into the mouth of Jesus against the latter seem to confirm this assumption. The contrast between the Law and the principle of love which forms the central idea of Paul's teaching is here still more stressed, so that John for the Church became the typical preacher of Love.

CHAPTER IX

THE GNOSTIC SECTS

The opening pages of the Bible, the first ten chapters of Genesis, says Ranke, the great historian, gave the world—of course, through the Greek translation—the idea of the common history of early mankind and thus actually reunited it in one. This idea forms the background of the writings of Paul and the fourth Gospel, despite their antagonistic attitude to the book of the Law, and it also captivated those Gnostic sects that were hostile to the Old Testament and to the God of Israel.

Certain it is that the Gnostic sects, called in the Talmud *Minim,* "Sectaries," are older than the Christian Church whose members also are named Minim there. As the name Gnosis—knowledge (of God)—indicates, they were not concerned with mere faith (*Pistis*), but instead endeavored to penetrate into the mysteries of God and Creation, and this was done, as we learn from the Talmud,[1] Philo, and the Christian writings, not so much by speculative reason as by ecstatic visions which made the soul feel as if it entered the innermost realm of heaven called "Paradise." [2] It was a practical study of cosmogony and theosophy, called *Maaseh Bereshit* and *Maaseh Merkaba,* such as was taught exclusively in strict esoteric circles by R. Johanan b. Zakkai and his pupils and pupils' pupils of the first and second centuries. There was the danger in those pursuits that the hypostatic forces, or secondary elements, might predominate and so put the absolute God on high, the Prime Mover above all the visible world, into the background and lead to the assumption of a secondary deity, a *demiurgos,* a creator of inferior rank.

Such dualism or pluralism, indeed, was the chief feature of the multiform Gnosticism, and, as it affected the leading spirits of Judaism, it became a disturbing factor and a real menace to the Christian Church in the second century. The Talmud [3] tells of four eminent teachers of the second century, Ben Zoma, Ben Azzai, Elisha ben Abuyah, called *Aher,* "the other" or "changed one," on account of his apostasy, and Akiba, all of whom "entered Paradise," the first two of whom were bewildered by what they saw; the third beheld *Metatron,* the divine Chariot-holder, in God's places, and became a believer in two divine beings and apostatized, no longer observing the Law of which he had been a prominent teacher; the fourth, Akiba, passed the crisis unscathed in body and mind and became, by his firm stand for the Law and the tradition, the great pillar of Talmudic Judaism. It appears that Alexandrian Judaism after Philo, who had persistently warned against those dangers of Gnosticism, succumbed to them and became the pitfall of the Christian Church. Under its influence many Gnostic leaders went far beyond Paul in their antagonism to the Law, declaring the God of the Old Testament to be accursed and, like the devil, the very personification of evil. The remarkable fact, however, is that these very Gnostics took ideas and names from the Old Testament, especially from the opening pages of Genesis, and made them integral parts of their system.

Without going into detail, let us glance at some of these Gnostic sects that go back to pre-Christian times. For, this much is certain, Gnosticism had its origin in the dis-

solution of the ancient pagan religions. The old gods
no longer satisfied the people and they craved for some
mystic power, for a redemption that would free them
from the base forces of evil and make them one with the
highest potency of life, such as Wisdom, or some similar
abstraction. Now, as far as we know, we meet the first
Gnostics in the Mandeans of the upper part of Syria,
who bore the Aramaic name for Gnostics, namely, followers of *Manda d'Haya*, "the Knowledge of Life."
Their system was a combination of Babylonian and
Persian systems, a dualism of light and darkness, or of
life and death, in which, however the Persian predominated, inasmuch as the seven Babylonian star deities
were turned into evil powers and the mother-goddess
Ishtar into a demon *Namrus*, the consuming noon-heat,
who, in opposition to the Jewish religion, was given the
name of *Ruha Di K'udsha*, "the Holy Ghost." In order to
conquer these evil powers Manda d'Haya has to descend
into hell to fight with Leviathan or Ur, the ruler, and
redeem the upper world, while using as weapons the staff
of living water and the crown of living fire which the
Mandeans still use in their ritual. Alongside of Manda
d'Haya appears the demiurgos *Ptahil*, apparently identical with the Egyptian creator *Ptah*. He creates *Adam*,
the first man, in the shape of a bodily column, *Golem*,
while Manda d'Haya breathes into him the soul emanating from above.[4]

It is difficult to say whether the Mandean Gnosticism
influenced the Hellenic, not to speak of the Hermetic lore,
which is, as the name shows, mostly Egyptian in origin.
Here we find first of all the *Ophites* and *Naasenes*, who
took their name from the Serpent—*Nahash, Ophia*—of
Paradise, the archfiend, transformed in opposition to the
God of the Scripture into the highest deity, the mother

of life, the incarnation of the divine Wisdom, bringing
to man the knowledge of good and evil. These Ophites
had their whole system construed upon tablets, *Gilionin.*[5]
It consisted in a celestial world of light and one of air,
forming the habitation of the seven archonts or world
rulers, four of whom bear the name of Yao, Sabaoth,
Adonai, and Eloha, and containing also the Paradise with
its tree of knowledge and of life; while the earthly world,
with its ten circles, was surrounded by the Biblical
Leviathan, as the all-encompassing soul. The first of
the seven world rulers was *Yulda Bahath,* "the son of
the Chaos," shaped as a lion and probably identical originally with the Babylonian Marduk and later with
Michael. Another of the archonts had the shape of an
eagle, identified with Gabriel; another that of the ox,
called Suriel; and a fourth that of a dragon, identified
with Raphael. Thus we see Biblical and post-Biblical
elements used in the construction of the Ophitic system,
and Friedländer has convincingly shown that both R. Tar-
phon and R. Ishmael, who lived when the Temple was
still in existence, and could hardly have had any knowledge of the Gospels (Evangelia), referred to those
Ophitic tables on which the names of God (Azkarot)
were written. Accordingly they must have been used in
Jewish circles at the time.

Similar to the Ophites, or Naasenes, there were the
Cainites, a Gnostic sect named after Cain to express
opposition to the Jewish religion and known already to
Philo. Similarly, the *Sethites,* called after Seth, were a
Gnostic sect opposed to Judaism. In fact, Gnostic sects
antagonistic to the God of Israel and His Law sprang
up like mushrooms during the first, second and third centuries, all under different leaders and with different systems; and, because of this antagonism to the Old Testa-

ment, most of them appealed to the Paulinian Churches, which at first joined with them.

These Christian Gnostics accepted the idea of the Demiurgos, the Creator, whom they identified with the God of the Jews who had proceeded from the Highest God, the unknowable source of all perfection, at an infinite distance, whereas it was Christ through whom the highest God was revealed, while he produced out of himself the world of light or the world of the blessed spirits with the help of whom men could free themselves from the fetters of the Demiurgos and of matter, the evil powers that ruled over heathenism. This freedom from the fetters of the Demiurgos led the ones to the most rigid abstinence and a contemplative life, the others, on the contrary, to libertinism, seeing they regarded the moral laws as the work of the Demiurgos. The latter class was known to the Rabbis of the Talmud and led to their designating the Christians also by the name of *Minim* or Gnostics. As these Gnostic Christians in their close association with the members of the Synagogue at a later time became a peril to the latter, all the more so as in their habits they differed but slightly from them, R. Gamaliel II instituted the *Birkat Ha-Minim,* the insertion of the prayer of execration of these Christians in the Eighteen Benedictions.⁶

Far more difficult was the stand to be taken by the Church, both the Judeo-Christian and the Paulinian, toward Gnosticism, since it undermined the very foundation of the belief in the Hebrew Scripture upon which Jesus and the Twelve Apostles stood; and it became the foremost task of the early Church fathers to denounce on behalf of the Church the innumerable heresies which had arisen under the collective name of Gnosticism. An extensive literature appeared. Only fragmentary parts of it, however, have been preserved, and they fail to give us a true insight into the Gnosticism they combated. But this very stand in defense of Christianity against its accusers led to a wholesome reaction, from which the Catholic Church, with a *regula fidei*, a fixed rule of faith, emerged, acknowledging the Old Testament as the basis of the New and beholding in it an earlier divine Revelation.

NOTES

BOOK I

CHAPTER I

[1] Herzfeld, *Geschichte des Volkes Jisrael von der Zerstörung des ersten Tempels bis zur Einsetzung des Makkabäers Schimon zum hohen Priester und Fürsten,* Braunschweig, 1847, V. I, 1, 381ff.; H. Graetz, *Geschichte der Juden von den ältesten Zeiten bis auf die Gegenwart,* Leipzig, II, 2, 155; N. Krochmal, *Moreh Nebuke Ha-Zeman,* Warsaw, 1894; Berlin, 1924, *passim;* Charles Taylor, *Sayings of the Jewish Fathers,* 2d ed., Cambridge, 1877, 110; Emil Schürer, *Geschichte des Jüdsichen Volkes im Zeitalter Jesus Christi,* 3d ed., Leipzig, 1898, II, 3, 355; B a c h e r , art. "Synagogue, the Great," in *J. E.,* XI, 640.

[2] See Josephus, *Contra Apionem,* II, 17; Acts 4:20; Targum J. to Ex. 18:20; to Judg. 5:2; to 2 Chron. 14:29; to Isa. 1:13, and to Amos 5:12.

[3] Immanuel Loew, *Gesammelte Schriften,* Szegedin, 1898, IV, 8, where Shab. 32 is referred to; Samuel Krauss, *Synagogale Altertümer, Berlin-Wien,* 1922.

CHAPTER II

[1] We must bear in mind that worship of the Deity without sacrifice and a consecrated priesthood was then unknown, and it is quite significant that the last of the prophets looking about him could say: "For from the rising of the sun even unto the going down of the same My name is great among the nations; and in every place offerings are presented unto My name; for My name is great among the nations, saith the Lord of hosts" (Mal. 1:11).

[2] Num. 28:4.

[3] I Meg. Taanith, 1, 1.

[4] Lev. c. 16.

[5] Lev. 16:2.

[6] Yoma 53b.

[7] Sifra, Aharè Mot, §3; Tos. Sotah 13, 5-6, 8; Yoma 19b.

[8] Num. 6:22; see Sifrè, Num., §39.

[9] Lev. 23:15f.

[10] Ex. 21:24.

[11] Josephus, *Antiquities,* XX, 9, 1: ". . . the sect of the Sadducees, who are very rigid in judging offenders above all the rest of the Jews."

[12] Num. ch. 19.

[13] Mishnah Parah 3, 7; Tos. Parah 3, 1-8.

[14] Ezek. 44:22; Kiddushin 4, 5; San. 4, 2; Josephus, *Ant.,* 13, 10, 6; Geiger, *Urschrift,* 115; Geiger, *Ges. Schriften* V, 127f.; 132f.; Schürer, *Geschichte,* II, 3, 412.

[15] Isa. 65:5; Assumption of Moses 7, 10 (in Charles' *Apocrypha,* 11, 420).

[16] Ed. Schechter, p. 26.

Chapter III

[1] Yoma 69b.
[2] Amos 7:17; Ezek. 4:13; 1 Sam. 26:19.
[3] Deut. 29:27.
[4] 20:40.
[5] Ex. 9:29, 33.
[6] 6:11.
[7] 1 Kings 8:23-53.
[8] 46-50.

[9] Herzfeld, *Geschichte*, I, 24; Graetz, *Geschichte*, II, 2, 15ff.; Wellhausen, *Isr. u. Jüd. Geschichte*, IV, 149 seq.; Schürer, *Geschichte*, II, 3, 428ff.
[10] Ps. 137.
[11] Isa. 40:1ff.
[12] 44:4; 48:1.

Chapter IV

[1] Gen. 25:21.
[2] Gen. 20, 7, 17; Nu. 11:2; 21:7; Deut. 9, 20, 26; 1 Sam. 7:5; 12:19; Isa. 37:4; Jer. 7:16; 11:14; 37:3; Job 42.10; cf. also Ps. 72:15.
[3] L. c. 147.
[4] *Kritischer Commentar zu den Psalmen, nebst Text und Uebersetzung*, Breslau, 1882, pp. 16-37.
[5] 1 Chron. 25:7; Ezra 8:16; Neh. 8:3, 9.
[6] *The Old Testament and the*

New Scholarship, London, 1901, p. 172.
[7] 42:9; 43:4.
[8] *L. c.*, pp. 20ff.
[9] עני und ענו in den Psalmen, Leipzig, 1891.
[10] For the meaning of *Hesed* cf. Hosea 6, 4, 6; and Ish-Hasideka, Deut. 33:8.
[11] Neh. 9:5; 8:4-9.
[12] Ezra 3:10; Neh. 11:17.

Chapter V

[1] Is. 66:2.
2 Cf. Salomo Jehudah Rapoport, *Erekh Millin*, Prague, 1852, I, 171; Herzfeld, *Geschichte*, III, 215ff.; *J. Q. R.*, VI, 1ff.; Müller, *Tractat Soferim*, pp. 181ff.; Elbogen, *jüd. Gottesdienst*, pp. 174f.
[3] Neh. 8:1, 13, 9:3.
[4] Cf. 17:18 and Jer. 2:8; 18:18.
[5] Tos. San. 4, 7 (ed. Zuckerman-

del, p. 421); San. 21b-22a; Zeb. 62a; Yer. Meg. 1, 71b.
[6] Ezra 7:12.
[7] Ezra 7:6-12; Neh. 8:3f.
[8] Geiger, *Urschrift*, *pp.* 308ff., 384ff.
[9] See J. Lauterbach, *Midrash and Mishnah*, New York, 1916.
[10] 1 Macc. 2:42; 3; 13:44-48; 7:12; 2 Macc. c. 14.

Chapter VI

[1] 1 Chron. 29:10ff.
[2] 2 Chron. 20:6ff.
[3] Ezr. 9:6ff.; Neh. 1:5ff.; 9:6-37.
[4] 2:19ff.; 9:4ff.
[5] Ps. 148:14; 149:1.
[6] Cf. Frankel, *Monatsch.*, 1851, pp. 405f.

[7] Taan, 3, 8; in Tos. Taan. 3, 1; he is simply spoken of as a *Hasid*.
[8] *Ant.*, XIV, 2.
[9] *Taan*. 23ab, where a number of others are also mentioned.
[10] See Midr. Tehillim to this verse.

CHAPTER VI—(continued)

[11] Neh. 8:6.
[12] Ab. Zar. 17b-18a and Mid.
Teh. to Ps. 36:11.
[13] Sanh. 10, 1; Tos. Sanh. 12, 9.
[14] Isa. 52:6.
[15] Ps. 91:14-15; see Midr. Teh.
ibid. and Pes. R. 22 at the close.
[16] Sotah 9, 15; Tos. Sotah 15, 5;
Sotah 49b.
[17] Ber. 33a; 34b; Jer. Ber. 5, 9d.

[18] Ber. 5, 5.
[19] Taan. 24b.
[20] Taan. l. c.; Tos. Ber. 3, 20;
Ber. 17b; Yoma 53b.
[21] Suk. 5, 4; Tos. Suk. 4, 2;
Suk. 51-53a; Jer. Suk. 5, 55a.
[22] Ber. 5, 1.
[23] Ber. 5, 1; Tos. Ber. 3, 20.
[24] Taan. 8a.
[25] Jer. Ber. 9, 9b.

CHAPTER VII

[1] About them see Wellhausen,
Die Pharisäer und die Sadducäer,
1874; Hanover, 1924; pp. 131-164;
Ryle and James, *Psalms of the
Pharisees,* Cambridge, 1891; Beer,
in Kautzsch's *Apokryphen und
Pseudepigraphen,* Tübingen, 1900,
II, 127.

[2] Pss. of Solomon, 8:28; 12:8;
13:9; 14:2, 7.
[3] Ib. 3, 8-10.
[4] 6:6.
[5] 5:1.
[6] 8:40.
[7] 10:7-8.
[8] 17:42.
[9] 5:2, 13; 10:7; 15:2; 18:3.

CHAPTER VIII

[1] Eccl. 7:16.
[2] 9:2.
[3] Pss. of Sol. 3:8-9.
[4] Tos. Ned. 1, 1; Ned. 10a; Ker.
6, 3; Tos. Ker. 4, 4.
[5] Num. 15:38; Menah. 40b.
[6] Nid. 38a.
[7] Shab. 121b.
[8] Shab. 150b; Pes. R. 23; Lev.
R. 34, 16.
[9] Tos. Shab. 13, 9; Jer. Shab.
15d.
[10] Darkè ha-Mishnah, 40f.; see
also Brüll, *Mebo ha-Mishnah,* 39f.
[11] *Dor Dor we-Dorshav,* I, 109f.
[12] Lev. 15:33.
[13] Sifra, Mezorah, at the close;
Shab. 64b; Jer. Git. 9, 50d; Baraita
Niddah, ed. Ch. M. Horowitz, 51;
Tos. Shab. 1, 14; Jer. Shab. 1, 3b.
[14] Lev. 19:4.
[15] Sifra, Kedoshim, at the begin-

ning; Shab. 149a; Ab. Zar. 50a;
Pes. 104a; cf. Hippolytus *Refut.
Haeres.,* IX, 13f., as to the Essenes.
[16] Tos. B. K. 2, 6; B. K. 30a.
[17] Tos. Hul. 2, 24; Hullin 44b;
Ab. de-R. Nathan II, ed. Schechter, pp. 8, 12; cf. Didache 3, 1.
[18] B. K. 7, 7; 79b.
[19] Ab. de-R. N. c. 8 (ed. Schechter, p. 38); Pes. R. 3 (ed. Friedmann, 9, 9b); Gen. R. 41, 5.
[20] Ab. de-R. N. *ibidem,* and Jer.
Demai 1, 21d; Shab. 112b; Hul.
5b; 7a.
[21] B. K. 99b; Mek. to Ex. 18, 20
(ed. Friedmann, p. 59b; ed. Weiss,
p. 68); cf. the story of Rab in
B. M. 83a with reference to Prov.
2:20 and B. K. 103b.
[22] Jer. Ter. 8, 46b; cf. Ab.
de-R. N., ed. Schechter, II, 52, 58;
Sifrè, Deut. 48.

CHAPTER IX

[1] Tos. Peah 3, 8.
[2] Tos. Peah 4, 19; B. B. 8b.
[3] 9:23.
[4] 4:24.
[5] Ab. de-R. Nathan ed. Schechter, 21, 22.
[6] Referred to in Peah 8, 7; Tos. Peah 4, 8-19; Tos. Meg. 3, 4; 4, 15; B. B. 8a-9b; Sanh. 17b.
[7] Semahot c. 12; Tos. Meg. 4, 15.
[8] Ed. Schechter, 36.
[9] Tos. Peah 4, 16, Tos. Shebiit 7, 9; cf. Bik. 3, 12.
[10] Sanh. 17b.
[11] See art. "Apostles" in .J. E., II, 19.
[12] Tos. Peah 4, 15; B. B. 8b.

[13] See art. "The Development of Jewish Charity," in my Hebrew Union College and Other Addresses, p. 239.
[14] Tos. Peah 4, 18; B. B. 11a; see Josephus Ant. XX, 2, 1-4.
[15] G. Uhlorn, in Die Christl. Liebesthätigkeit in der Alt. Kirche, Stuttgart 1882, failed to understand it.
[16] Midr. Teh. to Ps. 37.
[17] See my Introduction to the same in Semitic Studies in Memory of Alexander Kohut, Berlin, 1897, p. 270.
[18] Ket. 50a; Jer. Peah 1, 15b.

CHAPTER X

[1] III, 126ff.
[2] Isa. 45:1-3.
[3] Isa. 45:6-7.
[4] Fr. Spiegel, Erânische Alterthumskunde, Leipzig, 1871-3, III, 570, 590.
[5] Isa. 25:8.
[6] Isa. 11:4; cf. the Targum, which names him Angrimqinjus, corrupted into Angrimaljus, whence the name Armillus arose later on.
[7] Hagigah 2, 1; 13b f.; see art. "Merkaba" in J. E. VIII, 498.
[8] Prov. 25:2.
[9] Job 32:2ff.
[10] Cf. Enoch 60, 7; Baruch 29, 4 and Ezra Apocalypse 6, 52; B. B. 74b.
[11] Cant. R. 1, 4; Mid. Zuta Cant. 1, 4. As to these secrets of

God or of the Torah see Zunz, Gottesdienstliche Vorträge, pp. 174ff.
[12] Isa. 24:16.
[13] Suk. 28a; Meg. 3a; B. B. 134a.
[14] Tos. Hag. 2, 1f.; Hag. 14b.
[15] Tos. Hag. 2, 3-4.
[16] Cf. Paul in 2 Cor. 12:4.
[17] Ps. 116:15.
[18] Ch. 4, pp. 27-44.
[19] Ket. 106a.
[20] Jer. Shab. 1, 3c; Jer. Shek. 3, 47c; Ab Zar. 20b; Sota 49, at the close.
[21] Tos. Sotah 12, 5; 13, 2.
[22] Tos. Sota 13, 3-4.
[23] Gen. R. 37, 7; Sedar Olam, c. 1.
[24] Ed. Friedmann, p. 36.
[25] Sanh. 65b; cf. Sifrè, Deut. 173.

CHAPTER XI

[1] Sifrè, Num. 143.
[2] Deut. 10:8; 18:5, 7; Ps. 20:2, 8.
[3] See L. Loew, "Die Aussprache des vierbuchstabigen Gottesna-

mens," in Gesammelte Schriften, Vol. I, p. 187; Heitmueller, Im Namen Jesu, Goettingen, 1903; Dalman, Der Gottesname Adonai.
[4] 6:13; 10:20.

CHAPTER XI—(continued)

[5] Jer. 44:26.

[6] Nokeb Shem, Lev. 24:16; Sifra, Emor *ad loc.* and Sanh. 56a.

[7] Pes. de-R. Kah. 148a.

[8] Sotah 7, 6; Tam. 7, 2; Josephus *Ant.* II, 12, 4. See Sifrè, Num. 43.

[9] Sifrè, Deut. 306.

[10] Tos. Ber. 7, 23; Kid. 71a.

[11] See art. "Adonai" in *J. E.* 201; and, for the following, my art. "The Tetragrammaton and Its Uses," in the *Journal of Jewish Lore and Philosophy,* 1, 19ff.

[12] Sanh. 10, 1; Tos. Sanh. 12, 9; Ned. 7b; Abot de-R. Nathan 36 (ed. Schechter, p. 108).

[13] Kid. 71a.

[14] Jer. Yoma 40d has *Kesherim,* the "blameless ones," for *Z'nuim She-be-kehuna.*

[15] Abot 1, 13.

[16] Ed. Schechter, p. 56.

[17] Meg. 28b; Ned. 62a.

[18] See L. Blau, "Das Altjüdische Zauberwesen," in *Jahresbericht der Landes—Rabbinerschule,* Budapest, 1898, pp. 96ff.; 137ff.; and Zunz, *Die Synagogale Poesie des Mittelalters,* pp. 145f., where most of the things upon which the sacred Name is said to have been engraved are mentioned.

[19] Enoch 69:13-25.

[20] Cf. the Prayer of Manasses and Suk. 53ab; and, in particular, the Geonic Book of Enoch in Jellinek, *Bet ha-Midrash,* II, 116ff.

CHAPTER XII

[1] Deut. 6:4.

[2] *Uber Juden und Judentum,* Berlin 1910, p. 254.

[3] *Die gottesdienstlichen Vorträge,* 2 ed., p. 379.

[4] Ber. 33a.

[5] The casual remark in Ber. 21a that the Shema Yisrael is a Rabbinical statute puzzled Rashi, and it certainly is incorrect; see Tosafot. Cf. דרכה של תורה, Finneless, p. 20.

[6] *Ant.* IV, 8, 13.

[7] *Revue des Etudes Juives,* XXXI 181f.

[8] Isa. 45:7.

[9] Tamid 4-5.

[10] Ber. 9b; 25b-26a.

[11] Tamid 5, 1.

[12] *Jewish War,* II, 8, 5.

[13] *Bikkurè ha-Ittim,* X, 118f.

[14] *De Vita Contemplativa,* ed. Mangey, II, 475, 485.

[15] Fr. Spiegel, *Avesta,* Leipzig, 1852, II, 49:51; III, 7; 20, 2-7, and *Eranisches Alterthum,* III, 691; cf.

Graetz, *Geschichte der Juden,* II, 419.

[16] Yoma 3, 8.

[17] Pes. 4, 8. For the significance of the response to the pronounciation of the sacred Name, compare the story of the Patriarch Jacob (Sifrè, Deut. 31; Pes. 56a, and Targum and Midrash to Gen. 49:2).

[18] *Der jüdische Gottesdienst,* pp. 26, 514f.

[19] See Targ. to 1 Sam. 9:13, Rosh ha-Shanah 29b; Ps. 134:2.

[20] Meg. 4, 4-6.

[21] Suk. 5, 4; cf. Ezek. 8:16.

[22] Ber. 9b; 29b; Jer. Ber. 4, 7b.

[23] Ber. 21a.

[24] *L. c.,* p. 25.

[25] Num. 15:37-41.

[26] Ber. 11b.

[27] Ber. 13a.

[28] For the rest see Elbogen's work.

[29] Ber. 1, 3.

[30] Ber. 13ab.

CHAPTER XIII

[1] Ber. 14b.
[2] Deut. 6:8; 11:18.
[3] See Samuel ben Meir's Commentary to Ex. 13:9.
[4] *Ant.* IV, 8, 13.
[5] 159. In Charles' *Apocrypha*, II, 109.
[6] Matt. 23:5.
[7] Cf. Targum to Cant. 8, 3; Ber. 23b and Men. 33b for the Mezuzah.
[8] Ber. 23a; cf. Shab. 6, 2.
[9] Men. 36b; Mek., Bo, ed. Friedmann, p. 21b; Weiss, 27.
[10] Zeb. 19a.
[11] Men. *l. c.*
[12] Ber. 47b; cf. R. H. 17a.
[13] Men. 35a.
[14] Ber. 6a; Men. 35b.
[15] *L. c.*
[16] Darmesteter, *Avesta*, I, 191,
199; *Spiegel, Eran, Alt.,* III, 690, 700.
[17] Bundahish 30, 30.
[18] Suk. 28a; Taan. 20b.
[19] Jer. Ber. 2, 4c; and cf. Jer. Erub. 10, 26a about Hillel's maternal grandfather, if this be correct.
[20] Ex. 20:26.
[21] 2 Sam. 6:20f.
[22] Num. 15:38f.
[23] Men. 44a.
[24] Men. 38b.
[25] Men. 43b.
[26] Men. 41b.
[27] Men. 44a.
[28] Ber. 60b; Men. 43a.
[29] Ex. 34:6; R. H. 17b.
[30] Ch. Hilkot Zizit of his *Shulhan Aruk.*

CHAPTER XIV

[1] 11:13; Sifrè, Deut. 41.
[2] Ber. 26b; Jer. Ber. 4, 7a.
[3] Jer. *ibidem.*
[4] Pp. 2-3. *The Old Jewish-Aramaic Prayer, the Kaddish,* Leipzig, 1909.
[5] Ber. 26b.
[6] Ed. Buber, p. 127.
[7] C. 31 (ed. Buber, p. 138).
[8] Jer. Ber. 4, 8b.
[9] The beginning of the Prayer with praise and thanksgiving so as to give it the form of Benediction has its prototype in 1 Chron. 29:10 and, according to R. Simlai, it was suggested by the prayer of Moses (Deut. 3:24f.; Ber. 32a; 34a).
[10] *G. V.* II, 380.
[11] Tos. Ber. 3, 15; Tos. R. H. 4, 11.
[12] Ber. 33a.
[13] Meg. 17b.
[14] See *Schürer, G. J. V.* II, 3, 354f.
[15] See my art. "The Origin and Composition of the Eighteen Benedictions, with a Translation of the Corresponding Essene Prayers in the Apostolic Constitutions," in the *Hebrew Union College Annual,* I, 1924, pp. 410-425.
[16] Yoma 7, 1; Tos. Yoma 3, 18.
[17] *G. V. I.* II, 190f.
[18] *J. G.* p. 235.
[19] Taan. 2, 2-4.
[20] Tos. Ber. 3, 25; Jer. Ber. 5a.
[21] Ber. 28b.
[22] Ber. 4, 8a; Num. R. 18, 21.
[23] *R. É. J.* XIV, pp. 26-32.
[24] *Die Worte Jesu,* pp. 299f.
[25] *L. c.,* 42.
[26] After Ex. 3:15; Deut. 10:17.
[27] Ben Sira 51, 12.
[28] Ps. 89:6, 8; Job. 5:1.
[29] See Jer. Ber. 5, 9c; and Mas. Soferim 16, 12.
[30] Annotations to Singer's Prayer Book, LXI.

CHAPTER XIV—(continued)

[81] *G. V.* p. 381.

[82] Jer. Ber. 2, 4d, and Sifrè, *ibidem.*

[83] Shab. 12b.

[84] Jer. Yoma 5, 42c.

[85] Jubilees 12:17.

[86] *L. c.,* p. 33.

[87] *L. c.,* 33-35; 50f.

[88] Jer. Ber. 2, 5a; Meg. 17b.

[89] Jer. Ber, 4, 3 and Ber. 20a.

[40] Cf. Ben Sira 36, 1-17, apparently taken from another source, where verses 12-14 read:

"Have mercy upon the people that is called by Thy name,
Israel, whom Thou didst surname Firstborn.

Have mercy upon Thy holy city, Jerusalem, the place of Thy dwelling (Shekinah).

Fill Zion with Thy majesty,
And Thy Temple with Thy glory."

[41] Jer. Yoma 7, 44b.

[42] Tos. Ber. 3, 25.

[43] Ber. 29a and Jer. Ber. 4, 8a.

[44] *L. c.,* 39f.

[45] *G. V.* p. 381.

[46] See Abudarham.

[47] *J. G.* p. 73.

[48] Yoma 7, 1; Jer. Yoma 7, 44b.

[47] Cf. Ber. 5, 3, and particularly the corresponding Essene Benediction in the seventh Book of the Apostolic Constitutions.

[50] Cf. Sifrè, Num. 43.

CHAPTER XV

[1] R. H. 4, 5.

[2] *J. G.* p. 110.

[3] Pes. 117b.

[4] *G. V.* p. 371.

[5] Cf. Mek. Yitro 7; Pes. 106a.

[6] Tos. Ber. 3, 7.

[7] Cf. Sanh. 58b and B. Jubilees 2:16f.

CHAPTER XVI

[1] See 2 Kings 4:23; Isa. 1:13; 66:23; Amos 8:5; Lam. 2:6.

[2] Ex. 31:13-17 following Ezek. 20:11-24.

[3] Ex. 13:8; cf. 12:17.

[4] 12:42.

[5] R. H. 11a; cf. Jer. 23, 8.

[6] Shab. 86b.

[7] Men. 65a; Meg. Taan. 1, 1.

[8] The name Feast of Rejoicing is especially taken from Deut. 16:15; cf. also Jubilees 16:25-31.

[9] Cf. Zech. 14:16f.

[10] Lev. 23:24; Num. 29:11; cf. Num. 10:10.

[11] See Ezek. 40, 1 and Lev. 25:9-10.

[12] R. H. 32b.

[13] Zech. 9:14.

[14] Jer. R. H. 4, 59c; R. H. 27a; Jer. R. H. 1, 57a.

[15] See art. "Alenu" in *J. E.* I, 337f.

[16] *De Sept.* 28, II, 296.

[17] *J. Q. R.* VII, 128.

[18] Sifra, Ahare Mot. 8; Yoma 8, 9.

[19] *Studien zur Geschichte des jüdischen Gottesdienstes,* Berlin, 1907, p. 49.

[20] Lev. 16:21.

[21] The name *Selihah,*—Forgiveness,—refers to the words of God: *Salahti,* "I have forgiven" (Num. 14:20).

[22] Seder Olam Rabba c. 6; Taan. 30b, Rashi on R. H. 17b.

[23] Yoma 87b.

CHAPTER XVII

[1] 1 Kings 18:29; Dan. 9:21.
[2] Num. cc. 28-29.
[3] Suk. 53a; cf. Tos. Suk. 4, 5.
[4] Ber. 4, 7.

[5] Taan. 4, 1, 4.
[6] *Der jüdische Gottesdienst*, p. 115.
[7] Jer. Ber. 4, 8c.

CHAPTER XVIII

[1] Suk. 4, 8; Shab. 21b.
[2] Taan. 3, 9.
[3] Ber. 56a; Pes. 117a.
[4] Pes. 10, 6.
[5] Tos. Suk. 3, 2; Jer. Suk. 4, 54c; Taan. 28b.
[6] Arakin 10a.
[7] Tamid 7, 4.

[8] R. H. 31a.
[9] Jer. Taan. 4, 68b; Taan. 27b, Mas. Soferim 17, 5.
[10] Shab. 118b; Mas. Sof. 17, 11.
[11] Ber. 3b, 4a.
[12] Masechet Soferim, edited by Dr. Joel Müller, Leipzig, 1878.

CHAPTER XIX

[1] *Con. Apion.* 2, 18; *Ant.* XVI, 2, 3.
[2] *De Sept.* 6; *Opificio Mundi* 3; *Eusebius, Praep. Ev.* VIII, 7.
[3] Jer. Meg. 4, 75a; B. K. 82a; Mas. Sof. 10, 1.
[4] *Ant.* IV, 8, 12.
[5] Sota 7, 8.
[6] Cf. Sifrè, Deut. 160 and Tos. Sotah 7, 17, as to the extent of the reading from Deuteronomy.

[7] "The Reading of the Law and Prophets," in *J. Q. R.*, 1893, 420ff.; see the Bibliography in Elbogen, *Der jüdische Gottesdienstes*, pp. 155ff.
[8] Sifra to Lev. 23:43 (ed. Weiss, p. 103), and Sifrè, Deut. 127.
[9] *J. G.*, p. 157.
[10] Philo. II, 630; Yoma 7, 1; Jer. Meg. 4, 75a.
[11] Meg. 3, 4-6.

CHAPTER XX

[1] Ber. 33a.
[2] R. H. 4, 5.
[3] Yoma 7, 1.
[4] Neh. 8:6.
[5] Mas. Soferim 13, 8.
[6] Cf. Müller to Mas. Soferim. pp. 181-185.
[7] See Ber. 21a; 48b; Tos. Ber. 7, 1; Sibyll. 4, 25; Letter of Aristeas 184; Matt. 14:19, and elsewhere.
[8] Ber. 7, 1f., 48b.
[9] Even if a man ate by himself, he must recite the three Benedic-

tions; see Mekilta, ed. Friedmann, p. 31b; ed. Weiss, p. 38.
[10] Mek. Yitro 7; Pes. ch. 10; Ber. 8, 1; cf. Geiger's Zeitschr., VI, 116.
[11] Pes. 10, 6.
[12] Mas. Soferim 19, 9.
[13] Ket. 7b, cf. Tobit 8:6-17.
[14] Ber. 46b; Semahot cc. 12; 14.
[15] Shab. 137b; Tos. Ber. 7, 12-13.
[16] Tos. Ber. 4, 1ff. Ber. 35a; 40ab and 44a.
[17] Ber. 35ab.
[18] Ber. 9, 2; 58b-59b.

Chapter XX—(continued)

[19] Ber. 54b after Ps. 107.
[20] Tos. Ber. 7, 9ff.
[21] *He-Haluz.*, VII, 40ff.
[22] *Spiegel, Eran. Alterth.*, III, 691.
[23] Ber. 60b.
[24] Darmstetter, *Zend Avesta*, I, 193: "The cock announcing the dawn calls people to prayer."
[25] Tos. Ber. 7, 18; Jer. Ber. 9, 13b; Men. 43b.
[26] Diogenes Laertius I, 1, 7.
[27] David Kaufmann, in *Monatsschrift*, 1893, 14ff.

[28] Ber. 60b.
[29] Ber. 11b.
[30] Yoma 87b.
[31] Shibbale ha-Leket, ed. Buber, Wilna, 1886, p. 6 (Tephillah §6).
[32] See Rappaport, *Erek Millin*, p. 37.
[33] Referred to in Ginsberg's *Geonica*, II, 50f.
[34] See Yalkut to Deut. 836.
[35] Men. 43b.
[36] Num. R. 18, 21.
[37] Ber. 40b; Jer. Ber. 6, 10b.

Chapter XXI

[1] Tamid 7, 1.
[2] Tamid 7, 3; Ben Sira 50, 16-21.
[3] *J. G.* p. 73.
[4] See Solomon B. Freehof, "The Origin of the Tahanun," in *Hebrew Union College Annual*, II, 339ff.
[5] See Elbogen, *l. c.*, 73-78.
[6] See Kol Bo, Lemberg, 1860, §16, p. 9b.

[7] *G. V.* p. 386.
[8] *L. c.*, p. 80.
[9] *Ges. Schriften*, VI, 418.
[10] In his *Vindiciae Judaeorum*, IV, 2.
[11] On the abuse of the prayer by Christian maligners, see the article "Alenu" in *J. E.* I, 337f.
[12] Cf. Hoefling, *Taufe*, I, 381.

Chapter XXII

[1] Sota 49a.
[2] Cf. Macc. 1:3-5 for literal similarity.
[3] Ezek. 38:23.

[4] Pp. 8-9.
[5] P. 39.
[6] See art. "Kaddish," in *J. E.* VII, 401.

Chapter XXIII

[1] Men. 65a; Meg. Taan. 1.
[2] Taan. 4, 2; cf. Sifrè, Num. 142.
[3] Chron. 24:18; 23:6-24 and 25: 31.
[4] Taan. 4, 2-4; Tos. Taan. 4,

2f.; Taan. 27b; Mas. Soferim 17, 5.
[5] *J. G.*, p. 237.
[6] Taan. 27b.
[7] Meg. Taan. c. 12 and Mas. Soferim 21, 3; ed. Müller, p. 294.

Chapter XXIV

[1] Cf. 2:42; 3:13, 44; 2 Macc. 14:6.
[2] Ps. 149:6-7.
[3] Cf. Gen. R. 65, 22.

[4] 2 Macc. 14:3.
[5] Shal. 64b; Nid. 38ab; Ket. 61a; B. K. 82a; Sifrè, Deut. 237, 291.
[6] Compare with this the Zaddi-

Chapter XXIV—(*continued*)

kim and Hasidim of the twelfth of the Eighteen Benedictions.

[7] Josephus, *Ant.* XIII, 10, 5; cf. Kid. 66a, where Alexander Jannaeus is erroneously mentioned instead.

[8] Lev. 19:1.

[9] Sota 3, 4; 20a; 22b.

[10] Sota 22b; Jer. Ber. 9, 14b; Abot de-R. Nathan, text A, c. 37, text B, c. 45 (ed. Schechter, pp. 109, 124).

[11] Shab. 17b.

[12] Tos. B. K. 7, 8; Tos. Sanh. 5, 2, 5; Sanh. 25b; 26b; B. M. 61b; Jer. Peah 1, 16a.

[13] *Ant.* XIII, 5, 9; *J. W.* II, 8, 14; cf. R. Akiba in Abot 3, 19.

[14] Sifrè, Deut. 32; 53; Sifra, Shenimi I; Sifra, Kedoshim 2; Ber. 9, 5.

[15] Sifra to Lev. 22, 32.

[16] Ex. 34:6-7.

[17] Num. 15:39-40.

[18] Sifrè, Deut. 49; Sota 14a.

[19] Abot 1, 19 and elsewhere.

[20] Sifra, Behar 4; Tos. B. K. 7, 8; B. M. 58b; B. B. 88a-90b.

[21] B. M. 49a.

[22] Peah 5, 6; B. M. 60b with reference to Lev. 25:36.

[23] Lev. 19:18.

[24] Shab. 31a; in Tobit 4:15; and Philo II, 236; Ab De-R. Nathan, ed. Schechter, pp. 55, 60.

[25] Gen. R. 24, 8.

[26] Abot, 1, 12; 4, 12; Shab. 88b; Taan. 20b.

[27] Sifrè to Deut. 25, 4; Ber. 40a; Git. 62a.

[28] Num. 78; 157.

[29] Pesikta Rab. 24; Lev. R. 23, 12; Ber. 12b; Shab. 33a; Nid. 13a.

[30] Abot 1, 3.

[31] Cf. C. H. Toy, *Judaism and Christianity,* Boston, 1890, p. 260.

[32] Abot 4, 2.

[33] Lev. R. 22, 8.

[34] Moreh Nebukim 3, 32.

[35] 1, 239f.

[36] Kuzari II, 26.

Chapter XXV

[1] See below.

[2] *Ant.* XIII, 11, 2; *J. W.* 1, 3, 5.

[3] *Ant.* XV, 10, 4-5.

[4] *Ant.* XVII, 13, 3; *J. W.* II, 7, 3.

[5] *J. W.* V, 4, 2.

[6] *Hist. Nat.* V, 17.

[7] Pp. 471-488.

[8] Cf. Shab. 33b regarding the levity of woman: "Women are frivolous" (Nashim da'tan kalla).

[9] Cf. Eccl. 9:8.

[10] This direct reference to the Law and the Prophets and the Apocalyptic scrolls which emanated from the ancestors of the sect, compared with the vague statement of Josephus: "the writings of the ancients selected for the wel-fare of the soul and the body," proves the genuine Jewish character of our version.

[11] Cf. Wisdom of Solomon 7:20.

[12] See ch. 25 as to the purpose of the hatchet and also of the apron, both of which are based on the law of Deut. 23:10-15, while the white robe is to serve as the symbol of purity.

[13] Matt. 5:44.

[14] Deut. 23:15.

[15] Cf. Yoma 3, 2.

[16] Jer. Ab. Zarah 3, 42b; 43d.

[17] Ab. Zara 12a.

[18] Cf. Sanh. 59a.

[19] Cf. Josephus XVIII, 1, 6, who ascribes this to the *fourth*

CHAPTER XXV—(*continued*)

sect founded by Judas the Galilean.

[20] Sifrè, Num. 116; Pes. 72b-73a.

[21] Tos. Sota 13, 2, after Ps. 74:9.

[22] Luke 2:25, 30; 23:51.

[23] Midr. Lekah Tob to Deut. 5:37; Shab. 87a.

[24] Sifrè, Num. 99.

[25] See Taan. 2, 10; cf. Mid. Teh. to Pss. 36:8; 77:12; 91:2.

[26] Ed. Friedmann, p. 60a.

[27] *J. W.* II, 8, 9.

[28] See my art. "The Essenes and the Apocalyptic Literature," in *J. Q. R.* (New Series), XI, 163.

[29] See Mek. Yithro 2 (ed. Friedmann, p. 60b); Sifrè, Num. 78 and Deut. 352; Yalk. Judges I, 16; Abot de-R. Nathan I, c. 35 (ed. Schechter, p. 105); and especially Nilus, the Mount Sinai monk of the fifth century, quoted by Hilgenfeld (*Die Ketzergeschichte des Urchristenthums,* Leipzig, 1884,

138f.) and my article just quoted, 160f.

[30] Eccl. R. to 9, 9; Ber. 9b; Tamid 27b.

[31] Ber. 22a; Jer. Ber. 3, 6c.

[32] See Lam. R. 4, 1; Ebel Rabbati, in Brüll's Jahrbücher, I, 25, 44; Geiger, *Jüd Zeitschrift,* VI, 279.

[33] For further details see my art. "Essenes" in *J. E.* V, 224ff.

[34] Allusion to such healing power possessed by King Solomon is made in the Apocryphal Wisdom of Solomon 7:20.

[35] Translated from the Greek by Conybeare in *J. Q. R.,* XI, 1-45, and undoubtedly originally Jewish.

[36] *Ant.* VIII, 2, 5.

[37] Ber. 22a; Jer. Ber. 3, 6c.

[38] 1 Macc. 1, 62; cf. Frankel, *Zeitschr.,* III, 441; *Monatsschr.* II, 30; 61; and Darke ha-Mishna 14.

CHAPTER XXVI

[1] Neh. 8:1-8.

CHAPTER XXVII

[1] Hosea 2:1; Jer. 3:4; Isa. 63:16; Sota 9, 15; Yoma 8, 9.

[2] Abot 3, 13.

[3] Zech. 8:23.

[4] Deut. 4:6-7.

[5] Exodus Rabbah 1, 26.

[6] Cc. 17-18.

[7] Mal. 3:23; Ben Sira 48, 10f.

CHAPTER XXVIII

[1] Ps. 128:2; cf. Abot 4, 1.

[2] Abot 1, 18.

[3] Shab. 31a.

[4] Hul. 94a; Shebuot 39a; Tos. B. K. 7, 8-13; Tos. B. M. 3, 25-27.

[5] B. M. 4, 2.

[6] Suk. 30a; B. K. 94a.

[7] B. M. 83a.

[8] Jer. Sanh. 1, 18a; Babli Sanh. 64a.

[9] Sanh. 92a.

[10] Pes. 113b.

[11] B. M. 49a.

[12] Num. R. c. 11; Ukezim 3, 12.

[13] Jer. Peah 1, 16a; Derek Erez Zuta, Perek ha-Shalom.

[14] Lev. R. 34, 3.

[15] Gen. 1:28.

[16] Yeb. 61b-63b.

[17] Sanh. 106b.

CHAPTER XXVIII—(continued)

[18] Yoma 29a.
[19] Ned. 10a; Sifrè, Num. 30 with reference to Num. 6:11.
[20] Jer. Kid. 4, 66d.
[21] Ber. 32b after Deut. 4:9; B. K. 91b; Shab. 82a.
[22] R. Gamaliel, Shab. 151b; cf. Test. Zebulon 8, 3.
[23] B. M. 58b; Pes. 118a.
[24] Sifrè, Deut. 286; Sota 14a.
[25] Abot 1, 12; see the comment in Ab. de-R. Nathan I, c. 12; II, c. 24 (ed. Schechter, p. 48).
[26] II, ch. 4.
[27] Deut. 25:4.

[28] 1 Cor. 9:9.
[29] Deut. 22:6; Ex. 20:10; cf. Prov. 12:10.
[30] Gittin 62a based on Deut. 11:15.
[31] B. M. 85a.
[32] Lev. 22:32; Jer. B. M. 2, 8c.
[33] Sifrè to Deut. 6:5 (ed. Friedmann, p. 73a).
[34] Tos. B. K. 10, 15.
[35] Abot 1, 3.
[36] Cf. also the art. "The Historical Development of Jewish Charity," in Hebrew Union College and Other Addresses, pp. 229ff.

CHAPTER XXIX

[1] See Graetz, Geschichte d J., IV., 341, which refers to Julian's Epistles 30, 49.
[2] Abot 1, 2.
[3] Ex. 18:20.
[4] Mek. ibidem (ed. Friedmann, p. 59b) and B. K. 100a.
[5] Sanh. 17b.
[6] See Tos. Peah 4, 8-15; Peah 8, 7; Jer. Peah 8, 21ab.
[7] Kid. 4, 5; B. B. 9a-11a; cf.

Sifrè, Deut. 210; Sota 9, 6. Cf. also Josephus Ant. XX, 2, 5 and Tos. Peah 4, 20 and B. B. 11a with Matt. 6, 19-20.
[8] Tos. Gittin 5, 4; Jer. Gittin 47c; Jer. Demai 24a; cf. further the art. "Alms" in J. E. I, 435f., and "Charity," J. E. III, 667f. See also E. Frisch, An Historical Survey of Jewish Philanthropy, New York, 1924.

CHAPTER XXX

[1] Lev. 16:31.

[2] Deut. 31:10-14.

CHAPTER XXXI

[1] Hil. Melakim 8, 9-10.
[2] Lev. 19:34; 24:22.
[3] Ex. 20:10; Lev. 16:29; 17:10-15; 18:26; 24:16, 22.
[4] Ex. 12:48.
[5] See Kohler, Jewish Theology, p. 415.
[6] Ps. 4:6; Sifrè and Targ. to Deut. 33, 19.
[7] Mishnah Kerit. 2, 1; Babli Ker. 8b.

[8] Yeb. 22a; 48b; Gen. R. 39, 14.
[9] Ps. 115:11; 118:4; 135:20.
[10] See Bernays' Gesammelte Abhandlungen, 2 vols., Berlin, 1885, II, 74f.
[11] 165-167.
[12] Sota 12a; cf. Apocryphal book Asenath.
[13] Ker. 9a.
[14] Gen. R. 18, 5; Cant. R. 1, 4.
[15] Lev. R. 2, 9.

CHAPTER XXXI—(continued)

[16] Yeb. 47a; Mas. Gerim c. 1.

[17] Shab. 31a.

[18] Cf. also Harnack, *Die Mission und Ausbreitung des Christenthums, in den ersten drei Jahrhunderten*, 2 vols., Leipzig, 1915, I, 1-12.

[19] Isa. 14:1.

[20] Yeb. 47b; 109b.

[21] Tos. Ab. Zara 9, 4; Jer. Ab. Z. 2, 40c; Sanh. 56-57; Gen. R. 34, 8; 98, 9; Mid. Teh. (ed. Buber, p. 2), 5.

[22] Gen. 9:4, referred to also in the Book of Jubilees 7:20; the Ethiopic translation, however, is incorrect.

[23] See Seeberg, *Die Beiden Wege un d. Apostol. Decret*, p. 25.

[24] "Tie jüdischen Proselyten im Römerreiche unter den Kaisern Domitian, Nerva, Trajan und Hadrian," in *Jahres-Bericht des judisch-theologischen Seminars*, Breslau, 1884.

[25] Mid. R. to Gen. 12, 5; Ab. de-R. Nathan c. 12 (ed. Schechter, p. 53.) For further details see Kohler, Jewish Theology, pp. 408-423.

[26] See art. "Christianity" in *J. E.* IV, 49ff.

CHAPTER XXXII

[1] 12:1.

[2] Gen. 49:1.

[3] Tanhuma and Targ. *ibidem* and Pes. 56a.

[4] Deut. 11:21.

[5] Sanh. 90b; cf. the similar argument in Matt. 22:32.

[6] Ps. 37:11, 29.

[7] Sanh. 10:1; Kid. 1, 10; cf. Matt. 5:5.

[8] Ps. 116:9.

[9] Pes. R. c. 1 (ed. Friedmann, p. 2b); Jer. Kil. 9, 32c.

[10] After Isa. 26:19.

[11] Isa. 27:13.

[12] 4 Ezra 6:23; Ber. 15b; Targ. Jer. to Ex. 20:15; cf. 1 Cor. 15:52.

[13] Cant. R. 2, 1; cf. the similar Christian belief concerning Jesus.

[14] Tos. Sanh. 13, 2.

[15] Sifré, Deut. 329; Abot 4, 22.

[16] See Mek. to Ex. 17, 16 (ed. Friedmann, p. 56b); Pes. R. c. 1 and Sanh. 97a-99a.

[17] Sanh. 99a.

[18] Sanh. 91b; Ber. 34b.

[19] Mek. Shira 8 (ed. Friedmann, p. 41f.).

[20] Mek. Bo 14; ib. 16b.

[21] Tanh. VA'ERA, ed. Bubert, p. 15; Bo 6; 19.

[22] Gen. R. 98, 9; Targ Jer. Gen. 49, 12; Jer. Ab. Zar. 2, 40c, Mid. Teh. Ps. 21, ed. Buber, note 3).

[23] Cant. R. 7:5 after Zech. 9:1.

[24] Cf. Josephus *Ant.* XVIII, 4, 1; 2 Macc. 2:4-8; Yoma 52b and elsewhere.

[25] See my art. "Eschatology" in *J. E.* V, 209ff.

[26] Sanh. 91b.

[27] As in Isa. 66:15-16; Zech. 13:9.

[28] Tos. Sanh. 13, 3.

[29] *Ibidem*, 13, 5.

[30] Abot 3, 16; cf. Rev. 19:9; Luke 13:28f. and parallels.

[31] Enoch 60:7f.; Ap. Baruch 29, 4; 4 Ezra 6, 52; B. B. 74b, Mid. Teh. to Ps. 104, 26.

[32] Cf. Bundahish 30, 25, where other such primeval animals are mentioned.

Chapter XXXII—(continued)

[33] Ber. 34b; Sanh. 99a; Matt. 26:29.

[34] Ps. 78:25; Hagigah 12b; Tanh. Beshalah, 21; Sibyll. 3, 746.

[35] Ber. 34b.

[36] Isa. 64:3.

[37] Ber. 17a.

[38] See Kohler's *Heaven and Hell, with Special Reference to Dante's Divine Comedy.* New York, 1923, and art. "Eschatology" in *J. E.* V, 209.

Chapter XXXIII

[1] P. 5.

[2] Sanh. 10, 1.

[3] In *J. Q. R.* 1920, 145f.

[4] See my art. "Book of Jubilees" in *J. E.* VII, 301, and my "Introduction to the Testament of Job" in *Semitic Studies in Memory of Alexander Kohut*, p. 264f..

[5] Hag. 2, 1; Babli. Hag. 12-14; Jer. Hag. 2, 77b; Suk. 28a; Meg. 3a; Cant. R. 1, 29; Agg. Shir. ha Shirim, ed. Schechter l. 13 and elsewhere.

[6] Josephus *J. W.* II, 8, 7; cf. Jellinek's Introductions to his Bet ha-Midrash, II and III; and Hilgenfeld, *Jüd. Apocalypse*, 1857, pp. 243-283.

[7] In his Commentary, p. xxv.

[8] *Ant.* X, 11, 7.

[9] Cf. the Shammaites in Erubin 13b with 4 Ezra 4:12; Baruch Apoc. 10:6; 11:7 and elsewhere.

[10] See Beerman's Commentary, pp. xxvf.

[11] *Ant.* X, 11, 7.

[12] 8:19; 11:27, 35, 40; 12:4, 6, 9.

[13] 25:12; 29:10.

[14] Dan. 9:2, 24, 27.

[15] 8:25; cf. 2:34, 45.

[16] 7:25; 12:7.

[17] 12:11.

[18] 12:11.

[19] 2:35-45.

[20] 7:1-14.

[21] 7:13f.

[22] 12:1-3.

[23] Ezek. 14:14, 20.

[24] *Ibidem* p. 28, 3.

[25] Gen. 5:24.

[26] Zimmern in Schrader's *Keilinschriften und das Alte Testament*, 3d ed., Berlin, 1902-3, pp. 408, 533; cf. Bousset, *Religion des Judenthums*, 2d ed., Berlin, 1906, p. 559; 3d ed., Tübingen, 1926, p. 491.

[27] Enoch 10:4; Yoma 63b; Targ. J. to Lev. 16:22; cf. Jellinek, Bet ha-Midrash, VI, p. x.

[28] Shab. 149b; Enoch 27:1.

[29] Yalkut Bereshit 44; Jellinek, *l. c.*, IV, 127-128.

[30] Ch. 37-72.

[31] 68:1.

[32] Ch. 1-36.

[33] 10:17-19.

[34] Ch. 26-27.

[35] 32:2; cf. 25:4-5.

[36] Ch. 83-90.

[37] 90-93.

[38] 25:11.

[39] 2 Macc. 14:37f., where Razis is a copyist's error.

[40] 89:73.

[41] Num. 24:8.

[42] 14:8-25; ch. 17-19.

[43] Cf. *J. E.* art. "Merkaba."

[44] After Isa. 11:4.

[45] After Ps. 72:17; cf. Pes. 54a.

[46] Cc. 46-51.

[47] Ch. 60.

[48] See art. "Eschatology" in *J. E.*, and Bousset, *R. d. J.*, ch. 25.

CHAPTER XXXIII—(*continued*)

⁴⁹ See my synopsis in *Heaven and Hell,* pp. 67-70.

⁵⁰ Heb. Sira 44, 16; Greek: an "example of repentance."

⁵¹ See Charles' edition, London, 1908, p. lix.

⁵² 4:17.

⁵³ Cf. Enoch 12:1; 92:1.

⁵⁴ Gen. R. 25, 1.

⁵⁵ See *Heaven and Hell,* pp. 77-80.

⁵⁶ Gen. 15:7; see Targ. J.

⁵⁷ Cf. 4 Ezra 3:14 and Apoc. Baruch 4:4.

⁵⁸ Ch. 10; 15; 17.

⁵⁹ Sifrè, Deut. 338; Gen. R. c. 5.

⁶⁰ See art. "Merkabah" in *J. E.*

⁶¹ Jellinek, *B. H.* II, 115; III, 104.

⁶² Ch. 17. For other functions Michael has in common with Jahoel, see Apocalypse of Abraham, ed. Box, London, 1918, notes to ch. 10, pp. 47-49.

⁶³ Ch. 11.

⁶⁴ Ch. 10.

⁶⁵ Gen. 15:11, cf. Targ. J.

⁶⁶ Cc. 25; 31.

⁶⁷ Dan. 10:6; cf. Ps. 29:3.

⁶⁸ Ch. 12-17.

⁶⁹ Ch. 18.

⁷⁰ Cf. Gen. R. 44, 14.

⁷¹ Ch. 19-21.

⁷² Cf. Ber. 40a.

⁷³ Ch. 22-23.

⁷⁴ Pirke de-R. Eliezer, c. 13.

⁷⁵ Ch. 23-29; cf. 4 Ezra 10:45; 14:11.

⁷⁶ Ch. 30.

⁷⁷ See art. "Belial" in *J. E.*

⁷⁸ C. 25.

⁷⁹ 1:29.

⁸⁰ 25:27.

⁸¹ 15:33.

⁸² Sifrè Deut. 43 and elsewhere. See art. "Belial" in *J. E.*

⁸³ Issachar 5, 2; 7; 6; Dan. 5:3.

⁸⁴ Asher 1, 5-8; so also Reuben 4, 7, 11; 6, 3: Simeon 5, 3; Levi 3, 3; 18, 12; 19, 1 and elsewhere.

⁸⁵ Levi 18, 12.

⁸⁶ Judah 25, 3.

⁸⁷ As in Levi 10, 5; 16, 1; Judah 18, 1 and elsewhere.

⁸⁸ Introd. p. lix.

⁸⁹ Levi 5, 4; Asher 2, 10; 7, 5.

⁹⁰ Hag. 12b and elsewhere.

⁹¹ Dan. 12:2.

⁹² Charles ed., pp. 221-234.

⁹³ See Charles, Introd., pp. lxvi-lxviii.

⁹⁴ See Charles, Introd. p. xlii and notes to ch. 6, p. 8.

⁹⁵ 1, 12, 14; cf. 12, 7, and Philo, *Vita Mosis* III, 19; Pesik. R. c. 6; Ex. R. 3, 6; 6, 3; Deut. R. 3, 12 and elsewhere, where Moses is also spoken of as the Mediator—Sirsur.

⁹⁶ Deut. 34, 6.

⁹⁷ 11:5-8.

⁹⁸ *Ant.* IV, 8, 48.

⁹⁹ Bet Ha-Midrash II, Introd. p. vii.

¹⁰⁰ Josephus *J. W.* II, 8, 9.

¹⁰¹ See my art. "The Essenes and the Apocalyptic Literature," in *J. Q. R.* (New Series), XI, 163, note 4.

¹⁰² See Charles, Introd. p. l.

¹⁰³ Charles, p. li f.

¹⁰⁴ *J. Z.* 1868, pp. 45f.

¹⁰⁵ 8:1-5.

¹⁰⁶ *Ant. XIV,* 15, 5 and *J. W.* I, 16, 4.

¹⁰⁷ P. 36.

¹⁰⁸ 10:9-10.

¹⁰⁹ 12:6.

¹¹⁰ Both 4 Ezra 14:5, and Baruch 59:3 tell us of Moses' translation to heaven and his initiation into the mysteries of the future.

CHAPTER XXXIII—(continued)

[111] Ch. 10:12 and 1:18; cf. Charles' notes.

[112] Sanh. 97b, Seder Olam ch. 11, ed. Ratner, note 8.

[113] See Seder Olam, ch. 20.

[114] Ed. Friedmann, p. 131.

[115] See A. Mormorstein, *The Doctrine of Merits in Old Rabbinical Literature*, London, 1920.

[116] Erubin 13b.

[117] San. 98b; Mek. (ed. Friedmann), 50b, 51a and elsewhere; cf. Matt. 24:8 and parallels; the Baruch Apocalypse ch. 27 counts twelve such woes.

[118] See Schürer, III, 3, 305ff.

[119] Cf. 41:4.

[120] 72:2.

[121] 50:1; Charles' notes.

[122] See Bousset, *Die Religion des Judenthums*, last chapter, and art. "Eschatology" in *J. E.* V, 209ff.

[123] See Charles, notes 4 and 5 to Baruch ch. 29:4, and the art. "Eschatology" in *J. E.*

[124] The same is the case with the marvelous abundance of the crops, of wine and the heavenly manna, spoken of in B a r u c h 29:5-8; Charles' note 5; Shab. 30b; Mek. (ed. Friedmann), 50b, 51b.

[125] 15, 5; Charles' note; 77:15-16.

[126] Ch. 57.

[127] 59:4; see Charles' note.

[128] 54:15, 19.

[129] *J. W.* II, 8, 14.

[130] Abot. 3, 15.

[131] 23:5; cf. Gen. R. 24, 4; Lev. R. 15, 1. "The number of offerings" that determines the End (59:9) must be corrected to "the number of Jubilees," as stated in Sanh. 97b.

[132] 60:1; cf. Shab. 6, 10.

[133] 48:15; cf. Abot. 4, 22.

[134] Ch. 77-78.

[135] 4 Ezra 13:39f.

[136] Deut. 29:27.

[137] Josh. 3:16.

[138] *Ant.* XI, 5, 2.

[139] Jer. Sanh. 10, 29c; Gen. R. 73, 6; Pes. R. c. 31 (ed. Friedmann, p. 147a).

[140] *J. W.* VII, 5, 1; cf. Pliny *H. N.* 31, 2.

[141] *J. Q. R.* I, 21.

[142] 9:29-10:57.

[143] Notes to Baruch, p. 15.

[144] Cf. also 9:13-22.

[145] Matt. 22:14; 7:13-14.

[146] 7:116-131.

[147] 7:102-115.

[148] 9:12.

[149] See Box's note to 4 Ezra 5:23.

[150] 6:8f.

[151] Sanh. 96-98, and Mark 13, 4f.

[152] 5:1-13 and 9:1.

[153] 4:33-37.

[154] 7:79-87.

[155] 7:88-99.

[156] 9:26.

[157] See 9:23f.; 10:51-53; 12:51.

[158] 7:26-44; cf. 13, 32, 37; 14:9.

[159] 13:25f.

[160] 12:32.

[161] 13:32f.

[162] 13:39-50.

[163] Sanh. 99a; Pes. R. c. 1 (ed. Friedmann, p. 4a); Midr. Teh. to Ps. 90:15, where the tradition as to the name varies.

[164] 11:1-12:11.

[165] 11:37; 12:32; 13:3-Dan. 7:13.

[166] 11:1-12:34.

[167] 13:57-58.

[168] Cf. 12:37f. See Book II as to the relation of our Apocalypse to Paul's epistles and letters.

BOOK II

CHAPTER I

[1] 14:37; cf. verse 3.
[2] As stated in Book I, Ch. XXIV.
[3] Ex. 23:32; Deut. 7:2.

[4] Josephus *Ant.* XIII, 10, 5;
Kiddushin 66a.

CHAPTER II

[1] *Ant.* XVIII, 5, 2.
[2] II, 458.
[3] *Neutestamentliche Zeitge-
schichte,* I, 319.
[4] 1:16-17.
[5] 18:31.
[6] *Ibidem,* 36, 25.
[7] 13:1.
[8] Matt. 3, 4.
[9] Luke 3:17.
[10] 40:3.

[11] 3:23f.
[12] 3:4.
[13] Luke 1:5-25, 41-55, 57-80.
[14] Mal. 3:24.
[15] Luke 3:7-8.
[16] Luke 3:13-14.
[17] Matt. 14:1-2; Mark 6:16.
[18] Acts 19:1-7.
[19] See Brandt, *Die Mandäische
Religion,* Leipzig, 1889, pp. 137,
218, 228.

CHAPTER III

[1] 4:13.
[2] Mark 5:41.
[3] Mark 7:34.
[4] Mark 15, 34 and Matthew
27, 46.
[5] 23:46.
[6] Matt. 8:22.
[7] Cf. Gen. R. 23; 51; 85; Ex. R.
15, 26; Ruth R. 4, 7; 8, 3; Naz.
23b; Hor. 10b; Meg. 14b.
[8] Luke 2:49.
[9] Ps. 2:7.
[10] *Ant.* XVIII, 3, 3.
[11] See art. "Demonology" in *J. E.
IV,* 514.
[12] Mark 1:32; Luke 4:40.
[13] Mek. Ki Tissa, ed. Weiss,
p. 110.
[14] Luke 8:26f. and parallels.
[15] P. 266f.
[16] Isa. 35:5f.
[17] Matt. 6:26.
[18] Matt. 6:28f.; Luke 12:27.
[19] Mark 12:29f.

[20] Matt. 5:17-20.
[21] Luke 6:21f.
[22] After Deut. 15:11.
[23] Mark 10:19-31 and parallels.
[24] According to Luke 4:18.
[25] 16:19.
[26] Luke 15.
[27] Mark 2:17 and parallels.
[28] Mark 3, 22 and parallels.
[29] Matt. 5:20.
[30] Matt. 5:21f.
[31] Tos. Peah 4:18.
[32] Matt. 7:13.
[33] Mek. Beshallah, ed. Weiss,
p. 56.
[34] Mark 2:24; 3:1f. and parallels.
[35] Mek. Ki Tissa, p. 110.
[36] Luke 6:1.
[37] Lev. 23:11-14.
[38] 1 Sam. 21:5-7.
[39] Mark 7:6-23; Matt. 23:23f.
[40] Mark 7:15 and parallels.
[41] Acts 10:14.
[42] Nidah 13b.

CHAPTER III—(*continued*)

[43] Matt. 5:29.

[44] Seeberg, A., *Die Didache des Judenthums und der Urchristenheit*, Leipzig, 1908.

[45] Matt. 15:24.

[46] Matt. 10:5.

[47] Matt. 7:6.

[48] Luke 6:13f.; Mark 3:14; Matt. 10:2f.

[49] Matt. 20:28; Luke 22:30.

[50] 10:1.

[51] Mark 9:1; Matt. 16:28; Luke 9:27.

[52] 24-25.

[53] Luke 17, 20f.

[54] Cf. the מחשבי קץ.

[55] Thess. 5:2; 2 Pet. 3:10; Matt. 24:37.

[56] Matt. 24:42; Mark 13:35.

[57] Matt. 24:44-25:13.

[58] R. Eliezer and R. Johanan b. Zakkai Shab. 153a.

[59] בהיסח הדעת, San. 97a.

[60] Irenaeus *Adv. Haereses* V, 33f.

[61] Cf. also Ket. 111b.

[62] Matt. 10:34f. and Luke 12:49f.

[63] Mark 4:11; Luke 8:10; Matt. 13:11.

[64] Matt. 13:35.

[65] Matt. 13:39.

[66] Mark 12:13ff. and parallels.

[67] Ex. 3:6; cf. Sanh. 90b.

[68] Mark 12, 18ff. and parallels.

[69] Tos. Menahot 13, 21-23.

[70] See art. "Pharisees" in *J. E.*

[71] Luke 23:2-5.

[72] Mark 8:31; 10:33; 11:18; 14:43 and parallels.

[73] 18:28f.

[74] Mark 12:13; Matt. 22:15.

[75] Ch. 27.

[76] Luke 19:48; 21:38.

[77] Luke 23:48.

[78] Matt. 27:26; John 19:1.

[79] John 19:19-20.

[80] Mark 14:50.

[81] Mark 15:42; Luke 23:54; Matt. 27:62; John 19:31.

[82] 1 Cor. 5:7.

[83] Mark 14:12f.; Matt. 26:17f.; Luke 22:7f.

[84] Matt. 26:26f.; Mark 14:22f.; Luke 22:19f.

[85] See art. "Agape" in *J. E.* I, 230.

[86] Luke 23, 51.

[87] Cf. Ab. de-R. Nathan, ed. Schechter, p. 56: Beth Ramata.

[88] Mark 15:43.

[89] Mark 10:32f. and parallels.

[90] In 1 Cor. 15:5-8.

[91] 1 Cor. 15:14.

[92] 16:18.

[93] 51:1.

[94] Mark 7:27; Matt. 15:26f.

[95] Luke 10:25f.

[96] Mark 13:30f. and parallels.

[97] Mark 4:28f.; Matt. 13:18f.

[98] Matt. 11:27.

[99] Mark 12, 35f. and parallels.

CHAPTER IV

[1] Mark 16:7; Matt. 28:7; cf. verse 16.

[2] Matt. 16:13-16 and parallels.

[3] 1 Cor. 15:3-8.

[4] 1:4ff.

[5] Ch. 2.

[6] 1 Cor. 14.

[7] 3:1-3.

[8] 1 Cor. 15:3-8.

[9] 10:46; 11:15; 19:6.

[10] 1 Cor. 13 and 14.

[11] Acts 9:13, 32, 41; 26:10.

[12] Rom. 1, 7 and elsewhere.

[13] See *J. E.* VII, 68f.; also Spitta, *Zur Geschichte und Lit. des Urchristenthums*, 1896, II, 61-239, and

CHAPTER IV—(continued)

his *Der Brief des Jacobus*, Göttingen, 1896. Cf. also Acts 7:38.
[14] 3 and 4; Acts 2; 44f.; 4:32.
[15] 4:32f.
[16] 1 Cor. 16:1f.; 2 Cor. 9:1; Rom. 15:26.

[17] See also *Encyclopedia Brittanica*, IX, 870 (Eucharist).
[18] Acts 3:11; 5:12.
[19] Acts 3:1.
[20] Acts 4:13.

CHAPTER V

[1] Luke 2:25, 38; 23:51.
[2] See Kohler "The Essenes and Apocalyptic Literature," *J. Q. R.* (N. S.), XI, 145f., and *Heaven and Hell in Comparative Religion*, pp. 83ff.
[3] Mark 6:8-10; Luke 22:36.
[4] Josephus *J. W.*, II, 8, 4.
[5] Matt. 7:13; Luke 13:24.

[6] See the instructive works of Charles on the Enoch books and others.
[7] See art. "Didascalia" in *J. E.* IV, 588.
[8] See "Origin and Composition of Eighteen Benedictions," in *H. U. C. Annual*, I, 387f.

CHAPTER VI

[1] 9:4.
[2] Acts 12:2.
[3] Mark 3:17.
[4] Acts 9:31.
[5] Eusebius, *Hist. Eccl.*, II, 23.
[6] *Nazir Olam.*
[7] *Ant.* XX, 9, 1.

[8] Quoted by Eusebius, *Hist. Eccl.*, II, 23.
[9] Ps. 118:20.
[10] Acts 15:20.
[11] Rev. 2:14.
[12] Acts 11:26.

CHAPTER VII

I. THE DIDACHE

[1] J. Rendel Harris, *The Teaching of the Apostles*, London, 1887, pp. 78ff.
[2] C. Taylor, *The Teaching of the Twelve Apostles*, Cambridge, 1886, p. 6ff.
[3] Adolf Harnack, *Die Chronologie der Altchristlichen Litteratur*, Leipzig, 1904, II, 487.
[4] R. Pohanan b. Zakkai.
[5] Eusebius, *Praep. Evangelica*, VII, 7.
[6] Shab. 31b.
[7] Matt. 7:12; Luke 6:31.
[8] Shab. 31a.
[9] Deut. 4:2; 13:1.
[10] Ch. VIII.
[11] Ch. VII.

[12] Ch. XIV.
[13] See Apost. Const. VII, 36; II, 36, 59; VI, 23.
[14] Ps. 80:15.
[15] Cf. Ch. X: "Gather the Church together from the four winds." See Taylor, *Teaching of the Twelve Apostles*, pp. 70-72; and art. "Didache" in *J. E.*
[16] Ch. II.

II. THE APOSTOLIC CONSTITUTIONS

[17] Cf. Chs. IX and X.
[1] *Constitutiones Apostolorum*, Leipzig, 1862; Didascalia, 1854.
[2] *Gesch. des Kirchenrechts*, Giessen, 1843 I, pp. 148-177.
[3] Ch. III.
[4] 5:7.

CHAPTER VII—(*continued*)

[5] Lev. 19:18.
[6] Cf. Ab. de-R. Nathan, ed. Schechter, Chs. 15-16.
[7] Massek. Kallah and Massek. Derek Erez.
[8] Cf. Sifra, Ahare Mot, IX, 13.
[9] Ex. 20:14 is so interpreted by the Rabbis.
[10] 1 Cor. 11:3.
[11] Cf. Didache 4, 10.
[12] 1 Cor. 11:3.
[13] Apost. Const. III, 3.
[14] Cf. Philo *De Profugis* VI; Hag. 14a; San. 17a.
[15] 1 Cor. 9:7-9.
[16] Chs. V-VIII.
[17] Shab. 88b.
[18] IX-X.
[19] XIII-XLIII; XLVII.
[20] Portion of lost Midrash.
[21] Ch. XIV.
[22] Ch. 34.
[23] II, 26; III, 6, 7, 14.
[24] Luke 2:36f.
[25] See art. "Charity" in *J. E.* III, 667f., and in my *Hebrew Union College and Other Essays*, pp. 229f.
[26] Cf. Deut. 28:33.

[27] Ex. Rabbah, end of Ch. 45.
[28] Ch. 6.
[29] B. B. 10b; Sanh. 26b.
[30] Book II, 61-62.
[31] Cf. the more explicit passage in Book II, 53.
[32] Book II, 54.
[33] Book II, 57.
[34] *Lateinische und Griechische Messen*, 1850, pp. 22f., 33, 64.
[35] Apost. Const. VII, 26, 33; VIII, 40.
[36] *H. U. C. Annual*, 1924, pp. 387-425.
[37] VII, 40, 41.
[38] See Baring-Gould, *The Holy Eucharist of the First Three Centuries*, pp. 133-141.
[39] See C. Kayser, *Die Canones Jacobs von Edessa*, pp. 106, 167, 172.
[40] See my art. "Origin and Composition of the Eighteen Benedictions with a Translation of the Corresponding Essene Prayers in the VII Book of the Apostolic Constitution," in *H. U. C. Annual*, I, pp. 387ff.

CHAPTER VIII

[1] Acts. 11:19f.
[2] See Krenkel's *Beiträge zur Aufhellung der Geschichte u. Briefe des Apostels Paulus*, Braunschweig, 1890, ch. 4.
[3] I, 11f., II, §2.
[4] Isa. 42:8.
[5] 1 Chron. 29:11.
[6] 2:13.
[7] Rom. 7:7.
[8] 7:18.
[9] 10:4.
[10] 11:25.
[11] Deut. 21:23.
[12] Gen. 15:6.
[13] Gen. 17:5.
[14] 1 Cor. 15:28.

[15] 1 Cor. 1:23.
[16] Ch. 15.
[17] See art. "Didascalia" in *J. E.*
[18] Acts 17:19f.
[19] Matt. 26:26f.; Mark 14:22f.; Luke 22:19f.
[20] Cf. Heb. 8:6-13; 9:15ff.
[21] Heb. 7; cf. Ps. 110:4.
[22] See art. "Saul of Tarsus" in *J. E.* XI, 79f.
[23] John 3:14; 12:32f.; 17:5.
[24] John 1:29.
[25] 13:34.
[26] Lev. 19:18.
[27] 7:13; 8:40-59; 10:31 and elsewhere.
[28] 8:44.

CHAPTER IX

[1] Hagigah 13a where Ben Sira, 3, 20, is quoted.

[2] Hag. 14b, cf. Paul in 2 Cor. 12:2.

[3] *L. c.*

[4] See Brandt, *Die Mandäische Religion*, Leipzig, 1889.

[5] See Friedläender, *Der Vor-* *christliche Jüdische Gnosticismus,* pp. 83f.

[6] On this point the otherwise valuable work of Friedländer, *Der Vorchristliche Jüdische Gnosticismus,* Göttingen, 1898 (see pp. 93f.), must be corrected.

THE JEWISH PEOPLE

HISTORY • RELIGION • LITERATURE

AN ARNO PRESS COLLECTION

Agus, Jacob B. **The Evolution of Jewish Thought**: From
Biblical Times to the Opening of the Modern Era. 1959

Ber of Bolechow. **The Memoirs of Ber of Bolechow**
(1723-1805). Translated from the Original Hebrew MS. with an
Introduction, Notes and a Map by M[ark] Vishnitzer. 1922

Berachya. **The Ethical Treatises of Berachya, Son of Rabbi
Natronai Ha-Nakdan**: Being the Compendium and the Masref.
Now edited for the First Time from MSS. at Parma and Munich
with an English Translation, Introduction, Notes, etc. by
Hermann Gollancz. 1902

Bloch, Joseph S. **My Reminiscences.** 1923

Bokser, Ben Zion, **Pharisaic Judaism in Transition**: R. Eliezer
the Great and Jewish Reconstruction After the War with Rome.
1935

Dalman, Gustaf. **Jesus Christ in the Talmud, Midrash, Zohar,
and the Liturgy of the Synagogue.** Together with an
Introductory Essay by Heinrich Laible. Translated and Edited
by A. W. Streane. 1893

Daube, David. **The New Testament and Rabbinic Judaism.** 1956

Davies, W. D. **Christian Origins and Judaism.** 1962

Engelman, Uriah Zevi. **The Rise of the Jew in the Western
World**: A Social and Economic History of the Jewish People
of Europe. Foreword by Niles Carpenter. 1944

Epstein, Louis M. **The Jewish Marriage Contract**: A Study
in the Status of the Woman in Jewish Law. 1927

Facets of Medieval Judaism. 1973. New Introduction by
Seymour Siegel

The Foundations of Jewish Life: Three Studies. 1973

Franck, Adolph. **The Kabbalah, or, The Religious Philosophy
of the Hebrews.** Revised and Enlarged Translation [from the
French] by Dr. I. Sossnitz. 1926

Goldman, Solomon. **The Jew and The Universe.** 1936

Gordon, A. D. **Selected Essays.** Translated by Frances Burnce
from the Hebrew Edition by N. Teradyon and A. Shohat,
with a Biographical Sketch by E. Silberschlag. 1938

Ha-Am, Achad (Asher Ginzberg). **Ten Essays on Zionism and
Judaism.** Translated from the Hebrew by Leon Simon. 1922.
New Introduction by Louis Jacobs

Halevi, Jehudah. **Selected Poems of Jehudah Halevi.**
Translated into English by Nina Salaman, Chiefly from the
Critical Text Edited by Heinrich Brody. 1924

Heine, Heinrich. **Heinrich Heine's Memoir**: From His Works,
Letters, and Conversations. Edited by Gustav Karpeles;
English Translation by Gilbert Cannan. 1910. Two volumes in one

Heine, Heinrich. **The Prose Writings of Heinrich Heine.**
Edited, with an Introduction, by Havelock Ellis. 1887

Hirsch, Emil G[ustav]. **My Religion.** Compilation and
Biographical Introduction by Gerson B. Levi. **Including
The Crucifixion Viewed from a Jewish Standpoint:** A Lecture
Delivered by Invitation Before the "Chicago Institute for
Morals, Religion and Letters." 1925/1908

Hirsch, W. **Rabbinic Psychology:** Beliefs about the Soul
in Rabbinic Literature of the Talmudic Period. 1947

Historical Views of Judaism: Four Selections. 1973

Ibn Gabirol, Solomon. **Selected Religious Poems of Solomon Ibn
Gabirol.** Translated into English Verse by Israel Zangwill
from a Critical Text Edited by Israel Davidson. 1923

Jacobs, Joseph. **Jesus as Others Saw Him:** A Retrospect
A. D. 54. Preface by Israel Abrahams; Introductory Essay by
Harry A. Wolfson. 1925

Judaism and Christianity: Selected Accounts, 1892-1962.
1973. New Preface and Introduction by Jacob B. Agus

Kohler, Kaufmann. **The Origins of the Synagogue and
The Church.** Edited, with a Biographical Essay by H. G. Enelow.
1929

Maimonides Octocentennial Series, Numbers I-IV. 1935

Mann, Jacob. **The Responsa of the Babylonian Geonim as a
Source of Jewish History.** 1917-1921

Maritain, Jacques. **A Christian Looks at the Jewish Question.** 1939

Marx, Alexander. **Essays in Jewish Biography.** 1947

Mendelssohn, Moses. **Phaedon; or, The Death of Socrates.**
Translated from the German [by Charles Cullen]. 1789

Modern Jewish Thought: Selected Issues, 1889-1966. 1973.
New Introduction by Louis Jacobs

Montefiore, C[laude] G. **Judaism and St. Paul:** Two Essays. 1914

Montefiore, C[laude] G. **Some Elements of the Religious
Teaching of Jesus According to the Synoptic Gospels.** Being
the Jowett Lectures for 1910. 1910

Radin, Max. **The Jews Amongs the Greeks and Romans.** 1915

Ruppin, Arthur. **The Jews in the Modern World.** With an
Introduction by L. B. Namier. 1934

Smith, Henry Preserved. **The Bible and Islam;** or, The Influence
of the Old and New Testaments on the Religion of Mohammed.
Being the Ely Lectures for 1897. 1897

Stern, Nathan. **The Jewish Historico-Critical School of the
Nineteenth Century.** 1901

Walker, Thomas [T.] **Jewish Views of Jesus:** An Introduction
and an Appreciation. 1931. New Introduction by Seymour Siegel

Walter, H. **Moses Mendelssohn:** Critic and Philosopher. 1930

Wiener, Leo. **The History of Yiddish Literature in the
Nineteenth Century.** 1899

Wise, Isaac M. **Reminiscences.** Translated from the German and
Edited, with an Introduction by David Philipson. 1901